RosaLee

Leon Dash was a staff reporter for the investigative and special projects department of the *Washington Post*. While interviewing male and femal convicts in Washington's DC jail looking for a family to write about, he met Rosa Lee Cunningham. For four years (1990-94) he followed the lives of her and her children. When his series of articles, 'Rosa Lee's Story', was published in the *Washington Post* 4,600 readers phoned the paper in response. It won numerous awards including the Pulitzer Prize and the Robert F. Kennedy Journalism Award. Leon Dash is now Professor of Journalism at the University of Illinois.

Dedicated to unfettered inquiry.

Rosa Lee

Leon Dash

with a foreword by
Gary Younge

P

PROFILE BOOKS

First published in Great Britain in 1997 by
Profile Books Ltd
58A Hatton Garden
London EC1N 8LX

This edition first published in 1998

First published in the United States in 1996 by
BasicBooks, a division of
HarperCollins, Publishers, Inc.

Copyright © Leon Dash, 1996, 1997, 1998
Cover Photo © Lucian Perkins, The Washington Post
Foreword © Gary Younge, 1997

The moral right of the author has been asserted.

All rights reserved. Without limiting the rights under copyright reserved
above, no part of this publication may be reproduced, stored or
introduced into a retrieval system, or transmitted, in any form or by any
means (electronic, mechanical, photocopying, recording or otherwise),
without the prior written permission of both the copyright owner and the
publisher of this book.

Printed in Great Britain by
St Edmundsbury Press Ltd, Bury St Edmunds, Suffolk.

A CIP catalogue record for this book is available from the
British Library.

ISBN 1 86197 079 X

Contents

Foreword

Monday morning outside King's College hospital in Camberwell, south-east London. A night's clubbing and a morning's weeping has left glazed and bloodshot eyes. The man they called 'Blue' had died. Slain by gunfire in a nearby night club during the early hours. Three others had been injured and while almost everybody could tell you what happened nobody could say why. It appeared that a relatively minor argument some months earlier between two young men had 'gotten out of hand'.

So they wait, with sadness and rage, in the hospital forecourt for news from the morgue and the operating table. Still dressed in their clubbing clothes they stand in the early morning sunshine and shake their heads in disbelief. The women in large clumpy boots and hot pants and skimpy tops with their hair lacquered to the sides of their faces; the men in designer jeans, expensive trainers, perforated T-shirts and close cropped hair.

Around them the world still turns. But it is revolving at an altogether slower and more predictable pace. After all it is Monday morning. While Blue and his friends were getting ready to go out the evening before most people were having an early night so they could start their working week refreshed. Now they are running for buses, dropping off children and buying newspapers. Gearing up for another day of work, they cast fleeting glances towards the commotion outside the hospital. It barely acknowledges them.

There can be few more graphic examples of the relationship between the so-called 'underclass' to the rest of British society than the parallel universes which passed each other in mid-orbit on that Monday morning in Camberwell. It illustrates the extremities of social dislocation far better than any academic could ever describe. Without cases of human tragedy such as this rubbing shoulders with the mundaneness of everyday life, the very term 'underclass' could become little more than an elusive abstraction. But in the fresh light of a new week it seems horrifically real.

Apparently defying a universally accepted definition, the underclass is so overloaded with ideological baggage that it makes any exploratory journey into its root causes both uncomfortable and arduous. By the very nature of their predicament those who belong to it are not in a position to articulate their plight. They have no public voice, no spokespersons and no organisational network. Conversely, the political class – politicians, policy makers and pundits – who are about as far removed from the underclass as anyone can be, allude to them more often than almost any other section of society. When they are talking about welfare reform, lone parents, long-term unemployment, low educational standards or moral meltdown in the inner cities the spectre of the underclass is never far from their minds.

Being constantly talked about but unable to speak for themselves, the underclass are left prostrate at the feet of misinterpretation. Still, there are a few generalisations that can be made with some confidence.

First of all, the key definer of what makes the underclass is not individual poverty. Indeed it is often the case that those in the underclass have far more disposable cash than people in work. Nor, contrary to what the eugenists would have us believe is its membership hereditary although its attributes are often passed down through the generations.

It is about a set of values, aspirations and cultural codes determined in part by social mores that lie outside the mainstream and below what has been decreed as 'normal' and 'civilised'.

It is about a lifestyle, stubbornly and often irretrievably entrenched on the fringes, where few established support mechanisms like the family, full-time paid employment or a basic standard of education exist.

It is about staggering from crisis to crisis to get through the day with the weight of society's moral opprobrium bearing down on your shoulders while the parameters for what is right and reasonable are constantly shifting.

In short it is a condition, rooted in social poverty and characterised by long-term unemployment, petty crime and low educational achievement. But it is not defined by them – given the number of people who fit all of those descriptions but still do not make up the underclass. As such the underclass do not so much stand at the bottom of a country's social heap but outside it altogether.

Social environment clearly provides the raw material for that condition. Value systems do not come from nowhere; nor are they immutable or absolute. If your parents have no work, take drugs, do not value education as a means of social advancement and supplement their welfare cheques with the proceeds of petty crime, prostitution and burglary the likelihood is that you will do the same.

One of the greatest strengths of *Rosa Lee* is that it bypasses the sterile debate about nature versus nurture that seeks to heap responsibility, in its entirety, either on society or the individual. It also avoids the temptation to play God and apportion either blame or praise on the actors in the melodrama that is Rosa Lee's life.

In many ways these are debates most people in Britain believed would never reach our shores. For a long time the underclass was one of the few American phenomena which British society took pride in not mimicking. As the antithesis of social cohesion, the very notion of an underclass in Britain was an anathema to the post-war consensus that had provided the financial and ideological backing for a comprehensive welfare state.

That consensus started to break down in the eighties. As Margaret Thatcher, former prime minister, notoriously declared in 1987: 'There is no such thing as society. There are individual men and women and there are families.' Thus the safety net that was supposed to catch the poor and dispossessed disintegrated. The emphasis shifted from collective to individual responsibility and those who could not keep up were left behind to fend for themselves.

Like America the swelling ranks of this new class were urban and concentrated in 'problem' council estates with 'problem' schools where crime was rife, hard drugs freely available and social decay endemic. It is there, however, that comparisons with America end. Unlike America, Britain does not have the kind of gun culture that took the life of Rosa Lee's grandson Reco, although the scene outside the Camberwell hospital indicates that we are getting there.

Across the Atlantic the underclass is predominantly black. The legacy of slavery, sharecropping (which was in effect a form of bonded labour) and institutionalised racial discrimination has ensured that a substantial number of African-Americans, like Rosa Lee, remain excluded.

It is easy to forget that until relatively recently – forty-five years ago – huge areas of the most economically developed country in the world was an apartheid state where the very principle of segregation was defended by the Supreme Court. Until twenty years ago in most of the South the economic and political subjugation of blacks was – if not *de jure* then at least *de facto* – a feature of everyday life. It took almost two centuries to make things that bad. While a vibrant African-American middle class has emerged over the past thirty years it is not unreasonable to predict that better times for many are still a long way off.

Conversely the British underclass is mostly white. The first fifty pages of any Dickens novel will provide sufficient evidence to confirm that regardless of the good intentions of policy makers, this is not a new thing. Then they were called the 'undeserving poor' – as opposed to the 'deserving poor' – whose supposed indigence did not qualify them for either Christian charity or human sympathy. But times have changed since the era of the Artful Dodger and many characteristics of the underclass have changed with them.

Nowadays most are the products of the economic restructuring of the eighties that saw the rapid and almost complete demise of many labour-intensive industries like mining, shipbuilding and steel. With nothing to replace them, concentrated pockets of human desolation emerged sometimes on the edges of cities but often as self-contained communities cast out in the hinterland. 'When I was young nearly everyone worked in shipbuilding. Now there's nothing. There nothing else for the kids to do but lounge around. There's no work for the bairns – and no future,' said one mother from the rundown Pennywell estate in Sunderland.

In July 1995, an editorial in the *Daily Telegraph* following the disturbances in housing estates in Luton, the Ely estate in Cardiff and Blackbird Leys in Oxford read: 'A predominantly white underclass is engaging in flagrantly criminal behaviour and resents police attempts to check it.'

A year later the Chief Inspector of Schools, Christopher Woodhead, announced that white boys from working-class families performed worse at school than any other racial group. More of them leave school earlier, with fewer qualifications, than blacks, Asians – or girls of any description. Mr Woodhead referred to 'alienation', 'disadvantage' and 'parenting' as possible causes and asked: 'Do we have a culture among white working-class boys which is deliberately and explicitly anti-educational?'

There are several reasons why Britain's black population escaped the underclass for so long, one of the most compelling being basic arithmetic. The non-white population of Britain is only 5.5 per cent of the total population whereas African-Americans alone make up around 12 per cent of the United States. This scarcely leaves enough black Britons to make up a predominant part of any class.

Moreover, the vast majority of black people who came to Britain came as economic immigrants looking for work in the fifties and sixties that white Britons would not do. It was the promise of work and the hope of a better life (if only for a few years) which brought them across the oceans. While discrimination has always made sure unemployment rates were still higher among blacks than whites the fact remained that they arrived as the working poor – the lowest strata of the working class but working all the same. Nor were they concentrated in the industries most severely hit by the eighties restructuring.

Since the third generation of black Britons are only now making their way through school there has been less opportunity for black communities to be embroiled in the spiral of the underclass basically because there has been less time. Alan Wells, director of the Basic Skills Agency, the government quango charged with improving literacy and numeracy levels, has greater faith in what academic achievement can provide. 'There is a tendency among the white working class to see education as a waste of time. Their attitude is that it doesn't guarantee a job and it doesn't guarantee wealth. Minority communities, however, see it as a way of getting their children on.'

But the underclass is becoming blacker with every passing day. Britain's black population is concentrated in the poorest urban areas. Four of the five boroughs with the highest concentration of African-Caribbeans in the country are in the top ten most deprived districts in the country. African-Caribbean boys are four times as likely to be excluded from school than their white peers. Blacks between the ages of sixteen and twenty-four are twice as likely to be unemployed as whites in the same age group. In London 62 per cent of young black men are unemployed.

As Herman Ouseley, the chairman of the Committee for Racial Equality, notes, 'it seems that if you are black and grow up in certain urban areas of this country the system has decided that you are going to fail.'

Herein lies the true power of *Rosa Lee*. Leon Dash has transformed these statistics into people. Real people who love, hate, laugh and cry. Out there in the socio-political ether they may be part of a class; but in this book they are principally human beings, warts and all. Their weakness in the face of drug addiction and crime frustrates; the sheer resilience that gets them through each day is awe-inspiring. And the tragedy, that provides the backdrop to every passing hour, is as compelling as it is disturbing. Rather than patronising us with solutions Dash has shown how far we have to go before we can truly understand the extent of the problem.

Gary Younge
London, 1997

Prologue

OVERLEAF: *Rosa Lee Cunningham at her apartment window* (© *Lucian Perkins*—The Washington Post).

Rosa Lee Cunningham is thankful that she doesn't have to get up early this morning.

She is dozing, floating back and forth between sleep and drowsiness. Occasionally, she hears the muted conversations of the nurses and doctors puttering about the nurses' station outside her private room, but their muffled murmurs don't keep her from sleeping. She's tired and worn down. She could barely walk when she reached the emergency room four days earlier and wants to take full advantage of her hospital stay. A full night's sleep and daylong quiet are rare luxuries in her life. This is the closest she ever comes to having a vacation.

Rosa Lee welcomes the solitude of Room 13 on the fifth floor of the north wing of Howard University Hospital in Northwest Washington, D.C. It doesn't bother her when the doctors and the nurses periodically wake her to ask her how she is feeling or take her blood pressure. She relishes the attention. Any attention she gets seems to satisfy her. And in between she sleeps. Sleeps for hours.

Her birthday was eleven days ago, but there was no celebration. No gifts. No cards. Nothing from any of her six sons and two daughters, or her thirty-odd grandchildren. She tells everyone that it doesn't matter, but her eyes can't mask her hurt.

There are lots of grandmothers in America who complain of inattention from their children and grandchildren, but Rosa Lee is not your typical senior citizen. In fact, she is not a senior citizen at all. She is fifty-two years old, a longtime heroin addict with a long record of arrests for everything from petty theft to drug trafficking. Her eight children—the eldest of whom she bore at age fourteen—were fathered by six different men, and six of the children have followed her into a life of teenage parenthood, drugs, and crime. By any definition, Rosa Lee is a member of the urban underclass, the segment of the poor population trapped in a cycle of social dysfunction, deprivation, and misery. Though scholars and pundits may argue among themselves about who falls into the underclass, the definition that makes the most sense to me is the one used by the Urban Institute, a Washington, D.C., think tank, which undertook extensive studies to determine that a family belongs to the underclass if, like Rosa Lee's, it is headed by a single female and its members are welfare dependent, marginally educated, chronically unemployed, and engaged in repeated patterns of criminal deviance.

Rosa Lee's life story speaks volumes about why this group on the bottom rung of society is growing rather than shrinking.

Rosa Lee is convalescing in Howard University Hospital not because of any illness that you or I might contract. She is there because her body has been so racked by heroin that it is shutting down. Though she recently enrolled in a drug-treatment program, Rosa Lee has no intention of ending her heroin use. She simply wants the methadone that the program provides. The methadone, a synthetic drug that acts as a substitute for heroin, keeps her from going into withdrawal when she doesn't have enough money to buy the illicit opiate. The methadone is free. A quarter-teaspoon packet of heroin (a "billy") is forty dollars. She can't always raise that amount.

A few days ago, Rosa Lee woke up feeling achy and feverish, and her condition only worsened as the day wore on. Even her morning meth, as she likes to call it, failed to help. By midday, she found herself in the emergency room.

Rosa Lee didn't have long to wait after she registered with the receptionist because the nurses on Howard Hospital's emergency room staff know her. Rosa Lee's medical records show a thirteen-year history of drug abuse; the drugs she has used include heroin, amphetamines, and cocaine.

A blood test revealed that she is still using heroin. The emergency room physician asked Rosa Lee if she ever shared needles with other addicts, and she admitted sharing needles with her two daughters. What she omitted is that she shares needles with two of her sons.

"I didn't want to tell him all that the first evening he met me," she protests when asked why she wasn't completely truthful with the doctor.

She remembers being taken by wheelchair late that night to her fifth-floor room and wearily climbing into the welcoming hospital bed. She dozed off and on for the next three days. Her doctor reduced her daily methadone dose from fifty-five to twenty-five milligrams.

The smaller methadone dosage doesn't hinder Rosa Lee's ability to sleep. She is in a deep sleep Tuesday morning when she hears a familiar baritone voice. At first, the voice sounds far away. Then she recognizes who is talking.

Suddenly, she is fully awake. Today will not be another day of rest. The drug world she lives in has followed her. It is right outside her hospital room door.

She had forgotten last night's telephone call. The lie she had told.

A flash of fear washes over her and settles in her stomach when she hears Darrold's loud voice again. Darrold is at the nurses' station asking for her room. A nurse is telling him that he cannot visit anyone in the hospital at eight o'clock in the morning unless he is on a list of family members. Two other men are with Darrold, and they begin to argue with the nurse. They tell her that they are here to see Mrs. Cunningham because her daughter is in trouble. The nurse responds that whatever the problem is, they still cannot visit Mrs. Cunningham before 11 A.M., the time visiting hours begin. The three men insist on seeing her.

Rosa Lee sits up in bed. Her mind begins to race, searching for a plausible tale to tell Darrold, something that will cover why she doesn't have his $500, the money she told him over the telephone that she was holding for him in the hospital. He is now here to collect money she does not have. Money she never had.

Rosa Lee lied to keep Darrold from beating and possibly killing her thirty-year-old daughter, Patty. Darrold is a street drug dealer who employs addicts to sell heroin and cocaine. The week before, he gave Patty a ten-pack of heroin and a ten-pack of cocaine to sell for him. Normally, after selling both ten-packs, Patty would have paid Darrold $350 for the heroin and $150 for the cocaine. Patty's take would be $100, a profit of fifty dollars from each ten-pack.

But instead of standing on the sidewalk doing the hard and dangerous work of drug dealing, Patty slipped away to her boyfriend's apartment. The pair used up the drugs during a three-day binge.

Rosa Lee knew this when Darrold called her at the hospital last night. Darrold had caught up with Patty in the neighborhood and was holding on to her while he talked to Rosa Lee over the telephone.

"I could hear Patty in the background yelling," recalls Rosa Lee. "She said, 'I told you my mother had your money! You didn't have to track me down!' I had to tell Darrold I had his money. If I didn't, he would have hurt Patty."

Rosa Lee is still searching for something to tell Darrold when she hears a male physician intervene in the argument between Darrold and the nurse, telling him and his two henchmen that they will not be allowed to see Rosa Lee until eleven o'clock. Period.

Muttering to themselves, the three men turn and walk back to the bank of elevators. Rosa Lee is relieved when she hears the heavy, deliberate steps recede down the hallway. She has worked for Darrold selling heroin for several months herself. She knows that within an hour or two Darrold will be preoccupied with the quickening flow of morning drug sales. She is counting on him being too busy to return to the hospital today.

Rosa Lee's knowledge of the street drug trade does not relieve her anxiety about Patty's safety. If the "jugglers," the addicts who sell drugs on the street, learn that Patty ripped off Darrold for $500, he will have to retaliate. If he does not, then the other jugglers working for him will do the same thing. He may order his men to beat Patty unconscious or even kill her. Darrold will want the other jugglers to know he will do the same to them if they run off owing him money.

Rosa Lee is too agitated to go back to sleep. She wishes Patty would call her so she can know that she is all right.

I have met many people like Rosa Lee Cunningham in the course of my thirty-year career at the *Washington Post*. In many ways, her background could not be more different from mine: When Rosa Lee was struggling to take care of her eight children in the early 1960s, I was a teenager attending high school in Manhattan. When she was serving her first prison term for theft in 1966, I was earning a bachelor's degree at Howard University and working for the *Post* as an intern. When she was selling heroin on the streets of Northwest Washington in the mid-1970s, I was writing about the devastating effects of heroin trafficking on some of those same streets.

My interviews with Rosa Lee and her family grew out of a reporting project exploring the creation and growth of the urban underclass. I wanted to take a close-up look at the interrelationships among racism, poverty, illiteracy, drug use, and crime, and why these problems sometimes persist from generation to generation. I first met Rosa Lee in 1988 in the D.C. jail, where she was serving seven months for selling heroin; a jail counselor who was aware of my project had suggested that I talk to her. "She was arrested for selling drugs to feed three of her grandchildren," the counselor told me.

As Rosa Lee answered my initial questions, it was apparent that her life was an intricate tapestry, each thread reflecting issues that have absorbed and frustrated experts on urban poverty for years. Born in Washington on October 7, 1936, the daughter of North Carolina sharecroppers who had migrated to

the city, she grew up poor on the fringes of a Capitol Hill neighborhood. At thirteen, she got pregnant and dropped out of
school without having learned to read. At sixteen, she married to
get away from her mother. Within months, her husband began to
beat her and she moved back to her mother's. Most of the men
she met, including the six who fathered her children, came from
the same poor D.C. neighborhoods where she lived; some of her
pregnancies were the result of a desperate but futile attempt to
hold on to the men.

She raised her children by herself, supporting them as best she
could by waitressing in nightclubs, selling drugs, shoplifting, and
working as a prostitute. Uncertainty and instability became a
fact of everyday life: Since 1950, when her eldest child was born,
Rosa Lee has moved eighteen times, always within the District of
Columbia, twice to shelters for the homeless. Since 1951, when
she was first arrested for stealing, she has gone to jail twelve
times, serving a total of five years for theft or drug convictions.
Now, some of her children were cycling through the D.C. prison
system, repeating patterns set by their mother. On the other
hand, two of them consciously rejected her lifestyle and today
live conventional lives, hold down steady jobs and have never
been involved in drugs or crime.

The more I learned about Rosa Lee and her family, the more
I felt that spending time with her offered a chance to get beyond
the stereotypical notions that seem to dominate discussions
about poverty in America. Some friends and colleagues doubted
that I would learn much that was new. But I had written extensively about the District of Columbia's poorest communities
since the late 1960s and had found that I learned the most by
forgetting what I thought I knew and immersing myself in the
subject as deeply as I could.

Poverty is a phenomenon that has devastated Americans of all
races, in rural and urban communities, but it has disproportion-
ately affected black Americans living in the nation's inner cities.
As someone who grew up in a black middle-class family in
Harlem in New York, I have always been perplexed by the different outcomes for African Americans who migrated in massive

numbers in the first half of this century from fields of rural poverty in the South to cities across America, looking for factory jobs and a better life. How is it, I wondered, that many children and grandchildren from migrant families have prospered against considerable odds while some, like Rosa Lee, have become mired in lives marked by persistent poverty, drug abuse, petty and violent crime, and periodic imprisonment?

All of them carried out of the South the debilitating history of racial oppression, economic exploitation, and segregation. Once in the city, they still faced pervasive racial barriers in employment, housing, and education. Many managed to overcome these roadblocks, while others remained locked in desperate circumstances. Why did Rosa Lee and six of her children take one path, while two children managed to make it into the middle class and working class, never got involved in drugs and never went to jail?

Soon after we met at the jail, Rosa Lee asked me to read aloud a letter she had received recently from an eleven-year-old granddaughter. The letter read:

> *Dear Granny,*
>   *You know that I love you, right? The reason why I said [that] is because I want you to come out of jail. Why can't they just send [you out], put you on trial, or do what they have to do?*
>   *Granny, I love you so much that I will do something bad so that I can come in the Jail with you.*
>   *Granny, it is hard living with [my uncle] and [my aunt] because I almost all the time get in trouble. But don't talk to [my uncles], or nobody else about what I am talking about in none of my letters. I don't want you to talk to [my uncle] or [my aunt] for me no more. I will write why in my next letter.*
>   *Well, I will write to you later. I love you, Granny.*

Not long after our interviews began, I asked Rosa Lee for permission to spend time with her after she left the jail. She was eager to cooperate. She wanted her story told. "I'm not saying I'm going to change," she told me. "But maybe I can help some-body not follow in my footsteps if they read my life story. There have been some good times. Some real good times. But it's also been rough. Lord knows, it's been rough!"

I told her I was skeptical that her story would reach or influ-ence those who might be in danger of following in her footsteps.

"That's all right," she replied. "You never know who you may help. You write it like I tell it."

It's early Monday afternoon and Rosa Lee is getting dressed to leave Howard Hospital. A month has gone by since she entered the hospital's emergency room. She wanted to leave before now, but her doctor insisted that she was too weak. She had had a serious bout with pneumonia, and he wanted to be sure it was completely cleared up before he released her.

Thanksgiving is four days away. The holiday is not on Rosa Lee's mind, though; she's still worried about Patty. All this time she's been anxious about Patty's safety. Darrold did not return to the hospital, which is just as well. Rosa Lee doesn't have his $500.

Her youngest son, Ducky, has brought her daily reports about Patty. He's heard she's moving from apartment to apartment, but he hasn't seen her. Patty hasn't called, so Ducky's reports are the only thing that have given Rosa Lee a small amount of peace. Ducky is living in Malcolm X Park, down the street from the homeless shelter where Rosa Lee and a five-year-old grand-daughter had been staying. Every day Ducky came around the 11 A.M. start of visiting hours and begged her for some of her lunch. He stayed until the evening and begged her for some of her din-ner.

She's grateful that Ducky's lengthy stays in the hospital room are over now. She wishes Ducky would get a job and stop rely-ing on her to feed and look after him. She doesn't understand how a twenty-eight-year-old man can expect her to provide him with food. Every day?

"It doesn't make sense," says Rosa Lee to anyone who will listen. She repeats this one expression several times a day when referring to the behavior of her six drug-addicted children. "How can these grown-ass children rely on me all the time? I'm their mother, yes. But I'm not raising them anymore. They're grown!"

A churchgoing family friend with a car picks up Rosa Lee to drive her over to the homeless shelter. On their way there, Rosa Lee spots Darrold at the intersection of 14th and W Streets, N.W., in the heart of Washington's drug corridor. She lets herself out of the car, telling the churchgoing lady that she has a personal matter to look after. The friend has known Rosa Lee for sixteen years. She drives off without a word or a backward glance. She knows the personal matter is related to the clusters of drug dealers, addicts, and jugglers standing on all four corners of the intersection.

Rosa Lee walks directly over to the northwest corner, where Darrold is standing. He doesn't see her coming. He is intently watching a juggler on the northeast corner. The addict is working for him. Darrold does not want him to slip away as Patty had.

Rosa Lee steps in front of him. Darrold smiles. Over her shoulder, he keeps his eyes on the juggler across the street while he talks to her. He doesn't have a "beef" with Rosa Lee, known in the 14th Street drug culture as "Mama Rose." His beef is with her daughter. When he catches Patty, he intends to have her severely beaten. Immediately after the beating, he'll force Patty to work right in this intersection until she pays off the debt. Something Mama Rose says changes his plans.

"I know Patty still owes you for the dope and 'caine," she says. "I don't want you to hurt her, so I'll work it off right now."

Darrold gives Rosa Lee a ten-pack of heroin. Each billy is tightly wrapped in clear plastic wrap. Ten billies are held together with a rubber band.

Rosa Lee finds it easy to carry a ten-pack in her bra as she walks around from corner to corner in the intersection. She has done this many times. First, clockwise. Then, counterclockwise. As she walks among the clusters of jugglers and customers, she shouts the street brand name of Darrold's heroin, "MASERATI! MASERATI!" Each dealer gives his heroin a name to distinguish it from other dealers' heroin. Other jugglers are shouting "RATTLE-SNAKE! RATTLESNAKE!" or "747! 747!" or "EYE ROCK! EYE ROCK!"

Maserati, named after the Italian racing and luxury car, is selling well today at forty dollars a billy. On the average, Rosa Lee can "flip," or sell, a ten-pack of heroin in twenty minutes. This afternoon the Maserati is moving faster. Addicts whose faces she knows are coming up to her. They want to know where she's been and exchange small talk. She tells them she's been in the hospital and she doesn't have any time for talk.

"Do you want some dope?" she asks, getting quickly to the point. "No discounts today. Forty dollars or nothing. You got the money? Good. Here."

The money and the heroin change hands so fast that the uninitiated would barely believe that a transaction has taken place.

Mama Rose has never been known for selling "bad" dope, heroin so weak it would not even get a novice drug user high. Her heroin continues selling at a fast pace. At the rate she moves Darrold's heroin, she knows she will not have to be out on the street all night.

She does not keep the five dollars she would normally earn from each billy, but turns all the money over to Darrold. He gives her another ten-pack.

Now, if only the "jumpouts" don't catch me, she thinks, I can pay off Patty's debt and make me some money. The jumpouts are plainclothes narcotics officers, especially those who screech to a halt at an intersection in an unmarked car, jump out, and arrest as many street dealers with drugs on their person as they can find. That was how they busted Rosa Lee a year ago. They found four billies in her bra.

By 8 P.M., Darrold tells her to start taking out her share. Shortly before 10 P.M., Darrold tells her she has "squared" Patty's debt. Rosa Lee stops to count her money. She's made seventy dollars. She decides that's enough. She's going to pick up her granddaughter at the churchgoing lady's apartment and go to her room in the shelter.

Her young granddaughter, whom she hasn't seen since entering the hospital a month ago, greets her with a scream of joy and hugs her around her legs. Together, they walk the two blocks west to the shelter. In their room, the granddaughter begins to chatter, trying to bring Rosa Lee up to date on the events she has missed. Rosa Lee stops her.

"Grandma is very tired," she tells the irrepressible little girl. "It'll have to wait 'til morning."

As Rosa Lee drifts off to sleep, the last things she remembers seeing are the clock—it is 11 P.M.—and the back of her five-year-old granddaughter, who is sitting at the foot of the bed watching a late-night television movie.

One Crisis After Another

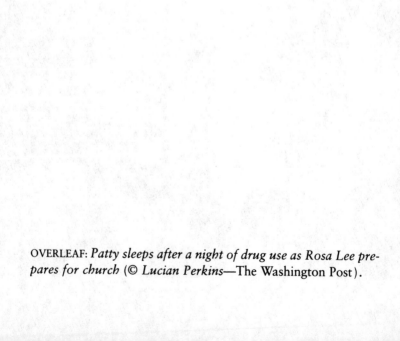

OVERLEAF: *Patty sleeps after a night of drug use as Rosa Lee prepares for church* (© *Lucian Perkins*—The Washington Post).

If ROSA LEE is bothered by the crowded, chaotic scene in her apartment on the morning of September 5, 1990, she doesn't show it. Most mornings she doesn't have time to worry about her "grown-ass" children and their daily bickering over money and drugs.

Even if she wants to stay in bed, she can't. Stomach pains awaken her early every morning, as they do many heroin addicts. The cramps begin at 6:30 and linger until she can get to the city drug-treatment clinic for her 55-milligram dose of methadone.

She doesn't mind getting up early. It gives her a little extra time to make herself look nice. She has "collected" a considerable wardrobe. She favors bold earrings, necklaces with gold crosses, and colorful paste-on fingernails that she chooses to match the stylish pantsuits she likes to wear. Long before I knock on the brown metal door of her two-bedroom apartment, part of a low-income housing complex near Washington's southeastern border with Maryland, she is dressed and ready for our first major interview since she was released from prison.

There are so many people living with Rosa Lee that I never know who might answer the door; this time it is thirty-nine-year-old Bobby, the eldest of Rosa Lee's eight children.

He leads me to the living room, his home for the past few months. It is 9 A.M. and the day is bright and sunny, but the shades are drawn, leaving the room in shadows. Ducky, thirty, exhausted from a night of cleaning ovens at a Kentucky Fried Chicken outlet followed by several hours of smoking crack, is asleep on one of the two sofas. Patty, thirty-two, emerges from the bedroom she shares with Rosa Lee and her seventeen-year-old son, Junior. I ask Patty why she looks so grumpy, but she just grunts and says she doesn't feel like being cheerful. Her son is still asleep on the floor in the same bedroom. He's been living at Rosa Lee's for several months, ever since his release from a group home for juvenile delinquents in Pittsburgh.

Rosa Lee's other daughter, twenty-nine, occupies the second bedroom along with her three children, aged seven, eleven, and thirteen. She's just completed eleven months in the D.C. jail for cocaine possession. She is trying to overcome her drug addiction and find a job; later, when she succeeds, she asks that I not identify her.

That nine people from three generations can get along in such cramped conditions is a tribute to Rosa Lee and her housekeeping skills. She's a compulsive cleaner, often jumping up during conversations to snatch a dirty dish, straighten the plastic Disney figurines that she keeps on the glass table in her living room, or wipe a dustless spot.

Rosa Lee is a safety net for most of her children. Bobby, Ronnie, Richard, Patty, and Ducky live a kind of nomadic existence, bouncing from friends' apartments to jail, to the street, to Rosa Lee's. All five are addicted to heroin or cocaine, or abuse both drugs. On this particular day, Ronnie, thirty-eight, is staying with one of Rosa Lee's younger brothers; Richard, thirty-six, is in jail on a parole violation.

Rosa Lee's two other sons, Alvin, thirty-seven, and Eric, thirty-four, don't need her safety net. They have jobs, families, and homes of their own. They are the only two of the eight who don't have prison records. They don't use or peddle drugs, and they despise what drugs have done to their mother and their siblings. "I'm tired of you living off Mama," Alvin often yells at Patty and Ducky. "I'm sick and tired of you worrying Mama about money and drugs."

Alvin always comes through for Rosa Lee, but he does so reluctantly, knowing that he is indirectly supporting the drug abuse of his addicted siblings. Eric does not give money, but he provides shelter when needed for Rosa Lee and some of her grandchildren when one of his siblings has gone to jail. One recent day, Alvin threatened to clear Patty and Ducky out of the apartment with a baseball bat. His threat stopped the pair from bothering Rosa Lee for money for two days.

As our relationship begins in earnest, Rosa Lee insists on calling me Mr. Dash, although I ask her to call me Leon. I ask if I can call her Rose and she says she prefers that I do so. All of her children follow her lead in calling me Mr. Dash, even though I ask them to call me by my first name. They tell me that whenever Rosa Lee speaks of me, she says "Mr. Dash," and they have become accustomed to calling me that. I address all of them by their first names.

Rosa Lee readily invites and accepts my daily involvement in her life, but at the outset of the project her children find my presence in their underworld lives a strange and awkward intrusion. The five drug-using children are especially wary, being unaccustomed to sharing with any outsider their personal histories and daily behavior. Their first response was to see me as a potential financial resource for their drug use. Patty even propositioned me in an unsuccessful effort to get five dollars.

I lay down ground rules: I will buy them meals and even cigarettes, but I will make the purchases. I explain I will never give or lend any of them any amount of cash. I know from past experience that drug users go to considerable lengths to collect small amounts of money from many people until they gather enough to buy drugs. The drug users among Rosa Lee's children boast to her that they will eventually get some money out of me. They are sorely disappointed. They try all sorts of subterfuges and invent emergencies to get me to break my rules, to get me to give them any amount of cash—even as little as two dollars for bus fare. Eventually, they drop their attempts, realizing I will not give them as much as a penny.

Rosa Lee and I are sitting on the second sofa in her living room, trying to decide what to do. Bobby has left us alone to talk, Patty has gone back to her bedroom, and Ducky is still asleep on the other sofa. I had planned to take Rosa Lee to the methadone clinic and then to a restaurant so I can interview her for several hours in relative quiet. Rosa Lee has other ideas.

She wants to go to the office of Pepco, the electric company, so she can talk to someone about restoring the electricity; it's been off for four months because Rosa Lee has fallen behind in her payments. Patty has been cooking meals on a neighbor's stove, and she's tired of bringing food back and forth. And now that summer's almost over, it will be getting dark earlier, and they will need the lights again.

Rosa Lee pulls from her purse a set of tattered, rolled-up papers, slips off the rubber band and leafs through them. They are her most important papers—her apartment lease, medical records, Medicaid documents, and bills and letters of all sorts. Rosa Lee hands me the pile. She wants me to figure out just what is owed on her electricity bill and what is the minimum she must pay to have the electricity turned back on.

Outside the Pepco building on Martin Luther King, Jr. Avenue, S.E., Rosa Lee is eager for me to come into the office with her. My suit and tie, she believes, might give her greater authority with the bureaucracy. I tell her that I'm a reporter and can't get involved in her affairs. But I see from her puzzled expression that she doesn't understand what I'm talking about.

I separate her electricity bills from the other papers. Rosa Lee returns the sheaf of papers to her large pocketbook while holding on tight to the electricity bills.

It's hard to imagine Rosa Lee having trouble getting someone's attention if she wants to. Her face is long and handsome, and she has learned how to smile or cry whenever it's necessary. Her hips are broader than they once were, but her 145 pounds settle easily on her 5-foot–1-inch frame, and she likes to boast that her narrow waist still turns men's heads. Her hands are firm and strong, the result of washing countless baskets of laundry on a scrub board when she was a child.

I wait in my car while she goes inside. Half an hour later, she comes out with a Pepco bill counselor. The counselor explains that she had finished with Mrs. Cunningham twenty minutes ago, but that Rosa Lee was confused and went back into the customer waiting room. Noticing that Rosa Lee hadn't left, the counselor reminded her that she had said a Mr. Dash was waiting outside for her. Rosa Lee told the woman she did not know why she had returned to the waiting room and she had forgotten I was waiting.

Rosa Lee's short-term memory seems to have deteriorated severely, I note silently, wondering why.

The somewhat exasperated counselor tells me that Rosa Lee doesn't understand her bill. She explains the situation: Rosa Lee owed $528 when the electricity was cut off. She had applied for emergency aid, so the D.C. Emergency Energy Office had paid $150 and the D.C. Department of Human Services had paid $238, but Rosa Lee had to pay half of the remaining $140 to get the electricity restored.

Rosa Lee says she doesn't have seventy dollars. We drive downtown to the energy office, but an official there says Rosa Lee isn't eligible for another emergency grant until January.

It's minutes after noon now and the methadone clinic is closed until 1 P.M. Over lunch in nearby Chinatown, another crisis emerges. Rosa Lee needs to renew the prescription for medication she's been taking and she can't find her Medicaid identification card, which allows her to pay fifty cents per prescription. As we discuss the lost card, I realize that Rosa Lee has not complained about having stomach cramps although she missed her morning methadone dose. That could only mean that she used heroin this morning. It also strikes me that she received her welfare check on either Friday, August 31, or Saturday, September 1. Now it's September 5, and she is broke. She must be spending money on drugs; perhaps she is even supporting Bobby's and Patty's drug habits since neither of them is working.

Suddenly, she begins to cry. Distracted, I decide not to ask about her drug use right now.

Through her tears, she tells me that she has the AIDS virus, that she is HIV positive. So are Patty and Bobby. Rosa Lee says she found out about her own status about two years earlier, Patty and Bobby a little more recently. So far, none of them has full-blown AIDS. Perhaps her infection is the cause of her short-term memory loss.

 · She doesn't know for certain how they got the virus. But they fit the profile of those most at risk for HIV: All three have shared needles with one another and with other addicts while injecting heroin. And all three have engaged in prostitution.

I ask why she didn't tell me she was HIV positive when she found out.

"I was afraid to tell you," she says. "Because I felt you wouldn't come around me."

No, I assure her, I have no intention of staying away. She seems relieved. She stops crying, wipes away the tears and begins eating her shrimp fried rice, her favorite Chinese dish.

On our way to the methadone clinic after lunch, several questions come to mind: Are Patty and Bobby still prostituting themselves? Are they taking precautions with their sex partners? If Rosa Lee is using heroin again, is she supporting their drug habits as well as her own? Rosa Lee is talking fast. She is so wound up, so emotional, that I again postpone asking her.

After Rosa Lee drinks her methadone at the clinic, we drive to Howard Hospital, where Rosa Lee hopes to see Dr. Winston Frederick, the internist who is treating her HIV condition. She doesn't have a telephone at home and whenever she tries to reach him from a pay telephone, the secretary puts her on hold. I wait outside while she goes into the hospital. Forty-five minutes later, Rosa Lee returns to the car with six prescriptions.

"I try to get as much medicine as I can so I can share the AIDS medicine with Patty," Rosa Lee explains. "She needs to get registered with welfare again so she can get her Medicaid card and get her own medicine, Mr. Dash. I'm tired of doing this."

Patty's welfare and Medicaid eligibility lapsed in 1983, when Junior was taken away from her by Washington's family court. Ever since, Patty has lived through prostitution, in jail, or off Rosa Lee.

We drive to a pharmacy where the pharmacist knows Rosa Lee and has a record of her Medicaid card. He agrees to fill Rosa Lee's prescription for AZT, a medication that sometimes delays the onset of AIDS. A monthly supply of 100 pills costs $147.95, so she could not possibly afford them without Medicaid.

When we finally return to Rosa Lee's apartment, she asks me to look through her papers to see if she is behind in her rent. In the past, when she was a young woman and lived in public housing, her rent payment was taken out of her welfare check before she received it, she explains. She doesn't know if the same is being done for this apartment and suspects that either she is paying double the monthly amount or her $350 monthly welfare stipend should be larger. I realize that she is drawing me into her survival network, but I offer to take the thick sheaf of papers home and sort them.

On my way home, I feel anxious and exhausted. Rosa Lee's daily life consists of one crisis after another. And this is just the first day of what will occupy me for many days to come.

She never seems to have a clear grasp of where she stands with any of her bills. Those of her children who live with her don't seem to know how to cope with life outside of prison either, and they could not care less about practical matters. Rosa Lee says none of them will lift a finger to try to get the electricity turned back on, to find out what the situation is with their rent, or buy any food for the household. They are all adults, yet they expect her to do everything. Patty even assumes Rosa Lee will get enough AZT for the two of them to share.

Yet three of the four children living with her expend enormous amounts of time and energy every day doing anything that comes to mind to get the money to buy cocaine and heroin. It is clear that Rosa Lee and most of her children have significant survival skills for life within the criminal and drug underworld. It is just as clear they do not have the basic skills to live in the conventional, bill-paying world.

Rosa Lee says her short-term memory loss is a recent development, something her children began pointing out to her a couple of months ago. She doesn't understand why it is happening, but it frightens her. She wonders if it is tied to her HIV infection, the stress of her daily life, or the methadone she's taking. She's asked the nurses at the methadone clinic and Dr. Frederick at Howard Hospital. They've told her they don't know, an answer that only increases her fears.

The next night, I return Rosa Lee's papers, divided into over-sized envelopes with bold, printed capital letters to help Rosa Lee recognize the words: WELFARE, MEDICAL, RENT, PATTY, BIRTH CERTIFICATES, and so on.

"I can't tell from your rent receipts whether there is a rent payment taken out of your welfare check," I explain to Rosa Lee. "You'll have to call the welfare office to find out if that is done. Otherwise, it looks like your rent is paid up. There's no problem there."

Patty, Rosa Lee, and I sit on the bed in Rosa Lee's bedroom. A crucifix is on a table next to her bed; often, when Rosa Lee is upset, she holds the crucifix close to her chest as she prays for relief or forgiveness.

Patty points to an envelope marked RICHARD. "What does that say?"

"Don't you know your own brother's name?" Rosa Lee says in disbelief.

Patty shrugs. Her reading skills, it turns out, are worse than Rosa Lee's.

They decide to draw up a plan to straighten out their tangled finances, and they ask me to write it down. Patty promises to reapply for welfare benefits. Rosa Lee's situation is more compli-cated. She has been receiving $350 a month in welfare and $280 a month in food stamps for herself and two of her grandchildren; now that her youngest daughter is out of jail, off drugs, and car-ing for her own children, Rosa Lee will lose some of that income. So she's going to find out if she is eligible for other assistance.

Their plan sounds good, but it's impossible to ignore this fact: Welfare payments and food stamps don't begin to account for all the money that comes and goes in the apartment.

Rosa Lee and I review her own and Patty's Medicaid status. Listening, Patty becomes aware that I know she is HIV positive.

"I didn't want him to know, Mama," she tells Rosa Lee angrily.

Rosa Lee stares at Patty, embarrassed that she's let out Patty's secret.

"It's all right, Patty," I say, trying to smooth out the moment. "I will not shun you or avoid you. Your mother has already told me other people are doing that. I will not."

Relieved, Patty smiles and says it's OK, then, that I know.

Bobby comes into the bedroom several minutes later. He's dressed in tan slacks and a dark brown sports jacket. I tease him about how well dressed he is for a man who does not have a job. He bets me that he'll find a cooking job by Monday or Tuesday of next week.

With his mother listening, Bobby tells me that when Rosa Lee woke up this morning she asked him why the electricity was not on. He reminded her that the electricity had been off for months. "Mama's memory has been going for months," Bobby continues. "What do you think causes that?"

I tell him I don't know, sounding calmer than I feel.

After Bobby leaves, we turn back to reviewing the paperwork Rosa Lee and Patty will take to the welfare office the next day.

"Don't forget to call your lawyer, Mama," Patty says.

"What lawyer?" I ask.

Now it is Rosa Lee's turn to glare at Patty. "Don't you think I can tell him about that when I'M ready to tell him, Patty?" she shouts at her daughter.

"Well, you'll have to tell him now." Patty laughs.

In August, Rosa Lee and Bobby went into the Hecht's department store in downtown Washington to shoplift bedsheets. Bobby was acting as lookout, but Rosa Lee was caught anyway. She pleaded guilty to larceny on August 29. In today's mail, she received a letter from her court-appointed lawyer, Elmer D. Ellis, telling her that sentencing is set for November. Bobby read the letter to her.

"We had a customer for the sheets, Mr. Dash," explains Rosa Lee. "I needed some money to put food in the house and Bobby needed some money for some dope."

Patty gives a cynical laugh.

Rosa Lee cuts her eyes at Patty. "Well, I might as well tell you. We all needed some money for some dope."

"Mr. Dash," Rosa Lee says one day in early October. "Why is it I can't find a place with no drugs?"

She is standing in her living room, her hands spread in a gesture of frustration and resignation, her voice competing with the sound of an afternoon soap opera on television.

"I don't know why you ask me a question like that, Rose," I respond. "Poor people sell drugs to make money, and as long as you're living in public or low-rent housing there will be people around you selling drugs. You told me that."

Rosa Lee shakes her head, acknowledging that she knew the answer before she asked the question. "I know, I know," she says. "I just hope one day I can find a place to live where they don't sell drugs."

Within a week of moving into this newly renovated apartment in the Washington Highlands neighborhood six months earlier, Rosa Lee ran into several drug dealers she had known for years. As broken ties were renewed and new relationships were formed, heroin and cocaine began to flow into the apartment, just as they had flowed into her previous apartment and into innumerable other apartments for years before that.

In recent months, she tells me, she has cut back her drug use to just an occasional speedball, or mixture of heroin and cocaine, which she lets Patty inject under the skin on the back of her hand. "The dope I don't need," she says. "It's the 'caine. The 'caine gives you a rush. It stays with you a little while, and it makes you want more. You want that rush again. If I go get a ten-dollar bag of 'caine and shoot it all by itself, ZOOM!"

She says these infrequent lapses don't make her an addict, but I don't think she's being candid with herself. Her eyelids have begun to droop noticeably during our conversations and she constantly rubs the back of her swollen hands. When I ask her about these symptoms, she insists she hasn't gone back to full-time drug use.

On this morning, Rosa Lee begins crying about Patty. Dr. Frederick has told her he cannot continue to double her medication so she can share it with Patty. Patty will have to register with the welfare office and get a Medicaid card so she can get her own AZT, something she has still not done despite the plans I discussed with her and Rosa Lee.

"But she won't go to the welfare to get nothing," cries Rosa Lee. "See how it gets me upset now. She knows she's worrying me."

Rosa Lee had previously told me that before the electricity was restored in late September, Patty had been using sex to pay for the privilege of cooking on the neighbor's stove. Around the first of every month, when he receives his Social Security disability check, the same neighbor sometimes pays Patty cash for their sexual liaisons, money that Patty uses to buy drugs.

I ask Rosa Lee how many men Patty is prostituting herself with.

"Oh, my God," she says. When Patty wants a "rock" of crack, "she goes out and gets one of them little, young boys. One of them boys that has money from selling crack. If they don't use a condom, it's OK with Patty. She just don't care. I tried so hard to love my children and make them right. Patty is the only one that gives me so much trouble."

Rosa Lee's shoulders shake and she begins to wail, her bottom lip trembling. "She done told everyone round here that she has the virus. The AIDS virus. When Patty gets drunk, she just runs off at the mouth. 'Well, I'm not worried about you hurting me 'cause I got the virus. I got the AIDS virus.' Like it ain't nothing. I tell her to shut up. Stop telling everybody her business. She don't pay me no mind at all. Patty, she's so embarrassing."

About a year earlier, Patty's "business" had landed Bobby in the hospital. Early one winter morning, Patty stood out in the courtyard drinking Scotch whiskey from a cup. She had found the bottle of Scotch in Rosa Lee's apartment and was drinking because she did not have money to buy crack. Rosa Lee was getting dressed "to go get my meth," and Bobby joined Patty in the courtyard.

Patty began hounding the three or four teenage crack dealers who were in the courtyard for crack on credit. All of them refused. She continued to beg and drink, getting progressively drunker. One of the boys told Bobby, "You better get your sister. She's meddlin' in our business." Bobby spoke to Patty, but she wouldn't leave.

She offered one of the dealers sex in exchange for crack. He turned her down. She persisted.

Patty was still offering the teenager sex for crack when the lieutenant for the drug dealer the boys worked for showed up. The lieutenant, a man in his mid-twenties, complained to the teenagers that they were not moving the crack fast enough, and said they would have to work harder. He noticed Patty's begging and suggested that if she was not buying anything she should "move along." Patty refused.

Rosa Lee was coming out of the building, on her way to the methadone clinic, when she heard a very drunk Patty cursing the lieutenant, calling him "a tired motherfucker." When Rosa Lee stepped into the courtyard, the lieutenant was trying to get to Patty, but Bobby had jumped in front of his sister. One of the teenagers swung at Patty with a large stick.

"Patty ducked and Bobby caught it right here," recalled Rosa Lee, indicating the front of Bobby's mouth with the palm of her right hand. "Bobby fell. The boy hit Bobby again." The lieutenant and all the dealers, except one, ran.

The teenager who stayed told Rosa Lee, "Miss Cunningham, I'm sorry, but I think your son is dead."

Bobby was not dead, but his jaw was broken in three places. He was taken to D.C. General Hospital, Washington's hospital for the indigent, where it was discovered he was an Army veteran. They transferred him to the Veterans Administration hospital. At the veterans hospital, they pulled out all of his teeth and wired up his jaw. Several days after Bobby was admitted, a doctor informed him that he was HIV positive.

The first time I met Bobby was in 1988, when he was in prison, serving a thirty- to ninety-month sentence for the street sale of heroin. He was in the Central Facility prison, the largest of Washington's seven-prison complex at Lorton, Virginia.

Bobby expressed mild shock when we shook hands in the conference room of the prison's administration building. In the fifteen years Bobby had been revolving through Washington and federal prisons, he had only once received a visitor: his younger brother Ronnie visited him at the D.C. jail in 1973.

"You came to see me?" asked Bobby, his mouth hanging open. "You know my mom? When they called me out of the dorm, I started not to come. I just knew that they had the wrong Cunningham. I didn't think I'd ever have someone come see me in here."

Bobby spoke in a singsong voice. His complexion was light brown, something he inherited from his father, "who was almost white." He was a slim man with a small frame, large horn-rimmed glasses dominating his round face. There were dark circles under his eyes, and his skin had a sickly cast.

The conference room was hot and stuffy, the building's heat up high to stave off the chill of a rainy April morning. He kept a hooded jacket on over his blue jumpsuit in spite of the heat. He continually pulled the hood forward to cover his head and sat hunched over the table to keep the hood from falling back. After an hour of this, I asked him whether he wouldn't be more comfortable if he took off the jacket. He looked up at me and then swept the hood back. His wavy hair was done in a woman's style. He pulled the jacket off over his head. The effort to hide his hairstyle now behind him, Bobby sighed and sat up in the chair.

When I had told Rosa Lee that I was going to see Bobby, she said, "You'll find he's different from the rest of my sons. I think I put too much housework on him when he was a boy." Now her enigmatic remark came back to me.

Bobby had been Rosa Lee's "little man" as far back as he could remember. By the time he was eight, Rosa Lee had turned over to him the task of raising her younger children. Under the tutelage of an older boy and later the adult heroin addict who fathered Ronnie, burglary became an adolescent passion for

Bobby. At age twenty, he started smoking opium and the following year began the intravenous use of heroin. His first adult
arrest was for stealing a car.

"We were kind of late starting school because, you know, it
was a large family," responded Bobby to a question about the
marginal educational achievement of most of his brothers and
sisters. "Then again, Mom wasn't too bright on getting us
started. She didn't have enough education to help us with our
homework. Then again, she did not emphasize homework or
anything like that when we were coming up."

As a child, Bobby noticed that his uncles often came to see his
mother on the day the welfare check was delivered. "We didn't
have much money but when my mother got her welfare check
everybody was hugs and smiles. My uncles were always begging
her with sympathetic and loving eyes and mouths. She loaned
them money. That's the only way she could buy their love."

None of the fathers of Rosa Lee's eight children made anything like regular financial contributions to the family, so Bobby
took on the role of provider. It is common for the eldest boys in
similar families to play this role. Sometimes the mothers know
what their sons are doing to bring additional money into the
household. Sometimes the mothers do not know and do not ask.
Rosa Lee clearly knew that Bobby was burglarizing homes,
stores, schools, and churches when he was as young as thirteen.

Rosa Lee acted as the fence, or salesperson, for the musical
instruments Bobby and three of his friends stole from a music
shop in one of his first successful burglaries. She split the profits
from the sale of the instruments with Bobby and his three
friends, and kept some for herself. Thereafter, Bobby turned over
some of whatever money he made from his burglaries to Rosa
Lee.

"I always shared what I made with Mom." He smiled. "That
was most of the reason for doing it. So we could all have food to
eat. She was taking care of eight of us by herself and the welfare
money never was enough. We were always out of food the last
week of every month as far back as I can remember."

Our conversation drifted to his youngest niece, the five-year-old daughter of his youngest sister. I told Bobby that nine months earlier, when his niece was four, she was living in the apartment of her father's girlfriend. When Rosa Lee went there the night after her latest release from jail and knocked on the door, no one answered. She later found her granddaughter's father and his girlfriend in a nearby cocaine den smoking crack. The woman went back to her apartment with Rosa Lee and let her in.

The apartment was dark. Rosa Lee found the child curled up in bed with a two-year-old boy, the woman's son. Rosa Lee called her granddaughter's name. The child jumped out of the bed and ran to Rosa Lee. There was a stocking cap on the girl's head, and Rosa Lee yanked it off. Underneath, the child's head was a mass of scabs and matted hair.

Rosa Lee took the girl with her. She washed her hair, but that did nothing to relieve the infection. The next morning she called Alvin, who took the child to a doctor. The doctor and a nurse had to tie the child to a chair while they cut off her hair and then scrubbed her scalp.

"It was very painful," I told Bobby. "You hadn't heard any of that? No one had been looking after her but crack addicts. You hadn't heard any of that?"

"No," Bobby answered, hanging his head. Heavy tears rolled down both cheeks and dripped into a puddle on the conference table's shiny waxed top. "My little nieces and nephews out there going through changes. You really know how to come in here and change my day, don't you?"

"I'm sorry," I replied. "It's not a pleasant story. I'm sorry."

"I'm going to be up all night," he said.

It is a Wednesday afternoon in late November, and Rosa Lee is stretched out on a bed in the emergency room at Howard University Hospital, telling me about the seizure that has landed her there. Actually, she's not telling me much, because she blacked out and she can't remember exactly what happened.

The room is cool, and she has pulled the blankets up to her chest, exposing only the shoulders of her white hospital gown and her drawn, tired face. She looks awful.

This is her second seizure in two days, her third in two months. The doctors don't know the cause of the seizures, so they have been putting Rosa Lee through a series of tests, which don't bother her nearly as much as the telephone calls from Patty and Ducky to settle minor squabbles over food and who can sleep in Rosa Lee's bed. "Why are they worrying me, Mr. Dash, while I'm in the hospital?" she asks.

The doctors suspect that Rosa Lee's drug use has something to do with triggering the seizures. On Monday afternoon, Rosa Lee and Patty shared a billy of heroin. Immediately afterward, she had a mild seizure that sent her to the emergency room but didn't require a hospital stay. Still, I thought she seemed shaken enough by the experience to stay away from heroin for a while.

Not shaken enough.

On Tuesday afternoon, she and Patty bought another heroin billy at an "oil joint," an apartment where heroin users can gather in privacy and relative safety when using the drug. Patty gave herself a hit, then Rosa Lee. As they went outside to hail a taxi, Rosa Lee suddenly went limp and her eyes rolled back in her head.

Patty struggled to keep Rosa Lee from falling and heard a man shout from across the street. It was Alvin. Her brother was on duty, driving a Metrobus north on Georgia Avenue, when he saw Patty trying to hold Rosa Lee. "Get Mama to the hospital," he yelled from the window of the packed bus.

Patty, still high from the heroin, maneuvered Rosa Lee into a taxi. At Howard Hospital, Dr. Frederick was furious. "If you suffer another one of these seizures, we may not be able to bring you back," Rosa Lee remembers him saying.

When she goes home on December 10, she vows to herself that her heroin days are over. But home is still the same apartment where Bobby, Patty, and Ducky spend much of their time in pursuit of their next high.

While in the hospital, Rosa Lee learned that her seizures were the source of her short-term memory loss. A young doctor told her she probably had suffered several mild seizures before the major occurrences.

Rosa Lee is still weak after her release from the hospital, so I follow a routine of picking her up every morning and driving her to the methadone clinic. As we often do, we have breakfast at the nearby McDonald's.

While we're eating one morning, Rosa Lee suddenly volunteers that she used her five-year-old granddaughter to ferry heroin through a street drug market when the little girl was in her care in the summer of 1988, a year after rescuing the child from the darkened apartment of her father's girlfriend.

Up to this point, I thought I understood Rosa Lee pretty well, but I see I clearly don't. "Why did you do that?" I ask, holding myself tight to keep the anger and judgment I am feeling out of my voice.

"Well, I figured if the jumpouts came they wouldn't search her," says Rosa Lee. "They'd search me, but they wouldn't find nothing."

Rosa Lee kept the billies of heroin hidden in an alley. She would accept cash from a customer. Then, on a signal from Rosa Lee, the granddaughter would stop playing on the sidewalk, go into the alley, retrieve a billy, and hand it over to the customer.

"I told her she had to help Grandma so we both could eat," Rosa Lee says.

Without any instructions from Rosa Lee, the granddaughter periodically moved the hiding place of the heroin. Rosa Lee asked her why. The child explained that she figured others were watching her go to the same spot in the alley. They might try to steal the drugs when she and Rosa Lee were not looking.

"She's smart, isn't she, Mr. Dash?" Rosa Lee smiles.

"Yes, she is," I acknowledge.

There it is. Rosa Lee has introduced her granddaughter to the drug trade as a way to earn enough money to eat.

"Boy, what a night," Rosa Lee says, settling into the front seat of my car. Eleven days have passed since she told me about using the granddaughter's help in her drug sales. It's Christmas morning.

Recovering drug addicts don't get holidays off. If Rosa Lee wants her daily dose of methadone, she still has to make the crosstown trek from her apartment in Southeast Washington to the clinic in Northeast, a distance of five miles. On the best of days, it's a thirty-minute trip requiring two buses; the holiday bus schedule makes it an uncertain journey that can last more than an hour.

When I arrive at 8:30, Rosa Lee is ready as usual, but everyone else is asleep, including her grandchildren. Unopened gifts lie waiting under an artificial tree decorated with yellow plastic garlands, candy canes and colored glass bulbs. Patty is stretched out on a living-room couch, her left forearm bandaged in white gauze.

As we drive through the deserted streets, Rosa Lee explains why everyone's exhausted.

It all started with Ducky's paycheck. Late on Christmas Eve afternoon, Ducky brought home $270 from his job at Kentucky Fried Chicken, gave $150 to Rosa Lee for his share of the rent, food, cable TV, and utilities, and left to buy crack with the rest of the money.

Ducky owed Patty twenty dollars, and Rosa Lee gave her the money, setting off a chain reaction that lasted all night long. Patty spent the twenty on crack, smoked it and wanted more. She begged Rosa Lee for another twenty dollars. "I just gave her ten dollars," Rosa Lee says.

As soon as the ten dollars were gone, Patty was pleading for more. Instead of saying no, Rosa Lee asked Patty to buy her some ice cream and handed over another twenty dollars. A few hours later, Patty returned with one of her regular tricks—men who trade drugs or money for sex. The man prepared a mix of powdered cocaine in Rosa Lee's bedroom, gave himself a hit and offered some to Rosa Lee. She said no. "I didn't even hesitate, Mr. Dash," she says. "I was so proud of myself."

Patty left and Rosa Lee fell asleep with the TV set on. About 2 A.M., she heard someone banging on the door. It was Patty's latest boyfriend, Howard, demanding to know where Patty was. Rosa Lee didn't know.

At 6 A.M., Ducky woke Rosa Lee to say that Howard and Patty were fighting in the hallway. Ducky pulled Patty, strung out from smoking crack and drinking liquor, into Rosa Lee's apartment. Patty's left forearm was bleeding. She told Rosa Lee that she had cut herself with a knife when she became distraught during an argument in Howard's apartment. Two paramedics arrived and bandaged Patty's arm. Moaning that she still loved Howard, she cried herself to sleep as Rosa Lee held her.

Patty has cut herself many times before when drinking, says Rosa Lee. "I think that's to get attention." Patty began using this type of manipulative attention-getting when she was nine, explains Rosa Lee. "She saw me threaten to kill myself or pretend to drink poison to keep a young man from leaving me. I had a lot of young men then, younger than me, who would move in and just as quickly move out. I'd threaten to kill myself to try to hold on to them. It never worked. They'd wait until everything got quiet and then sneak off. But I know Patty thought this was one way you tried to hold on to a man 'cause she saw me do it. Many times."

Now the fruits of Rosa Lee's lessons to her children are with her every day.

As I drop Rosa Lee off at her apartment, I try not to think about what awaits her inside.

"Merry Christmas, Rose," I say softly as she opens the car door. "I'll see you next week."

"Merry Christmas, Mr. Dash."

Just Trying to Survive

OVERLEAF: *Before taking the items to a fast-food restaurant to sell, Ducky and Rosa Lee assess the salability of sweaters and shirts that Ducky stole in a burglary; Patty talks on the telephone* (© *Lucian Perkins*—The Washington Post).

Rosa Lee guided her eleven-year-old grandson through the narrow aisles of a thrift shop in suburban Oxon Hill, Maryland, past the crowded racks of secondhand pants and shirts, stopping finally at the row of children's jackets and winter coats. Quickly, the boy selected a mock-leather flight jacket with a big number on the back and a price tag stapled to the collar.

"If you want it," Rosa Lee said, "then you're going to have to help me get it."

"Okay, Grandmama," he said nervously. "But do it in a way that I won't get caught."

Like a skilled teacher instructing a new student, Rosa Lee told her grandson what to do. "Pretend you're trying it on. Don't look up! Don't look around! Don't laugh like it's some kind of joke! Just put it on. Let Grandma see how you look."

The boy slipped off his old coat and put on the new one. Rosa Lee whispered, "Now put the other one back on, over it." She pushed down the new jacket's collar so that it was hidden.

"What do I do now?" he asked.

"Just walk on out the door," Rosa Lee said. "It's your coat."

Four days later, Rosa Lee is recounting this episode for me, re-creating the dialogue by changing her voice to distinguish between herself and her grandson. It is January 1991. By now, I have spent enough time with Rosa Lee that her shoplifting exploits no longer surprise me.

The previous November, Rosa Lee took her eight-year-old granddaughter into the same thrift shop on a Sunday morning to steal a new winter coat for the girl one week after they were both baptized in a Pentecostal church. On the Sunday of the shoplifting lesson, Rosa Lee had decided she did not want to take her granddaughter back to the church because her winter coat was "tacky and dirty."

In the thrift shop, Rosa Lee told her granddaughter to take off her coat and hang it on the coatrack. Next, she told the grinning child to put on the attractive pink winter coat hanging on the rack.

"Are we going to take this coat, Grandma?" asked the skinny little girl.

"Yes," Rosa Lee told her. "We are exchanging coats. Now walk out the door."

A month later, a week before Christmas, Rosa Lee was searching for something in a large shopping bag in her bedroom and dumped the contents onto the bed. Out spilled dozens of bottles of expensive men's cologne and women's perfume, as well as leather gloves with their sixty-dollar price tags still attached. She leaves the tags on when she sells the goods as proof of the merchandise's newness and quality.

"Did you get all this in one trip?" I ask.

"Oh, no," she says. "This is a couple of weeks' worth."

In Rosa Lee's younger years especially, shoplifting was a major source of income, supplementing her welfare payments and the money she made during fifteen years of waitressing at various nightclubs. With eight children to feed and clothe, stealing, she says, helped her survive. Later on, when she began using heroin in the mid-1970s, her shoplifting paid for drugs.

She stole from clothing stores, drugstores, and grocery stores, stuffing items inside the torn liner of her winter coat or slipping them into one of the oversized black purses that she carries wherever she goes. When her children were young—the ages of the grandson and granddaughter—she taught them how to shoplift as well.

"Every time I went somewhere to make some money, I would take my children," she said. "I would teach them or they would watch me. 'Just watch what Mama does. I'm getting food for y'all to eat.'"

In supermarkets, she could count on her children "to distract the security guard while I hit the meat freezer. The guards would always watch groups of children before they'd watch an adult."

Her favorite targets were the department stores. One of her two older brothers, Joe Louis Wright, joked with me one day that Rosa Lee "owned a piece" of Hecht's and had put Lansburgh's out of business. "Man, she would get coats, silk dresses," he recalled. "A cloth coat with a mink collar. She got me a mohair suit. Black. Three-piece. I don't know how the hell she'd get them out of there."

Her stealing has caused divisions and hard feelings in her family, and is one reason why Rosa Lee's relationships with several of her brothers and sisters are strained. They see Rosa Lee's stealing as an extreme and unjustified reaction to their impoverished upbringing. And her sons Alvin and Eric have always refused to participate in any of their mother's illegal activities.

Rosa Lee has served eight short prison terms for various kinds of stealing during the past forty years, dating back to the early 1950s. Her longest stay was eight months for trying to steal a fur coat from a Maryland department store in 1965. She says that she went to prison rehabilitation programs each time but that none had much of an effect on her. "I attended those programs so it would look good on my record when I went before the parole board," she says. "What they were talking about didn't mean anything to me. I didn't have the education they said would get me a job. I couldn't read no matter how many programs I went to."

Nothing seems to deter her from shoplifting, not even the specter of another jail term. On the day she directed her grandson in stealing the flight jacket, she was four days away from sentencing at the city's Superior Court for stealing the bedsheets from Hecht's the previous summer.

"I'm just trying to survive," she says.

Rosa Lee had chosen her clothes carefully for her appearance before Commissioner John Treanor in November. She wanted to look as poor as possible to draw his sympathy.

She wore an ill-fitting winter coat, gray wool overalls and a white wool hat pulled back to show her graying hair. She had removed her upper dental plate to give herself a toothless look when she smiled. "My homey look," she calls it. "No lipstick. No earrings. No nothing!"

Rosa Lee did not expect to go home that day. She saw a heavyset female deputy U. S. marshal move into place behind the defense table when the courtroom clerk called her name. It was a certain sign that Treanor had already decided to "step her back" and send her to jail. She hastily handed me her purse with all her documents.

"Hold on to these papers for me, Mr. Dash," she whispered. "Looks like I'm going to get some jail time. Tell my children where I'm at. You better come see me!"

Her lawyer's statements matched her downtrodden look. Rosa Lee's life was a mess, Elmer D. Ellis told Treanor. She was addicted to heroin, a habit she had developed in 1975. She was HIV positive. She was caring for three grandchildren because their mother was in jail.

Rosa Lee told Treanor that she was trying hard to turn herself around. She was taking methadone every day to control her heroin addiction and had turned again to the church. "I got baptized Sunday, me and my three grandchildren," she said, her voice breaking. "And I'm asking you from the bottom of my heart, give me a chance to prove that I'm taking my baptize seriously, 'cause I know I might not have much longer."

Tears ran down her cheeks. "I'm asking you for a chance, please," she begged Treanor. "I know I have a long record."

Rosa Lee was stretching the truth. Yes, she had been baptized, and yes, she was taking methadone. But no, she wasn't caring for her grandchildren alone. Their mother's jail term had ended in July, and she had returned to Rosa Lee's two-bedroom apartment to take care of the children, with help from Rosa Lee.

Treanor looked unimpressed with Rosa Lee's performance. He glowered at her, and Rosa Lee braced for the lecture she knew was coming. Both had played these roles before.

"Every time you pump yourself full of drugs and spend money to do it," he said, "you're stealing from your grandchildren. You're stealing food from their plates, clothes from their backs, and you're certainly jeopardizing their future. You're going to be one of the youngest dead grandmothers in town. And you're going to have three children that will be put up for adoption or going out to some home or some junior village or someplace."

That had been Rosa Lee's opening. "Can I prove to you that my life has changed?"

"Yeah, you can prove it to me, very simply," Treanor answered. "You can stay away from dope. Now I'll make a bargain with you. . . . You come back here the end of January and tell me what you've been doing, and then we'll think about it. But you're looking at jail time. You're looking at a cemetery."

Rosa Lee had won. Treanor postponed the sentencing. The marshal, who had moved in closer behind Rosa Lee at the start of Treanor's lecture, moved back. Treanor, red-faced with anger, called a ten-minute recess and hurriedly left the bench. Ellis shook Rosa Lee's hand.

Rosa Lee came over to me, her cheeks still tearstained but her face aglow. "Was I good?" she asked.

"Yeah," I said, startled at her boldness.

"Thank you," she said, smiling.

The marshal walked up to Rosa Lee. She too was smiling. She had escorted Rosa Lee and her daughters to the jail several times in the not-so-distant past. "You were going to jail, honey," she said to Rosa Lee. "You stopped him with those three grandchildren. He didn't want to have to deal with making arrangements for those children if he had sent you to jail. Is their mama still over the jail?"

"Yes, she is," Rosa Lee lied, putting on a sad face.

Five days before the hearing Rosa Lee was teaching her granddaughter how to shoplift. Through most of November and

December, Rosa Lee stole cologne, perfume, gloves, and brightly colored silk scarves to sell to people who used them as Christmas presents. The day before her court appearance, she and a fellow drug-clinic patient, Jackie, were shoplifting in a drugstore one block from the Superior Court building shortly after they had drunk their morning meth.

When she returns for sentencing on January 22, a transformed Rosa Lee enters the courthouse. She looks good. She has a clean report from the methadone clinic. She stopped injecting heroin and cocaine in November, after her last seizure. She seems to have done everything Commissioner Treanor asked.

She always dresses well, but she has outdone herself today: she's wearing a two-piece, white-and-gray cotton knit suit with tan leather boots and a tan pocketbook. A gold-colored watch on a gold-colored chain hangs around her neck, both items she stole from the drugstore.

Before they enter Treanor's courtroom, Elmer Ellis has a word with Rosa Lee. "Please don't cry, Mrs. Cunningham," her lawyer says gently. "If you start crying again, you're only going to make Treanor angry." Rosa Lee laughs and agrees not to cry.

"What would you like to say, Mrs. Cunningham?" Treanor asks Rosa Lee when she stands in front of him.

"Well, Your Honor, I know I haven't been a good person. I know it," she begins.

Treanor cuts her off. His demeanor is softer, his words more sympathetic than in November. "Wait a minute, now. Why do you say that? . . . You're taking care of those three grandchildren, isn't that right?"

"Yes, sir," Rosa Lee says, keeping up the pretense.

"All right," he says. "Now you've raised one family, and now you have another one."

"Yes, sir," she says.

"Which is really too much to ask of anybody, so I don't think you should sell yourself short. You're doing the Lord's work. Your daughter's in jail for drugs, right?"

"Yes, sir," Rosa Lee says.

"And you have or have had a bad drug problem yourself."

"Yes, sir."

Then Treanor launches into another lecture about drugs. He doesn't ask Rosa Lee why she steals. "You steal to support your habit," he says. "It's as plain as the nose on your face."

But it isn't that plain. Rosa Lee began stealing long before she became a drug addict.

Finally, Treanor announces his decision: no jail. Instead, he gives her a suspended sentence and one year of probation with drug counseling. "Now, don't come back here," he says.

Rosa Lee sometimes puts on a public mask, the way she wants the world to see her. She fudges a little here, omits a little there, even when she is trying to be candid about her behavior. By her account, her stealing started when she was a teenager. It was her eldest brother, Ben Wright, who told me that Rosa Lee's stealing started when she was nine years old. Her target: the lunch money that her fourth-grade classmates at Giddings Elementary School kept in their desks.

"JESUS, BEN!" Rosa Lee shouts when I ask her about it.

"What's the matter?" I laugh. "You said I could interview Ben."

It is a late afternoon in January, not long after her court appearance. We are talking in my car, which is parked outside Rosa Lee's apartment. We watch the teenage crack dealers come and go, making the rounds of the low-rent housing complex. Two of Rosa Lee's grandchildren are playing nearby on a patch of dirt where the grass has been worn away. The sun is beginning to sink behind the buildings as she tells me about her first theft.

The year was 1946, and Giddings's imposing red-brick building at Third and G streets, S.E., was a bustling part of the District's then-segregated education system. The school served black children living in Capitol Hill neighborhoods; some, like Rosa Lee, came from poor sharecropping families who had moved to Washington during the Depression, and they did not have the new clothes and spending money that their better-off classmates did.

Rosa Lee's father, Earl Wright, never made much money. He worked for a paving contractor as a cement finisher but he was never given that title; instead, he was always classified as a "helper" and paid a lower wage. Eventually, drinking became the primary activity of his life. Rosa Lee's mother, Rosetta Lawrence Wright, brought in most of the family's money, working as a domestic on Capitol Hill during the day.

"She used to call it 'day work,'" remembers Rosa Lee. "That's what she used to do down in the country" in North Carolina. "Clean white people's houses."

Rosetta also sold dinners from the family's kitchen in the evening and on weekends, always for cash. "She wanted cash because she was getting a welfare check for us," says Rosa Lee. The welfare payments began several years before her father's death because he spent all his time drinking and did not work. After he died, Rosetta had four additional children by another man. "Back in those days, they gave you a check for each child. Seventeen dollars a check. You never want the welfare to know how much money you got. They'll cut the check."

Ben contends that his sister's memory is faulty, that the family did receive monthly deliveries of surplus government food in this period, as did all of the poorest families in Washington, but his mother did not receive a monthly welfare stipend.

Whatever the truth, Rosa Lee and Ben agree that their family—there were eleven children in all—was poor. For much of her childhood, they lived in a ramshackle wooden row house within a mile of the Capitol, since replaced with a public housing project. None of the houses they rented over the years had electricity. The toilet for each dwelling was an outhouse along the edge of the property in the back yard. Water came from a standpipe spigot in the center of the yard.

"I hated them!" says Rosa Lee of the houses, her mouth turning down in a grimace. "No privacy. People knew what you were doing when you went into" the outhouse. "No bathtub. I was always afraid of the kerosene lamps. I was scared they'd turn over and we'd all burn up in those houses."

Other girls came to school with change to buy "brownie-thins"—penny-apiece cookies that the teachers sold to go with the free milk at lunch. Rosa Lee's family was too poor to spare even a few pennies. Rosa Lee was determined to steal her classmates' money so she too could buy cookies. And she did. She knew it was wrong to steal from her classmates' desks, she says. But she couldn't stand being poor, either.

Rosa Lee soon found that she had plenty of opportunities to steal, if she were daring enough. During the summer of 1948, a sinewy Rosa Lee was the only girl among the many "roughneck" boys selling the *Baltimore-Washington Afro-American* newspaper door-to-door on Tuesday and Thursday evenings. She was eleven. The newspaper sales were timed to catch middle-class black people—low-level federal and city civil servants—when they had just come home from work.

Rosa Lee was not concerned about tough neighborhood bullies taking her money or trying to force her off the blocks where an *Afro* seller was sure to be successful. "Rosa Lee would fight quick," remembers Ben. "Fight anybody! Beat up most girls and a good many boys. I don't remember ever having to stick up for her."

Selling the *Afro* also gave Rosa Lee a chance to slip into neighborhood row houses and rifle through the pocketbooks that women often left on the dining room table or the living room couch. Washington was a safer place in those days, and Rosa Lee discovered that many families would leave their front screen doors unlatched while they chatted in their back yards, trying to cool off on hot summer evenings after returning home from work.

"I would walk down Fourth Street," says Rosa Lee, in front of the row houses across from Mount Joy Baptist Church, where her family worshipped. "I would go and knock on their screen door. 'Afro! Anybody want an *Afro*?' I would open the screen door and if no one answered, I'd go in. I could look through the house and see them out back," she remembers. "Some people would leave their pocketbooks on the chair in the front room or on their table. I would go into so many peoples' houses."

After she took the money, Rosa Lee would ease back out the

screen door and knock on it loudly, as if she had just arrived. Her customers often tipped her when they bought the paper "because I was the only girl out there selling the paper." Often, she sold out her first batch of *Afros* and went back to the distribution center for a second bundle.

But she was still the only girl in her neighborhood among a large crew of boys who sold the *Afro*. When her girlish figure began to fill out with the onset of puberty, Rosa Lee became uncomfortable hawking the paper from house to house. The paperboys looked at her differently and started making sexual comments to her. She decided she was "too grown" to be selling papers, that it was something "a young lady shouldn't be doing," and stopped.

In the fall, she found a new source of money: Mount Joy Baptist Church. She had started serving as a junior usher during Sunday services and was assigned to help in the coatroom. She noticed congregation members often left money in their coat pockets. "I felt like if they wanted it, they wouldn't have left it in their damn pocket," she says.

Rosa Lee says she would wait until the "singing and praying" started before going to the racks of coats, patting the pockets and listening for the jingle of coins. Once in a while she would find dollar bills. Her coatroom thefts continued undetected until one Sunday, when Mount Joy's minister, the Reverend Raymond M. Randall, announced to the astonished congregation that someone had stolen several dollars from a member's coat pocket during the previous Sunday's service. Randall offered forgiveness and asked the culprit to come forward. If the thief was hungry, he said, the church would try to help.

Rosa Lee could not bring herself to confess in front of her family and friends. "My mother would have KILLED ME! Do you hear me? KILLED ME!" she shouts at me as she recalls the scene. "And who is going to go up there and tell him that you're hungry? That would embarrass the hell out of you!"

For the next few weeks, Rosa Lee did not take any money—dollars or change—from the parishioners' coat pockets. When she started stealing again, she was careful to take only change.

She often did not know what to do with the money she stole. Her immediate needs were small and simple: thirty-five cents for the Saturday matinee at the Atlas Theater or a dime for the snow cones that she loved. She gave away small amounts to her brothers and sisters and friends, but never enough to attract her mother's attention.

One Sunday afternoon after church, Rosa Lee dumped two handfuls of coins on the kitchen table in front of Ben. She asked Ben, sixteen at the time, to help her count the money. The total came to a little over seven dollars, a large amount of money for a twelve-year-old to have. She gave half to Ben and kept half. Ben asked her where the money came from.

"I've been getting it out of church," Rosa Lee told him.

"WHAT?" she remembers a shocked Ben shouting.

"Coat pockets," added Rosa Lee, with a deadpan expression.

"Girl, you are going to be a survivor," Ben continued. "Anyone who can walk in and out of church and not feel anything. Sis, I don't see a frown on your face. You're just as cold-faced as ever. Out of church! Rose, you're cold."

Rosa Lee has held on to Ben's *survivor* characterization of her behavior. It is Rosa Lee's last defense when she becomes testy if close questioning about her criminal activity begins to block the rationalizations she so readily uses to escape responsibility.

Rosa Lee hid her stolen money from her mother. "I would roll it up in a stocking," she said, and put the stocking under a rug, or under her mattress, or in her underwear.

Forty years later, Rosa Lee still hides her money every night—not from her mother, but from her five drug-addicted children. Sometimes she goes to bed with a wad of bills stuffed into her sock or underpants. "If I don't hide it, they'd steal it," she says.

If Rosa Lee felt bad about not having a few pennies to buy cookies in fourth grade, she felt even worse about not having a stylish wardrobe to match those of her friends in seventh grade. She hated the secondhand clothes that her mother bought for her; they were almost always out of style.

Rosa Lee already felt at a disadvantage in attracting boys, and thought fashionable clothes might help. At thirteen, she felt she had a good enough figure but was perplexed when the boys she knew seemed more interested in her girlfriend Betty, who lived next door. She thought Betty was skinny and shapeless and bluntly told her as much. Betty told Rosa Lee that she was able to "pull" more boys because her complexion was a lighter brown. Betty explained to Rosa Lee the complexities of black American skin-color consciousness and the higher value placed on blacks who are light skinned. Rosa Lee began to feel bad about herself. "I was dark skinned," she says. "I wasn't like the girls with long hair and light skin. The boys always went for them."

Rosa Lee looked to clothes to do for her what she now felt her looks could not. One morning, Betty lent Rosa Lee a new gray skirt with a pocket on each hip, one of the latest fashions. "My mother would never buy me one," Rosa Lee told me, her voice still smoldering with resentment. Rosa Lee loved the way she looked in it.

During lunch that day, Betty asked Rosa Lee in front of some classmates if she could share her thirty-five-cent meal. "I wouldn't give it to her," Rosa Lee said. "I was hungry!" So she said no.

Betty blurted out, "I didn't say that when you borrowed my skirt!"

Rosa Lee's classmates howled with laughter. Rosa Lee could beat up almost every girl in the crowd individually, but she was paralyzed with embarrassment in front of the group. As she retells the story, I can see that time has not healed her wound. Her voice hardens, her eyes narrow, her expression conveys the raw power of the memory. "That hurt," Rosa Lee says. "I thought, 'God, this will never happen again to me.'"

Days later, Rosa Lee walked into a five-and-dime store on Pennsylvania Avenue. She picked out a pleated gray skirt with pockets on the hips and a white lace blouse. Rosa Lee folded them into two tight bundles, slipped them under the skirt she was wearing and slowly made her way out of the store. As she turned the corner, she crushed the skirt and blouse to her chest in glee. Tears ran down her face.

She hid the skirt and blouse from her mother. Emboldened, Rosa Lee branched out to other stores in the Capitol Hill area. "I was determined to have what other girls had," she said.

At a party—called a "belly rub"—in early 1950, she met a light-skinned boy who was attracting the attention of the other girls. Rosa Lee wanted to impress her friends by pulling the boy. Clearly she did so, since she enjoyed the other girls' envious looks when he asked to walk her home.

She thought having sex would cement their relationship. She had sex with him that very night and the next day while her mother was in church. "I haven't seen him since," she said.

When school officials found out she was pregnant, they told her she would have to leave school until the baby was born. She never went back. In November 1950, six weeks after her fourteenth birthday, she gave birth to Bobby.

Not long after Bobby was born, Rosa Lee decided to dress for church in one of her stolen outfits. She knew it was risky, but she was tired of wearing hand-me-downs when the other girl ushers usually came in stylish clothes. As soon as her mother spotted the gray pleated skirt, she confronted Rosa Lee.

"Where did you get this from?" Rosetta demanded.

"I stole it out of the store," Rosa Lee confessed. "Please don't make me take it back to the store, Mama!"

Rosetta was furious. "Oh, now I'm suppose to be stupid! I ain't going to say nothing to you now because you told the truth, but don't bring nothing else in here that you've been stealing! DO YOU HEAR ME?"

"Yes, ma'am," said Rosa Lee, trembling as she waited for the blow from her mother she was certain was coming.

But her mother just said: "Put it on. Let me see what you look like in it. What are you shaking for?"

"Mama, you must not hear yourself," Rosa Lee answered.

"Put it on!" Rosetta repeated. "And you're going to church. Stand up in church in a stolen skirt and stolen blouse!" she added sarcastically.

Rosa Lee asked her mother what she would have done if she had asked her for a new outfit to usher in.

"I'd have taken you to the Salvation Army or the Goodwill," responded Rosetta—exactly what Rosa Lee was determined to avoid.

After Rosa Lee dressed, Rosetta told her the clothes looked good on her. It was a rare compliment from her mother. Rosa Lee beamed.

Rosa Lee describes her relationship with her mother as conflictual from as far back as her childhood memory takes her. Her mother's way of dealing with her was to smack her in the mouth or "upside my head" whenever Rosetta was annoyed with her. "My mother would whup me for almost no reason at all, Mr. Dash," Rosa Lee whines at the memory. "I didn't understand it. I cried myself to sleep many a night. I promised myself that I would not treat my children the way I was treated."

Rosa Lee had no way of knowing, but her harsh upbringing by her mother was a common method of child-rearing in southern rural black families. Elizabeth Clark-Lewis, a historian at Howard University and author of the 1994 book *Living In, Living Out: African American Domestics in Washington, D.C., 1910–1940,* has studied women of Rosetta's generation who migrated from the South. "There was very serious, very serious discipline," Clark-Lewis emphasizes to me when I question her about Rosetta's reactions to some of Rosa Lee's more minor infractions. "So it's important that it is in the child's mind, and that it is lucidly clear in the child's mind, that there are very severe penalties that you pay for, as you call them, minor infractions. They are not minor!"

Sitting in my car in front of Rosa Lee's building one evening, Rosa Lee suddenly grows tired of my constant questions about exactly how her mother beat her. She grabs my right shoulder in her left hand and pulls me toward her. With the broad palm of her right hand, she repeatedly tries to smack me in the face with powerful blows. I had not known how strong she is until this moment.

I block her swings with my forearms until she stops, gasping for breath. "There," she says, in between short breaths. "That's how she used to beat me. I'm tired of you asking me about it. It seems like you're picking at me about it."

I begin laughing and can't stop. Rosa Lee joins me. Tears spring from our eyes. Her young granddaughter sees us from the dining room window of their ground-floor apartment, comes outside and over to my open window. She stares at us as we laugh and wipe our tears. Each of us tries to stop to say something to the little girl, but before we can get out a sentence we begin laughing again.

Finally, Rosa Lee manages to tell her granddaughter that "we're all right. We're just sharing a joke." Relieved, the girl returns to the apartment.

Rosa Lee has no keepsakes, no mementos, no record of her parents or grandparents—except for a single black-and-white photograph of her mother and grandmother that somehow survived over the years. When I first saw it, it was lying loose atop a bureau in Rosa Lee's bedroom, unframed and unprotected, its edges torn, its emulsion cracking.

Her mother dominates the photo, much as she dominated Rosa Lee in her youth. Rosetta is sitting in a chair that is too small for her large body, dressed in what appears to be a white uniform, probably something she wore as a domestic worker. She dwarfs her own mother, Lugenia, who is sitting in an over-stuffed flower-print chair that seems to swallow her slight, almost frail body.

The memory of her mother, who died in 1979, stirs feelings of anger in Rosa Lee, not tenderness. There was the time, Rosa Lee remembers, when her mother accused her of stealing a check out of the mailbox. Rosa Lee was about nine. She ran to her grandmother's house, a block away. "She came around to my grandmother's house and whupped me. I mean really whupped me! . . . The next morning the mailman brought the check. My mother didn't say nothing. She just got mad at the mailman."

Most of Rosetta's children don't share Rosa Lee's view of their mother. They remember her as a woman working hard to keep her family together under difficult conditions. "She taught

me, 'If you want something, work for it!'" said Jay Roland
Wright, one of Rosa Lee's younger brothers. "I've always lived
by that." Jay Wright is fifteen years younger than Rosa Lee; her
memories go back to well before he was born.

As a little girl, she says, she became devoted to her father, who
doted on her. At dinner time on Fridays, Rosa Lee would walk
down to Earl Wright's favorite drinking place a couple of blocks
from the row house where they lived. He would lean on her on
the walk back home. Neighborhood children would laugh at the
sight. "It was embarrassing," remembers Rosa Lee. "He was a
winehead. Children used to throw it in my face so much. 'You
got a drunk father. Aaawww girl, I wouldn't be seen with that.'
It really hurt me."

When Rosa Lee was helping her father up the front steps, he
sometimes would tell her to reach into his pants pocket and grab
herself a handful of change. She always looked forward to that
moment. "My mother never gave me money. I never did believe
that she loved me, Mr. Dash. I did work that I ain't never seen
no children do. Them big tubs. Full with clothes. Sheets. I had to
wash those clothes on a rub board. My father loved me, though.
He used to sneak me money. All the time."

Rosa Lee even went to her father when she began her
menses at ten. She wasn't sure what was happening. She had a
vague idea that it had something to do with growing up, but
she doesn't recall anyone telling her about it directly. She
asked her father what she should do. Earl was embarrassed.
He told Rosa Lee to go talk to her mother. She refused. "Oh,
you know what she's going to say," she told her father. He
went to a nearby store and bought sanitary napkins for her,
and told her how to use them. "And that was that," says Rosa
Lee. "I never did discuss it with my mother."

Often, when Earl Wright was drunk he took his fists to
Rosetta, much as Rosetta took hers to Rosa Lee. "He'd go upside
her head, bam, all the time," she says. "He'd be drunk. She'd take
it dead out on me. I never did nothing. I was too scared."

Nineteen forty-eight was a pivotal year in Rosa Lee's life. She
turned twelve in October and lost her father in November. Earl

Wright, thirty-six, died of cirrhosis of the liver and Rosa Lee's childhood world fell apart. "When he died, it seemed like all hell broke loose. I didn't have nothing. I cried so much, I didn't know what to do. The first little boy I saw that showed me any kind of love, any kind of feeling, I just took my drawers off. I just took them off."

Rosa Lee ignored Rosetta's frequent orders to stop shoplifting. Whenever her mother questioned her about some new item, Rosa Lee just denied that she stole it. "My mother would tell me, 'Stop that lying,' and then let it go," Rosa Lee said.

But a judge wasn't so kind when fifteen-year-old Rosa Lee was caught shoplifting at a downtown department store, her first arrest. He sent her to a facility for juveniles for nineteen days in late 1951. But the lesson seemed lost on Rosa Lee; after her release, she went right back to shoplifting.

When Rosa Lee was away, her mother cared for one-year-old Bobby. Rosa Lee was pregnant with her second child, Ronnie. Rosetta had accepted Rosa Lee's first pregnancy, but she was angry that Rosa Lee was pregnant again. A few months earlier, Rosetta had forced Rosa Lee to have an abortion at D.C. General Hospital. "She felt that I was too young to be having these babies so fast," recalls Rosa Lee. "They were just coming one after another." Rosetta was furious when she learned Rosa Lee was pregnant again just months after the abortion. The father of the baby was another teenager in the neighborhood. "What do you think you doing, bringing all these babies in here?" Rosa Lee remembers her mother saying.

Rosetta demanded that Rosa Lee have another abortion, but Rosa Lee was finished with letting her mother tell her what to do—about babies, shoplifting, or anything else.

Anxious to win her mother's affection, Rosa Lee decided to steal something for Rosetta. One day after Rosetta came home from work, Rosa Lee took a multicolored cotton scarf from under her coat and handed it to her mother.

"What is this?" Rosetta asked. She took the scarf, turned it over in her hands and looked questioningly at her daughter.

"Mama, it's not a piece of rag," said Rosa Lee. "It's something I got for you."

Rosetta looked at Rosa Lee again, a question beginning to form on her mouth. Rosa Lee knew what the question would be. She waved both her hands, a sign to her mother not to ask where she got the scarf.

Her mother didn't. "Rose, I *never* had something like this!"

Rosetta threw her arms around Rosa Lee. "She grabbed me, and I grabbed her," Rosa Lee recalls. "I couldn't believe it!"

But the stolen scarf, and other stolen gifts that followed, did not bring Rosa Lee the close relationship that she craved. Rosa Lee says her mother didn't like her shoplifting and continued to badger her about it.

Ben feels their mother should have done more than badger Rosa Lee about her stealing. "I fault my mother," says Ben. "She never made Rosa Lee carry nothing back. She was almost like condoning it. Because, see, what Rosa Lee would do, if she found something that would fit my mother, she would steal *that!* By my mother not having a whole lot of money," Rosetta would accept the stolen item.

Nevertheless, the tension between Rosetta and Rosa Lee was always there, waiting to explode. One day, when Rosa Lee was twenty-two and raising five children in an apartment next-door to her mother's, it did.

Rosa Lee and a neighbor had a shouting match after the neighbor hit one of Rosa Lee's children. When Rosetta heard about it, she was angry at Rosa Lee. She stormed into Rosa Lee's home. Rosa Lee was standing at the kitchen sink cutting up chickens.

"She told me that all I am is a troublemaker," Rosa Lee recalls. "I told her that the neighbor shouldn't have hit my child. Mama said, 'You nothing but a damn nuisance,' and pow, right in my mouth."

Rosetta's blow with her right fist left her daughter with one visible legacy of their relationship: the upper denture she wears in place of the front teeth that Rosetta knocked out.

It also left a lasting impression on Bobby, who saw the confrontation. He was eight. Rosa Lee dropped the knife and the chicken parts in the sink. She staggered back, her right hand trying to stem the flow of blood from her mouth. The hand muffled her wails and cries from the pain and the discovery of several teeth in the palm of her hand.

"It was spooky," he told me. "Ain't nobody supposed to beat up Mom. As much as she went to get food and clothes for us. I don't care who it was."

Bobby glared at his grandmother. He did not see her swift and powerful right backhand coming until too late. He felt the sting of the blow on the entire right side of his face as he picked himself up from the floor on the opposite side of the small kitchen. "Don't look at me like that!" Rosetta told him.

A description of the scene doesn't surprise Rosa Lee's brother Joe Louis. "My mama knew how to whip your ass!" he says, chuckling.

Rosa Lee had just reached the suburban Maryland department store's exit door. She smiled to herself. She was seconds from getting away. Moments before, she had "exchanged" her "old, ratty brown wool coat" for the expensive fur coat she was wearing. She couldn't wait to show off when she got back to the small, crowded row house in Northeast Washington where she, her mother, and all their children—nineteen people in all—lived. This would be her first fur coat!

It was October 1965, a few days after Rosa Lee's twenty-ninth birthday, and she was using the same bold shoplifting technique she first developed as a teenager.

Months before, Rosa Lee had been caught and charged with shoplifting in a high-fashion women's department store on New York City's Fifth Avenue. Ben had come up from Washington at their mother's request and got her out of jail. A judge dropped the shoplifting charge when Ben promised him that Rosa Lee would not return to the city. "She had on an expensive suede cape that she had shoplifted in Washington, but the rest of the clothes she had on didn't match the quality of the cape," remembers Ben. "The store clerks spotted her the minute she walked through the door. They just waited for her to make her move and they made theirs."

That experience had not frightened Rosa Lee. In fact, nothing seemed to dissuade her from shoplifting. Whenever she was arrested, she accepted with a shrug of her shoulders that she was going to do some time in prison. Rosa Lee's New York arrest, it turned out, did not teach her much.

"I didn't know what I know now," she recalls. At the Maryland store, the clerks noticed her when she approached the fur-coat rack wearing her "raggedy" coat. The clerks also noted the "cheap" clothes she was wearing when she hung the wool coat on the rack. The second fur coat she tried on "fitted perfectly." As she admired herself in a full-length mirror, Rosa Lee told herself, "I'm going with this sucka."

Just as Rosa Lee's right hand reached to push the exit door handle, she felt a sudden grip inside the crook of each arm. "Miss, would you come with us, please?" a female voice asked as Rosa Lee turned to face three store detectives, two women and a man.

"They laughed at me," says Rosa Lee, her pride still wounded twenty-seven years after the arrest. "They told me that I didn't have a snowball's chance in hell of getting out of that store with the fur coat. I didn't look the part to have a fur coat on. I didn't think to look at myself."

She was held for sixty days in the Prince George's County jail. In the courthouse of the county seat, Upper Marlboro, she pleaded guilty to theft. The judge sentenced her to a year in prison. Standing at the defense table, Rosa Lee turned to look at her mother sitting in the first row of spectator seats. Rosetta was furious. "You're not going to forget this!" Rosetta yelled, waving her right forefinger at Rosa Lee. "You hear me? Leaving all those goddamn children! You're not going to forget this!"

On Christmas Eve, Rosa Lee entered the Maryland state prison for women in Jessup. "It was very nice, almost like college," she remembers. "They let you eat as much as you wanted. I worked on the prison farm in the spring and summer growing strawberries. It was like a vacation. It was relaxing. I was away from my children. I was away from *my mother!*"

Early in the new year, Rosetta brought all of Rosa Lee's children for a visit with their mother. In the prison's visiting hall, with the children gathered around Rosa Lee, Rosetta handed her the January welfare checks to endorse. There were eight checks. "Seventy-two dollars for each child," says Rosa Lee, a monthly total of $576. Rosa Lee signed them and handed them back to her mother. Rosetta cleared her throat. Immediately, Rosa Lee's guard went up.

"Rosa Lee," Rosetta began, "you know I got these children and the checks are still in your name. What do you expect me to do? I got your children."

"I just looked at her," Rosa Lee recalls. "I knew what the next thing was going to be. Turn the welfare checks over to her. She wanted me to sign some papers that I was an unfit mother. I told her, 'I don't want to sign my kids over. I love my children. I ain't going to do it!' "

"That's what's wrong with you!" responded Rosetta sharply. "That's why you're in here now!"

Each month, Rosetta traveled to the prison so Rosa Lee could endorse the checks. She brought the children out several more times in the spring and summer. When the weather was nice, they would all eat lunch at picnic tables set up for visitors.

Given time off for good behavior, Rosa Lee was released at the end of six months and twenty-four days in late July 1966 and moved back into the crowded house in Washington.

Before Rosa Lee's return, the District's welfare agency had begun to put Rosetta's name on the checks. "The checks were made out to Rosa Lee Cunningham in care of Rosetta Wright," Rosa Lee says. "That meant we both had to sign them. But after I got out, I wanted my mother's name off my checks."

Rosa Lee went to the welfare agency's office to be recertified. Rosetta went with her. A welfare supervisor told Rosa Lee that her mother had told them she was unfit to be the guardian of her own children. Rosa Lee looked askance at her mother, who was sitting next to her.

Rosetta, looking at the supervisor, spoke up. "My daughter steals. She's been in jail!"

Rosa Lee defended herself. "I'm not unfit! I just shoplift. Why don't you ask my children if I am unfit?"

The supervisor excused herself to retrieve some additional records. Rosetta jumped from her seat and backhanded Rosa Lee across her mouth. "That's for running your damn mouth."

Blood began dripping over Rosa Lee's lower lip. "You didn't have to do that," she whined.

When the supervisor returned, she noticed Rosa Lee trying to stop the bleeding. Rosa Lee asked if she could go to the bathroom. Rosetta "swelled up in the chair, looking like 'So, what! She's mine!' " says Rosa Lee.

After Rosa Lee returned from the bathroom, the supervisor asked her what had happened, but Rosa Lee would not tell her. Rosetta's name was removed from Rosa Lee's welfare checks. Three months later, Rosa Lee and her eight children moved into a roach-infested one-bedroom apartment in Northwest Washington. Rosa Lee was thirty years old and completely on her own for the first time in her life.

On the balmy Thursday night of April 4, 1968, a few hours after the assassination of Martin Luther King, Jr., looting and arson erupted in several of Washington's major commercial corridors.

Rosa Lee now had nine children to feed. She had informally adopted a months-old infant boy when his heroin-addicted mother was unable to care for him. He would live with Rosa Lee and her family until he was a teenager.

As the rioting spread, Rosa Lee watched as looters carried bags, boxes, and portable televisions past the house she was renting on L Street, S.E. "Where y'all get that stuff?" Rosa Lee called out from her porch.

"H Street," folks shouted back, referring to a commercial strip in Northeast Washington.

Rosa Lee did not have a television but she had heard about the civil rights leader's death that evening on the radio. She had also heard about the growing riot that had overwhelmed Washington's police force by 10:30 that night. She had a vague idea of King's efforts to improve life for African Americans, but she did not understand why blacks were rioting because he had been killed. "I didn't know how important he was," she says.

Still, the torching and trashing of businesses in reaction to his death did not disturb her. The shops, she says, were run by "greedy" merchants who gouged customers and took "whatever little money I had." So when Bobby, then seventeen, drove up in a Buick that Rosa Lee instinctively knew had been stolen, she didn't hesitate. "I didn't ask any questions. I didn't have to." She turned to the other children and said, "All right! Who wants to go?" As usual, Alvin and Eric, then fifteen and twelve, held back.

"Everybody was having a party" when they reached H Street, she says. "Everybody was grabbing everything they could get their hands on. We started grabbing too. Didn't know what we were taking. Just grabbing, grabbing, grabbing.

"We went to stores and got food!" Rosa Lee continues. "Anyplace there was a store, we went into it. Me and my sons. We had a back seat full with food."

They did not steal a television. All the portable ones had been taken and the sets that were left were too large to fit into the car. "We came in on the tail end. Most of the best stuff was already gone."

A couple of hours after midnight, H Street began to fill up rapidly with uniformed policemen. Rosa Lee knew it was time to go. She gathered her brood and they headed toward home in the stolen Buick. A liquor store was being looted on M Street, S.E., a block from their house. Her sons joined the looters. At the house, Rosa Lee hid the food and the liquor in the attic.

Early the next morning, before the second day of rioting began, the liquor store owner knocked on Rosa Lee's front door. People in her neighborhood told him that her sons had stolen a large amount of his liquor. "He was a white man," says Rosa Lee. He told her, "All I want is my liquor, lady." Rosa Lee thought, "I don't drink anyway," so she gave it all back to him.

When the looting started up again later that Friday, Rosa Lee kept her children home. "We already had so much stuff," she says. "There was no need to go out."

Rosa Lee and most of her nine living brothers and sisters were gathered in the narrow basement of their grandmother Lugenia Lawrence's house on Seventeenth Street, N.E.. They had come there to talk, drink, and eat after the 1977 funeral of Rosetta's younger sister, who had died of cancer. Rosa Lee's son Richard was also there.

The conversation that day eventually focused on Rosa Lee. Her brothers and sisters teased her about her many years of selling the clothes she shoplifted from Washington's department stores. Richard, then twenty-three, looked across the room to see how his mother was taking it.

Rosa Lee looked into his eyes. Richard saw pain and anguish. His throat tightened, but he remained silent. A broad-shouldered prison weightlifter, Richard is the biggest of Rosa Lee's sons and his reaction to his mother's torment frightened him. "The reason I didn't say anything, I was hurt *so* bad that I wanted to hurt someone," he recalls.

His mother hung her head and Richard wondered how long she would take the teasing. Suddenly, she looked up, her eyes bright with anger. Her face made a slow sweep of the room, looking into the eyes of all her siblings. "I put clothes on the backs of *everyone* in this room!" Rosa Lee shouted, her eyes filling with tears. "Don't you ever *forget it!*"

Rosa Lee's brothers and sisters fell into an embarrassed silence. She had dressed all of them, at one time or another, when there had been no money to buy even secondhand clothes. She had shoplifted clothes and shoes in the size of the family member most in need. There had been no teasing and laughing when she delivered the clothes without charge, only gratitude.

"You could hear a pin drop," remembers Richard.

Rosa Lee wasn't finished. "What I did may have been wrong," she said, "but what I did was worth it because nobody gave me nothing. I had to go get it." Then she turned on her heel and stomped up the basement stairs. Richard went up the stairs behind her.

There was not even a murmur from the others as the two climbed the stairs. The silence satisfied Richard, wiped away his pain. "Mom shook the house!" he said.

"Mr. Dash," Rosa Lee says as I am driving her to her apartment in February 1991, "stop at that High's so I can get a loaf of bread." I glance at her, and she knows what I'm thinking. "I'm not doing any shoplifting," she assures me.

I have told Rosa Lee that I cannot be a party in any way to her shoplifting. So when we pull into the convenience store parking lot, she makes a big show of leaving her oversized black bag on the seat. Wallet in hand, she heads for the store.

Fifteen minutes go by. My feet are getting numb from the cold, so I decide to see why she's taking so long. Her head is visible above the display counter of canned goods. When the elderly clerk is busy with a customer in the front of the store, Rosa Lee's head bobs down. She puts something into a large brown paper bag, too busy to notice I've come inside.

"ROSA LEE!" I shout.

She jumps at the sound of her name. She spots me standing near the smudged glass door. She crumples the top of the bag and walks toward me. I feel her cold anger as she breezes past.

"That's the last time I wait for you outside of a store!" I yell as we walk to the car. "You told me you weren't going to steal anything!"

She fires back, her words coming out in a steamy vapor from the cold. "I'm trying to feed my family and I don't have any money. We're just trying to survive!"

"That's dead!" I say. "Save that for the judges at Superior Court. You just threw away several hundred dollars buying dope and crack for your children."

"You know so goddamn much!" she snaps as I start the car. "I ought to go upside your head!"

"You threaten to go upside my head every other day." I laugh.

She laughs, and the tension evaporates. She shows me what's

in her bag: a loaf of bread that she bought, and the items she stole—two cans of spray starch and a can of baked beans.

I am angry with Rosa Lee for violating my trust, and I am angry with myself. The incident is a lesson for me: Why did I think that she would behave differently around me?

A few weeks after the shoplifting incident at High's, Rosa Lee and I are talking in her apartment. After spending so much time with her, I realize I don't always ask the questions that need to be asked.

"Rosa Lee," I say, "there's something I want to work out with you about how you look at the world."

I remind her of the times she took her grandson and grand-daughter to steal coats. In the instance with the granddaughter, they were on their way to church, but Rosa Lee thought the girl's coat looked ragged, so they went to the thrift shop to shoplift instead.

Rosa Lee nods.

"How do you put those two together?" I say. "One Sunday going to church to be baptized, and the next Sunday going to shoplift a coat?"

"I don't know," she says. "I didn't like to take her to church with that dirty-looking coat."

"But how do you take her out stealing then?" I say.

She protests that the thrift shop's white owner takes advan-tage of his customers, who are mostly black. "I don't understand how a thrift shop can charge so much for things," she says. "Do you know he charges $8.95 for stuff that don't cost that much brand new?"

"That's a rationalization, and it doesn't dance," I say.

"Yeah, you're right," Rosa Lee says, waving her hand at me in mock disgust. "But a [night]gown cost seven, five dollars. But you still think it's stealing? It's not brand new."

"I've seen you sell the things you steal out of there for the same price that is on the sales tag," I reply. "You charged one of your dope fiend buddies from the clinic five dollars for a gown from the thrift shop and the price tag on the slip was five dollars."

Rosa Lee looks genuinely embarrassed at having her rationalization turned around on her. "You know, I let you see and know too goddamn much," she sputters.

"The point is, it's stealing," I continue. "No one has told you that you have to spend your money in that shop. Is there nothing in the religion that you and your granddaughter were baptized into that tells you that what you were doing is wrong?"

Rosa Lee looks hurt. "So, you think that I should stop?"

"No, no," I respond. "I'm not getting into whether you should stop. I'm asking you how do you justify it?"

"I'm justified that these are donations and he has no right to charge what he wants," says Rosa Lee. "Maybe you're right, but I just don't feel it."

That night, I'm surprised to find a message from Rosa Lee on my answering machine in the newsroom, telling me that she has had "second thoughts" about taking her grandchildren to shoplift. The next day, she explains. "You gave me something to think about," she says. She told her grandchildren that our conversation had made her see that it was wrong to take them shoplifting, teaching them a way of life that has so damaged most of her own children.

Rosa Lee's granddaughter said, "Grandma, it was because I needed a coat."

"Well," Rosa Lee replied, "I should have paid for it."

Her granddaughter immediately went to the closet and got the pink coat that Rosa Lee had helped her steal. "What you want me to do with the coat?" she asked Rosa Lee.

"Keep it. Keep the coat. But we're not going to do any more stealing," Rosa Lee replied.

"Are you going to stick to that?" her granddaughter asked.

"So help me to God," Rosa Lee said. "I'm going to stick to that."

Rosa Lee looks at me, waiting for my reaction. If she stuck to her promise, I knew it would only apply to taking her grandchildren shoplifting. Rosa Lee had no intention of stopping shoplifting herself. I study her face. She seems sincere.

She's waiting for some sort of response from me and I search for one. "You have a powerful influence on those children," I say.

"I know it," she says.

THREE

Rosetta's Legacy

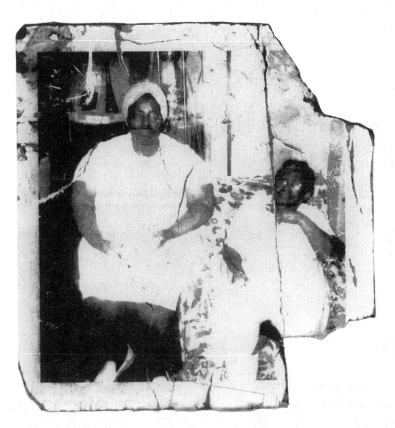

OVERLEAF: *The only photograph Rosa Lee has of her mother, Rosetta Wright (left), and her grandmother, Lugenia Lawrence (courtesy Rosa Lee Cunningham).*

ROSA LEE is so weak she cannot get out of bed.

I cradle one of her limp arms while Richard grips the other. Gently, we lift her up and support her as she tries to stand. She rocks unsteadily, groaning and whimpering from the exertion. We slowly lean her back against a tall wooden chest of drawers to brace her, but she slumps against it, banging the chest into the wall. We hastily return her to bed.

It is clear she needs immediate medical attention. She has been growing weaker and weaker since her release from Greater Southeast Community Hospital eight days ago. Rosa Lee's youngest daughter comes into the bedroom to dress her while Richard and I step out into the living room. I tell Richard that I am taking Rosa Lee to the Howard University Hospital emergency room. "An excellent idea," Richard declares.

Later that day, doctors began searching for the cause of her dangerously weak condition. After a blood test, the mystery unraveled.

Rosa Lee was a victim, it turned out, of her inability to read.

The blood test showed that she was overdosing on Dilantin, a medication that helps prevent seizures. She had twice the recommended level in her system.

She had been taking Dilantin only a few weeks. Doctors had

prescribed it for her after a seizure in February—her fourth since October—had landed her in the Community Hospital. When they sent her home, they gave her written instructions on how to take four medications they had prescribed for her. Under the word Dilantin, the instructions read "100 mgs 3X daily."

"No, I didn't tell the nurse I couldn't read," says Rosa Lee defensively. "She didn't ask me if I could read. I wouldn't have told her if she'd asked."

Rosa Lee didn't know that "100 mgs" meant 100 milligrams or that she was supposed to take one 100-milligram tablet three times a day. She thought she could take more than one pill if she wanted, as long as she took them three times a day. "Sometimes I would take two of them," she said. "Sometimes I'd get up in the night and take them."

It became an unending cycle: The extra Dilantin doses made her feel disoriented and weak; as she grew weaker, she would add another pill, thinking it would make her feel better. "I didn't know, Mr. Dash," she says, her voice reflecting pain and embarrassment. "I was trying to get well."

Rosa Lee can recognize certain words—enough to fool strangers —but the pages of a book look to her like a mass of gray, encrypted code. She can decode bits of it, spotting a word here and there that she knows, but she cannot make sense out of the sentences.

She often asks me to break the code for her. One morning at her favorite McDonald's, she asks me to explain a letter she has received from Washington's public housing agency. We are having breakfast after her daily visit to one of the two nearby drug-treatment clinics.

She rifles through the rolled-up sheaf of tattered papers she always carries in her pocketbook. The filing system I had set up for her a few months earlier has been abandoned. She scrutinizes each piece of paper for the housing agency's recognizable letterhead. The bulky stack is her portable filing cabinet, the place where she keeps all her documents, some dating back years. She never throws anything away, because she can't read well enough to decide what she needs and what she can discard.

Finally, she finds what she is looking for and hands it to me.

"This is the wrong letter," I say.

"No, it isn't!" she retorts. "Read the letter. It's from public housing!"

I shake my head and point to the date at the top of the letter: 1989. "This refers to public housing you lived in on Blaine Street two years ago," I say, "not to the application you have filed for a new apartment."

"Are you sure, Mr. Dash? Read it and make sure."

"This is not the letter. I've read it. In fact, you can throw this away."

"Don't you dare!" she says, snatching it. "I might need it."

It is infuriating that someone with such a sharp and quick mind is shut out from much of the world around her. She cannot find an unfamiliar street on a map of Washington, but she skillfully navigates the complicated bureaucracy of the city's public housing agency, repeatedly securing apartments for herself and her family ahead of other applicants who have been on waiting lists for years. Balancing a checkbook is out of the question, but she successfully handled large sums of money when she was dealing drugs in the 1970s and 1980s, satisfying customers and wholesale suppliers not known for patience.

She tries to hide her illiteracy by going on the offensive. Anyone spelling a name for her is ordered to slow down while she prints each letter in big, bold capitals. Sometimes, she casually hands over pen and paper and asks the person to write it for her, as if she were too busy to be bothered. She's so good at covering up her illiteracy that I find myself forgetting that she can't even read the few words on a medicine bottle label.

Saturday is my birthday. I stop by Rosa Lee's hospital room in the afternoon, dropping off a bunch of black seedless grapes for her, before going to celebrate. Since our visit to the Pepco office the previous September, this is the first time she has seen me in suit and tie.

"Where ya going all dressed up?" she asks, smiling, after we greet each other.

"I'm going out later. It's my birthday," I tell her.

"How old are you?" she continues.

"Forty-seven," I answer.

"Oh, you're an old, tired man. Over the hill." Rosa Lee laughs.

"Thank you," I reply with feigned anger. "I really need you to tell me that I'm an old, tired man and over the hill. On your birthday, I say, 'Happy Birthday, Rose.' But you talk about how old I am. I'll remember that. I seem to remember you being upset that no one remembered your birthday one of the last times you were in here. You wait 'til your next birthday comes around. I'll fix you good! In fact, I think I'll take my grapes back."

Rosa Lee continues to laugh at my empty threat. "There's nothing you can do can hurt me, buddy."

She's back to her feisty self.

I expect the same bouncy frame of mind when I call her Sunday morning. Instead, Rosa Lee begins crying into the telephone. "Richard's going to get me put out of here, Mr. Dash." This is just incredible, I think. It never stops. Rosa Lee remains stuck in perpetual turmoil and pain holding on to her adult children.

Richard had brought Rosa Lee's grandson, the boy she had taught how to shoplift a flight jacket, to visit her in the hospital on Saturday, shortly after I left. Rosa Lee was happy to see the boy when he walked into her room alone. She asked him how he'd gotten to the hospital. He told her he'd come by bus with his uncle Richard. In the hospital lobby, he continued, Richard gave him instructions on how to get to Rosa Lee's room and told the boy he would meet him there. "I got something to do," Richard announced.

Rosa Lee asked her grandson whether Richard had a tote bag with him. Yes, he replied, a big one, collapsed and folded up under his arm. Twenty minutes later, Richard walked into Rosa Lee's room holding the full tote bag by its handles.

"Richard, I hope you haven't been doing what I think you've been doing," Rosa Lee said, annoyed.

Richard played dumb. "Whatcha mean, Mama? I came here to see you. How are you feeling?"

Rosa Lee didn't say any more. She didn't want the patient in the bed next to hers to know that Richard had gone quickly around the hospital, slipping into empty rooms and stealing telephones.

In a dinner interview with Richard four days later, he insists that he has gotten off crack and, because of that, has dropped his practice of stealing from Washington's hospitals and office buildings. It's our second lengthy interview in a month and I'd rather he tell me the truth about his life, so I decide on a little shock treatment.

"Tell me how many telephones you got out of Howard on Saturday," I say.

Richard stops spooning up his seafood gumbo and sits back in the booth. "Great God almighty!"

"In a big tote bag," I continue.

"You know, I feel so bad about it, I'm not going to ever, ever do that again," he says, picking up his spoon.

"Tell me how many telephones you got," I repeat.

"Five," he responds. Normally, he says, he can sell them for forty dollars apiece.

"How much did you flip them for?"

He earned only forty dollars for all five telephones. He had to move them fast. He needed to buy some crack. "I sell them to people that I know. Beauty parlors. I got customers out there, Mr. Dash. Liquor stores. Restaurants. Chinese stores. They buy them."

It's clear Richard will soon be going back to prison. "The last time you went down to Lorton, you got busted over at the Washington Hospital Center stealing telephones," I remind him.

Richard keeps his head bowed over his gumbo and nods, indicating yes, he knows.

On the afternoon after her release from the hospital—a blustery March day that makes us welcome the warmth of her apartment—Rosa Lee and I are sitting on the plaid couch in her living

room. Howard Hospital has given her a new prescription schedule, and she has asked me to help her take the medicine correctly
this time.

I have a legal-size notepad of white, blue-lined paper. I intend
to write up a schedule in bold print using her physical descriptions of the medications with words she says she can read.

I pick up one of the amber-colored plastic containers. "This is
the phenobarbital. I notice they reduced the amount down to
thirty milligrams. When you left Greater Southeast, they had you
up to sixty milligrams." I shake several into my hand. "Now, do
you recognize this tablet? What do you see it as?"

Rosa Lee squints at it. "The little white pill. That's the kind
that makes me drowsy."

I print "LITTLE WHITE PILL" on the paper and hold up a
different pill. "Tell me what you see this pill as. This is the Dilantin."

"Is that one of the seizure pills?"

"Yes."

"A white-and-orange pill," she says. "That's the one I took so
many of."

"Right," I say. "That's what made you sick." I write "WHITE
AND ORANGE" on the list.

"Now this one," I say, displaying a folic acid tablet that she
takes as part of her HIV treatment.

Rosa Lee studies it. "Little white pill," she says tentatively.

"No, no, no. That's the phenobarbital. This pill is the yellow
pill. Here, look at it again."

"The yellow pill," she repeats, staring at the tablet.

"All right," I say, moving on to the last container. "This is the
retrovir, the AZT. This is for your condition of being HIV positive. Now, you tell me how you see this pill."

"My blue and white."

I show Rosa Lee what I am writing. "I'm putting down the
times you are to take each pill."

"Okay," she says, "but please put the P.M. and the A.M. for
me."

"I am. Now read this to me."

She read each word slowly, carefully, like a rock climber ascending a cliff. "Little white pill: 8 A.M., 1 P.M., and 6 P.M. The white and orange pill: 8 A.M., 1 P.M., and 6 P.M. The yellow pill: 8 A.M."

I interrupt. "You only take that once."

"Once. Okay. Blue and white pill: 8 A.M., 2 P.M., and 8 P.M."

"Right," I say. "Now, will that work for you?"

"Yes," she says.

Rosa Lee taped the list to the wall outside her bedroom so that her grandchildren, who read better than she does, could help her. As her strength returned and she spent more time away from home again, she took the medication schedule from the wall and stuck it in her pocketbook. After several weeks, she memorized the routine, and the list became just one more out-of-date item in her portable filing cabinet.

Rosa Lee has no trouble remembering when she began hiding her illiteracy.

It was 1953, and she was sixteen years old, separated from her husband of a few months and raising three children in her mother's house near Capitol Hill. It was the last place she wanted to be. Living in Rosetta's house meant living by Rosetta's rules, and those rules were choking Rosa Lee.

Rosetta and her family had come to Washington in the mid-1930s, seeking refuge from their harsh lives as sharecroppers in North Carolina and Maryland. While Earl was alive, and even more so after his death in 1948, Rosetta's domestic work brought in the household's most dependable income.

Just as Rosetta's mother had prepared her to be both a share-cropper and a domestic worker, Rosetta schooled Rosa Lee in domestic work. Long before Rosa Lee turned ten, her mother taught her to scrub laundry on a washboard, to wash a floor so it shined, to make a bed so it looked crisp and neat. Rosa Lee's apartment is a monument to those lessons; no matter how many people are living there, it is always tidy, clean, and well organized.

As the eldest girl, Rosa Lee was expected to do laundry for

everyone in the house: by the time she was in the third grade, she was spending hours at the scrub board every week, washing sweaters and shirts. "My mother didn't ask me did I have my homework done," Rosa Lee says. "When she came home from work, she'd say, 'Betcha didn't pull those sheets. Betcha didn't wash those clothes.' School wasn't important to her, and it wasn't important to me."

That was what Rosetta Wright's generation always called "training," says the historian Elizabeth Clark-Lewis. "It was a very bad reflection on the mother, the family, the broader community for a young woman not to be well trained. Training is reflected in what you can do with your hands, be it cleaning the house, washing expertly."

Since the early 1980s, Clark-Lewis has interviewed more than 120 black migrant women from the South. Eighty-three of them were of the same generation and out of the same southern rural traditions as Rosetta Wright. They came to Washington from all over the South in the 1920s and 1930s to work as domestics. About twenty, like Rosetta, were from rural North Carolina. "The reality of domestic work was all pervasive for black women of that generation," Clark-Lewis says.

As I spoke with Clark-Lewis, it became clear why education was such a low priority to Rosetta Wright. She had grown up in a time and place where hard work was the only way rural black sharecroppers could survive. What little education Rosetta managed to get in the segregated schools had not given her the wherewithal to sustain herself and her family. Especially not in Washington. Work did that. And if you were a black woman, work meant domestic work.

Rosetta's parents, Thadeous and Lugenia Lawrence, never had a school to attend, so they did not learn even the rudiments of reading, writing, and arithmetic. Both grew up in the isolation of the forests and swamplands of the Bishop and Powell Plantation near the hamlet of Rich Square, North Carolina, before marrying in 1916. When the white renter of the plantation, Joe Purvis, went broke in 1925, the Lawrences and their children moved to another farm ten miles north, where they sharecropped for its white owner, Charlie Lane, for four years.

Rosa Lee knows little about her grandparents or their experiences. She knows that they picked cotton in North Carolina before coming north a short time before Rosa Lee was born in Washington, but she doesn't know much else. "I don't know if my parents and grandparents came together or not," she says. "No one ever told me about that stuff and I never asked."

Thadeous Lawrence was a big man who almost never smiled. Rosa Lee remembers that, as a child, she thought her grandfather's serious demeanor was strange. "He wouldn't laugh or nothing, Mr. Dash," she recalls. "I just remember him sitting in a chair on his porch all day not doing nothing and not saying nothing." She once asked him why he never laughed, and she still remembers his reply. "We've had such a hard time down in them sticks" in North Carolina, he told her, "I don't see much to laugh about."

She didn't understand his response and still doesn't. "What do you think he meant by that, Mr. Dash?" she asks. "That's all I remember him saying."

I respond that her grandparents and parents lived in the South when segregation was rigidly enforced, rural blacks received little or no education, black men were routinely lynched, blacks had no legal rights, and their labor was exploited.

Rosa Lee says she understands what I've said. "I heard them talking sometimes about North Carolina and what they had to put up with, but I never really understood all of it," she continues. "Just bits and pieces."

On the Lane farm, the Lawrences settled into a ramshackle, weather-beaten two-story sharecropper's house on the northern edge of Quarter Swamp. The house is still occupied today, although it has been added on to and covered with dark green aluminum siding. The Lawrences sent their children, Ozetta, Rosetta, Joseph, and Jean, to the two-room schoolhouse at Cumbo, the nearest school available for black children, on the south side of the swamp.

The four Lawrence children were allowed to attend school

only when two circumstances converged: when there was no work to be done on Charlie Lane's farm and when the water in Quarter Swamp was low. That did not mean many days at school.

When the water was "up," the children could not use the two-mile-long footpath—a route cut by the longer-legged adult boot-leggers—which enabled them to get to school in little more than half an hour. The only alternative was to walk along five and a half miles of dirt road, which took them almost two hours—each way.

The water in Quarter Swamp was often up year-round, even in the cold of winter when there was little farmwork to be done. Rotting swamp vegetation keeps the bogs warmer than the surrounding land, and the running stream agitates the water so it won't freeze. Sometimes, Lugenia Lawrence sent her children along the longer dirt-road route, but most of the time she did not, according to Mamie Barnes, now in her mid-seventies, who attended the Cumbo School with all the Lawrence children. "That swamp didn't freeze over in the winter like you might think it would," remembers Barnes. "The water would be up from melted snow and ice."

Barnes's late husband's first wife was Lugenia Lawrence's sister. She knew all the Lawrences well and is close to Rosa Lee's brother Ben. She's never met Rosa Lee.

Compared to the Lawrences, Mamie Barnes was fortunate. She lived south of the swamp and did not have to contend with crossing the soggy morass at all. She was able to attend classes many more days than they did. She completed the seventh grade when she was fifteen, ending her education to take care of her ailing mother.

"We all went to that school together," says Barnes. "We all was in the same class." The Lawrences "didn't come to school too much 'cause it was too far to walk. And they didn't go to school too much in the winter. When it snowed, they had to stay home for a long time. If it rained, they stayed home."

Although Barnes was six years younger than Ozetta, and five years younger than Rosetta, the two Lawrence sisters missed so much school "that I went by them in grade. They even stopped school before they moved from Charlie Lane's farm" in 1929.

The white landlords of Rich Square had no interest in encouraging the black sharecroppers to send their children to school. Education was a threat to the sharecropping system that dominated much of the South when Rosetta was growing up in the 1920s; sharecroppers who could read and write might take their labor elsewhere. If they could do math, they might be able to tally up their own debits and earnings, and come to a different reckoning at the end of the harvest, a reckoning that would not leave them in debt to the white landowner.

The Lawrences were in the bottom tier of the three new post–Civil War class formations among African Americans in Northampton County, according to local amateur historian Samuel Glenn Baugham, who knew Thadeous Lawrence. The social hierarchy operated within the rigid confines of racial segregation and discrimination that affected all blacks.

The Lawrences were extremely isolated sharecroppers known as "river" or "swamp" blacks, who lived and worked on the plantations bordering the swamps along the Roanoke River. The river blacks were descendants of the slaves who had worked on the same plantations and, until the Depression, were cut off from even the small flow of humanity that passed through Rich Square. Generally, they had limited or no access to education.

Earl Wright came out of the "piney woods" blacks, the African American sharecroppers from around Rich Square who looked down on and generally ostracized the river blacks. Also the descendants of slaves, they lived in and among the pine tree lots far back from the meandering Roanoke River. They had easier access to education at an all-black school in Rich Square.

The descendants of the African Americans who were "free coloreds" before Emancipation were at the top of this hierarchy. They were better educated and had craftsmen's skills, such as carpentry and masonry, which the two lower groups lacked. Those among them who were not landowners were also the first to migrate North when urban factory employment opportunities first opened up for blacks during World War I.

By the time her son Ben was born in 1932, the fifteen-year-old Rosetta had worked in the cotton fields for a decade. The countless hours spent in the fields changed her body and shaped her soul, and taught her the importance of discipline and stamina. She developed quick, powerful arms and a tough, stern demeanor—a younger version of the grim, brooding woman in the photograph in Rosa Lee's bedroom.

There is no available record of the Lawrence "share" in 1932, no way to know whether the family earned enough to repay the white landowner for the money he had advanced them over the course of the year. According to family lore, Thadeous had a hidden source of income that kept the family from falling into irredeemable debt: a moonshine still. "My grandmother said my grandfather did a lot of bootlegging," says Ben. "He had plenty money! She said sometimes she would not see him for three and four months at a time. By bootlegging, he was able to pay off everything he owed" the white landowner.

Many sharecroppers, however, remained perpetually in debt, unable to make their share, yoked to the same landowner year after year. Most could not read or write, add or subtract, so they had no way to challenge the landowner's tally at harvest time. The Lawrences and Wrights were no different. Ben says his grandparents and father could not read or do arithmetic, but his mother could read a little.

Sharecropping for black farmers was a particularly harsh life, made even harsher by the effect the Depression was having on cotton farmers around Rich Square. In the space of three years, the price of a bale of cotton dropped from $500 to $250. So when Joe Purvis returned to Rich Square after the 1932 fall harvest and offered the Lawrences the opportunity to work with him on a dairy and tobacco farm in St. Mary's County, Maryland, the family decided to leave their friends and relatives and the land they knew so well. Rosetta, her six-month-old son, Ben, and her new husband, Earl Wright, joined the Lawrences on the journey.

Ben and Joe Louis vividly remember the stories that their mother and grandmother told them about their harsh life in southern Maryland. They had almost no money. Meals frequently consisted of whatever they could pick or trap. "They were eating a lot of muskrat and watercress," Joe Louis says. Watercress grew abundantly in the clear springs nearby, and muskrat was then a popular regional dish that the family never got used to. "My mother would say, if she ever got a job and made any money, she was never going to eat another muskrat," Joe Louis remembers. "Had to eat it, because that's all they could trap."

After the 1935 harvest, like thousands of other sharecroppers during the 1930s and 1940s, Rosetta and Earl Wright gave up rural life and headed for the city. The Lawrences stayed behind with three-year-old Ben, afraid that the boy might starve if his parents couldn't find work in Washington. Ben spent his entire childhood with his grandparents. "I was the oldest grandchild and a boy. They favored boys in those days. It was a different time. My mother was a fifteen-year-old teenager when she had me. She was still living at home. I used to call my grandmother 'Mama.' "

Six months after Rosetta and Earl moved to Washington, the Lawrences followed. The family's sharecropping days were over.

Washington in the 1930s was no land of opportunity for black migrants from the South, especially poor sharecroppers. It was a segregated city, but within the black community was a well-established and educated middle class that traced its roots to the freed slaves who stayed after the Civil War. Over the years, these families had built an extensive network of churches, schools, theaters, and other institutions. It wasn't a closed society, but neither did it reach out to embrace poor migrants from rural areas.

Some of the more fortunate newcomers had friends or family in the city to help them through resettlement. Others, like the Lawrences and Wrights, were on their own. Finding a job, any job, was a challenge.

Most of the jobs then open to blacks—as Post Office clerks and federal agency messengers and cafeteria workers and railroad station porters—went to middle-class blacks who had connections or education, says Portia P. James, the chief researcher at Washington's Anacostia Museum, one of the major repositories of black Washington's history. "You had to have certain resources to get those jobs," James told me. "Those jobs were very competitive. Low-level civil service positions were for the elite of black people. Those weren't considered just regular working-class jobs. Those jobs were considered highly desirable jobs." Middle-class blacks "knew how to take advantage of opportunity," she says. "That's how they got where they were."

For those migrating out of the rural South with farming skills and almost no education, employment opportunities were extremely limited. Thadeous and Earl became general laborers on construction projects, while Lugenia and Rosetta became domestics. This fit a familiar pattern, according to Elizabeth Clark-Lewis. "The middle class was not standing waiting for these people with open arms," she says. "There was a great deal of resistance to them. They had unrefined ways. There were color issues. There were all kinds of class issues. Education issues. Very few men could come in and get a government job, and for most poor, rural women, domestic work was the reality."

As the family grew—Rosetta gave birth to twenty-two children, ten of whom died before reaching adulthood—Rosa Lee became accustomed to bedrooms crammed with too many people and living rooms with no place for private conversation. But one thing that Rosa Lee could never understand was why her brothers could not chop the wood needed to heat the water to wash the endless tubs of sheets and clothes. "Why did I have to do all the work when my brothers could go out and play? I could see them in front of the house. My mother favored my brothers. It was like I was already a day worker and cleaning up behind them. They didn't have to do NOTHING! It used to make me mad! Mr. Dash, I didn't understand it." And she still doesn't understand it all these years later.

"They worshipped boys," agrees Clark-Lewis, explaining the values of Rosetta Wright's generation. "They absolutely adored sons. Sons are their joy." Women like Rosa Lee's mother, she continues, believed that "daughters are to be trained. They are to be worked. They are to be reared! But they are not to be indulged because life is not going to allow them to be indulged. It's part of being African American and female."

Rosa Lee remembers complaining to her mother about the number of chores she had to do and how young she was. "I was still in Giddings [Elementary] School when she gave me the whole house to clean, all the clothes to wash. Mr. Dash, it was just not fair! I told her, too. I stood out of reach of her arm when I did. Like on the other side of the room with something between us. Like a bed or something."

Rosetta Wright would look at her eldest daughter and shake her head, saying, "You're going to find out. This is the only kind of job we can find for black people."

As the first-born girl, Rosa Lee's role was set by the southern traditions that had shaped her mother. "For the older daughter, in particular," says Clark-Lewis, "the mother is so dependent on her carrying the household that the younger ones will have opportunities that the older one just won't have. By the time you are four, there are clear expectations that people have of you. By *eight*, you are considered dull or dim-witted if you cannot carry on almost all the functions of a household. Period!"

While Rosa Lee was still in the early years at Giddings, her smoldering resentment caused her to silently reject her mother's vision of her future. She was determined that domestic work was not going to be the way she survived. "I didn't tell my mother— she would have smacked me in the mouth—but I told myself that I wasn't going to work in white people's houses like she did. I didn't trust white people. I had never heard but that they had done us harm. Why would I want to work in their houses?"

The first-grade classroom at Giddings Elementary School that welcomed six-year-old Rosa Lee in the fall of 1942 was a long way from the Cumbo School that Rosetta Wright had first gone to seventeen years earlier in rural North Carolina. But there was one similarity between the schools that Rosetta and Rosa Lee attended: Both were part of the South's segregated school systems.

Rosa Lee's difficulty with reading and writing began in first grade. She does not remember getting any special help from teachers. "If you didn't learn it, you just didn't learn it," she said.

Then one morning at the beginning of fourth grade in 1946, nine-year-old Rosa Lee saw that school could be something more than a place of idleness and frustration. Although Rosa Lee's classroom was on the second floor, she followed a boy up to his third-floor classroom. "His name was Herman. I went up there and sat in the back. I meddled with the boy, but I saw he wasn't paying me a bit of mind. Then I got my mind off of him and started looking at how Miss Whitehead was teaching." Rosa Lee had heard Miss Whitehead did things differently in her classroom.

Within a few hours, Rosa Lee felt as if she had stumbled into a new school. On the second floor, she and her classmates rotated among four classrooms every day. But Miss Whitehead's students stayed all day in the same classroom and Miss Whitehead handled all the subjects. The students in Miss Whitehead's class had paper and pencils. Downstairs in her classroom, Rosa Lee was not required to write much of anything most of the time.

In Miss Whitehead's classroom, "the students didn't make a lot of noise. They didn't be in the back messing with each other. They were doing their work. I actually sat there and looked around. 'Well, I'll be derned.' This teacher acted like she really cared about her students."

On the second floor, the teachers seemed to spend a lot of time in the hall, talking to each other, while Rosa Lee and her classmates played and "meddled with each other." The teachers would "come back into the classroom if we got too loud. Tell us to be quiet. Then they went back out into the hallway." By contrast, Miss Whitehead's class seemed calm, orderly and exciting.

For three straight days, Rosa Lee climbed the stairs to Miss Whitehead's classroom and sat there, undetected. For the first time in her life, she found school fascinating. "She was teaching!" she told me. "She made you feel like you were learning something." Rosa Lee planned to stay upstairs forever.

Why weren't the children downstairs taught like that? she asked a girlfriend. The friend told her that the second-floor class was for "slow learners."

No one had told Rosa Lee that she was a slow learner. She remembers angrily cutting her friend off. "I don't want to hear that shit!" Rosa Lee forever felt the sting of the phrase *slow learner*. It was not true that she was slow, but no one ever told Rosa Lee anything different.

It seems difficult to believe, but Rosa Lee went unnoticed in the class for those three days. On the fourth day, she raised her hand to ask a question. Miss Whitehead asked, "Who are you and what are you doing in my class?" She asked Rosa Lee to stay behind during recess.

After the other students left, Miss Whitehead asked Rosa Lee where she was supposed to be, and Rosa Lee told her the name of her assigned teacher, adding that she preferred to be in Miss Whitehead's class. "But that's not the way we do things," Miss Whitehead told her. "You have to pass to my class."

Rosa Lee told her, " 'I can't read, but I can do number work.' I showed her my paper."

Miss Whitehead insisted that she return to her regular class-room.

"But I like the way you teach up here," Rosa Lee said. "Why won't you let me come up here?"

"You're not supposed to be up here," she remembers Miss Whitehead saying. "You're supposed to be downstairs."

Rosa Lee retreated to the second floor. "That was the most painful thing. I really wanted to stay up in her room. She was teaching and she made you feel like you were learning something."

Later that school year, Rosa Lee began skipping school frequently. When her teacher would turn her back to the classroom, "I would go right out that side door, Mr. Dash," Rosa Lee tells me one day as we stand inside her second-floor classroom at Giddings, which is now an adult education center. "I would go and get some other kids out of the room. Mr. Dash, I was a bad girl. We would hang on the back steps." On many mornings, she left the house as if she were going to school, but she spent the day roaming the streets of her Capitol Hill neighborhood instead. Rosa Lee says her mother was never notified about her absences. And despite her inability to read, she was promoted to the fifth and sixth grades.

At the end of her sixth-grade year, Rosa Lee's class was called to the assembly hall for its graduation ceremony. She knew she was not graduating so she sat in the last row, trying to hide. "I cried and cried, Mr. Dash," she recalls, sadly. "I didn't know what to do."

It was the spring of 1949 and Rosa Lee had been held back twice during her elementary school years. After the graduation ceremony, a schoolteacher came by her house. The teacher told Rosa Lee and her mother that Rosa Lee would be allowed to attend junior high school in the fall. "She told me I was being passed on account of my age," Rosa Lee said, "not because I had passed any of my classes."

Rosa Lee isn't sure how she made it as far in school as she did, considering her reading problems. Though she would have been allowed to return to seventh grade after Bobby was born, she never did go back to school. She had Ronnie at fifteen, and then, weeks after her sixteenth birthday, she married the father of Alvin, her third child.

Rosetta had insisted that Rosa Lee marry twenty-year-old Albert Cunningham. She told Albert if he didn't marry her daughter, she would report him to the police "on account of I was underage," says Rosa Lee. "I was only fifteen when I got pregnant by him." Rosa Lee didn't love Albert, but she was thrilled anyway. Marriage meant she could leave her mother's house forever. Four months after they married, she was back: her husband beat her after he found out that Rosa Lee had been sleeping with a neighborhood boy who lived in the house next-door to her mother's.

"My face was so swollen my mother didn't recognize me coming in the door," says Rosa Lee. "She told me, 'You don't have to go back to that man.'" Albert came by Rosetta's house that evening looking for Rosa Lee. Rosetta met him at the door and told him Rosa Lee was not ever going back to his house.

Yet those few months of independence made it hard for Rosa

Lee to return. She and her mother argued often about Rosa Lee's welfare checks. Rosa Lee wanted the money to come to her, but Rosetta said she was too young. "What are you going to do with it?" Rosa Lee remembers her mother saying. "You don't even know how to pour piss out of a boot."

"I never saw a penny of it!" recalls Rosa Lee. "If I even asked for ten, fifteen dollars so I could have something, I didn't get it."

Rosa Lee craved her mother's love and affection, but she also feared her. She looked at her mother's broad back and powerful hands, and could think only about how to avoid the stinging slaps Rosetta often delivered during their arguments. "My mother classified me as very dumb," Rosa Lee told me one day. "It was almost as if she was making fun of me. I never felt that my mother loved me."

The friction between Rosetta and Rosa Lee, the quick smacks and harsh beatings for any infraction, was not something unique to them; it was a common tradition from the rural black South. "Especially between mothers and daughters," says Portia James. The way Rosetta raised Rosa Lee "seems to be a very typical [southern rural] upbringing," as opposed to what would be expected in an urban culture.

Rosa Lee saw public housing as her escape. With the help of friends, and without telling her mother, she found her way to the public housing agency one afternoon. She asked a clerk there for help, telling him that she could not fill out the application by herself. The memory of his sneer still causes her mouth to tighten and her voice to thicken. "Back in those days, they didn't give you any sympathy when you said you couldn't read," she says. "It was like, 'So what? It ain't my fault.'" Humiliated, she trudged back to her mother's house. She vowed never again to reveal her illiteracy to someone she didn't know.

"Can you read?" she asked her then-current boyfriend, the boy who lived next-door to her mother. Of course he could read, he told her. Couldn't she?

No, Rosa Lee said defiantly. She sat next to him, brooding silently, while he filled out the applications to switch the welfare payments to her and to get Rosa Lee into public housing.

The showdown with Rosetta came four days later.

Rosa Lee was relaxing on the front porch, feeling good that she had completed her chores for the day, when she felt Rosetta's strong fingers jab her in the shoulder.

"Why didn't you tell me that you went and applied for welfare?" Rosetta demanded.

Rosa Lee had forgotten to check the mailbox. Now it was too late. She decided it was time to stand up to her mother. "I wanted to get me and my kids out of your hair," she remembers saying. "It seems like my kids were getting on your nerves."

Her mother's response was tinged with anger. "They're not the only ones getting on my damn nerves!"

Shaking her head at the memory, Rosa Lee stops narrating the scene for a moment. "My mother was very hard!" says Rosa Lee, before continuing.

Rosetta went on, "I don't know what this is going to prove. I've got to sign that I'm no longer taking care of them."

Rosa Lee had her response ready. "Mama, you're not taking care of them. *I'm* taking care of them. I take care of them all the time. Not only my children. I take care of my brothers and sisters. It's time for me to take my children and leave."

Rosa Lee was praying that this was as far as their conversation would go "because I was scared. She was ready to hit me because I was taking income from her."

Rosetta wanted to know more. Who helped her? How did she know where to send the application?

"I got somebody to help me! You wouldn't help me!" Rosa Lee retorted.

"Who are you talking to like that?" Rosetta said in the tone that Rosa Lee knew well.

"Mama," Rosa Lee pleaded, "you would not help me fill it out."

"How am I going to help you fill it out when I can't even read it myself?" Rosetta shouted.

Rosa Lee was stunned. She had assumed that her mother could read, and did not know that Ben helped Rosetta whenever there were any forms to fill out.

"Why didn't you tell me you couldn't read, Mama?" asked Rosa Lee.

" 'Cause I thought it was none of your damn business!" Rosetta said.

It is a January morning and Rosa Lee is fretting over her telephone bill. She stares at the eight pages, trying to figure out how her bill could be $241 when her monthly service costs $15.38.

She thrusts the bill into my hands. "Read it for me, Mr. Dash," she says, her lower lip trembling as it always does when she's upset.

As we talk, Ronnie, Richard, and Ducky are in the living room. They are watching a movie on cable, which Rosa Lee had installed for them. Patty is asleep on the couch after an all-night crack cocaine binge. None of them is working at the moment, and no one is helping Rosa Lee to pay the sixty-four-dollar monthly rent, the electricity and phone bills, or the cable.

Rosa Lee has the only steady income. The legal part is the $437 a month she receives from the Supplemental Security Income program for the disabled poor; the government considers her disabled because her medical problems and lack of skills limit her job prospects.

Money never lasts long in the Cunningham household, so when the phone bill arrived in late December, Rosa Lee was frantic. The words on the first page—"Message Units" and "Federally Ordered Subscriber Line Charge"—meant nothing to her. The subsequent pages, each showing totals and subtotals, confused her even more. She couldn't check the numbers, much as her sharecropping grandparents could not check the landowner's math when he added up their share after each harvest.

She put the bill aside. Three days after Christmas, the phone company disconnected the line. When her disability check came after New Year's, Rosa Lee paid $140 and the service was restored. But with $101 unpaid, Rosa Lee is worried. Her worries grow when D.C. Cablevision threatens to cut off its service as well.

I'm not eager to get caught up in her personal affairs again. I suggest she call Alvin. She can trust him to take care of it.

"NO, NO, NO!" Rosa Lee screams at me, tears trickling down her face. "Alvin's going to be angry and fuss at me for letting these grown-ass children live off of me! No! You've got to help me! You've got to call the phone company. If I call them, I'll only get flustered, and they'll find out I can't read. These bills are kicking my butt, and I'm not getting any help to pay them. *Please? Please?*"

"Okay, okay, okay," I reply, my head pounding, "but they won't be able to hear me if you're crying."

I scan the bill, which shows a balance of $137 from November, and quickly notice several problems.

Someone has been making calls to 900 numbers that charge four dollars a minute for sexually explicit conversations. After checking with Rosa Lee, I ask the phone company to put a block on the line that will prevent any more calls to 900 numbers.

There also are thirty-eight calls to directory assistance, at a cost of $9.88. That makes sense: Only Richard reads well enough to use the printed phone book, so everyone else uses directory assistance to find phone numbers.

And there are 511 message units for local calls outside the District—to phone numbers in Maryland and Virginia. This is a mystery: Rosa Lee, who didn't realize that she had to pay extra for such calls, says she doesn't know who might be making so many calls.

As I get an explanation of the charges from the billing office, I look at Rosa Lee accusingly. The 511 message units were all calls to the *same* number in Prince George's County. This was on top of 340 calls made to the number in November. What is going on? I ask.

Rosa Lee looks both surprised and sheepish. She has been letting a young woman down the hall use the phone to call her boyfriend in Prince George's County. The woman's phone has been disconnected for several months. But Rosa Lee had no idea the woman has been making so many calls.

It doesn't make sense. Why would the woman call her

boyfriend 511 times in one month, an average of seventeen calls a day? And how does she do it without Rosa Lee's knowledge?

The answer, it turns out, is drugs. Rosa Lee finally tells me the woman's boyfriend is a crack dealer, and the woman has been relaying orders for neighborhood teenagers who work for him. She makes most of the calls during the day, when Rosa Lee is out. One of Rosa Lee's children lets her in.

Rosa Lee is upset to learn the woman has taken advantage of her. But she is reluctant to cut off her use of the phone.

"What?" I say. "Why?"

"Sometimes I need some bread," Rosa Lee says. "Sometimes I need some sugar, or something . . . and I ask her to get it for me."

When Rosa Lee's arthritic knee is too painful for her to walk to the store, she would rather send her neighbor than one of her own children. "They spend my money on crack and don't come back with my change or my food," Rosa Lee says.

She gets up and begins nervously cleaning up her spotless bedroom, aimlessly opening the drawers in her bureau. Her bottom lip trembles, and tears begin to fall. I've been through this scene more times than I can count, so I get up to leave. "NO!" she shouts. "Don't leave! Stay with me a little while!"

She picks up the large brass crucifix that she keeps on top of her television, clasping it to her chest. "I need somebody to stand by me!" she says loudly, her voice reverberating off the walls. Her bedroom door is open. I know her children in the living room can hear every word. "I don't have nobody. I don't have nobody. I can't do it by myself."

For more than an hour, Rosa Lee continues her monologue, interrupted occasionally by a question from me. "I stick with my children. I try to do everything I can. I even give them my money, give them a place to live. I don't care what I do for 'em. It seems like they still walk over top of me."

I speak to her very softly, trying to get her to calm down again. "You don't have to shout."

She shouts again. "I WANT THEM TO HEAR IT!"

I finally get up to leave, telling Rosa Lee I'm exhausted. She says she understands and she won't wear me out like that again.

When I step into the living room, Richard is sitting in a chair watching television. He avoids eye contact with me. Patty is snoring on the couch. She's slept through all of Rosa Lee's shouting. I ask Richard where Ducky is. "Ducky left when Mama started crying," he replies. I walk back to the kitchen. Ronnie is in there cleaning it, although it is spotless.

FOUR

A Hell of a Rush

OVERLEAF: *Patty smokes crack while Ducky waits his turn* (© *Lucian Perkins*—The Washington Post).

A CROWD is milling around the bank of aluminum mailboxes that sits on a grassy island outside Rosa Lee's apartment building. The midday sun is warm on this spring day in 1992, and my car windows are open as Rosa Lee and I pull into the parking lot.

"Has the mailman come yet?" Rosa Lee shouts to her neighbors.

"No," comes the reply.

Ordinarily, the mailman's whereabouts don't generate much interest at the Southeast Washington housing complex where Rosa Lee lives. But today is the first of the month, the day when government checks are due to arrive.

Standing off to the side, surveying the scene, is a group of teenage boys who sell crack cocaine in the Washington Highlands neighborhood. They too are waiting for the mailman. As soon as the checks are cashed, they will begin their rounds, making new sales and collecting old debts.

Even before Rosa Lee reaches the door to her second-floor apartment, it flies open and Patty sticks out her head. "MAMA, HAVE THE CHECKS COME IN YET?" Patty asks in a loud voice, stuttering nervously through the question.

"Patty, you don't have to shout," Rosa Lee says. "You know the checks don't come until one o'clock."

We step into the living room and the reason for Patty's fear becomes clear: Seated on the couch are two teenage crack dealers, known to me only as "Two-Two" and "Little Man." Between them sits Ducky. The three of them are staring at the television, watching a soap opera.

Two-Two and Little Man have come to collect from Patty and Ducky. The teenagers know they have a better chance of getting their money if they show up early, before Rosa Lee and Patty have cashed their checks. I have seen this ritual played out many times before with Rosa Lee's family. Two-Two and Little Man barely acknowledge my presence with a slight nod of their heads. I give a slight nod in return.

Rosa Lee greets them by name. The boys nod, their facial expressions masks of cool indifference. They are dressed in hip-hop style: oversized jeans, baggy shirts, expensive sneakers, and baseball caps. Rosa Lee has asked Two-Two and Little Man several times not to sell crack to Patty and Ducky on credit, but they ignore her. Two-Two is a high school dropout who shows up in front of Rosa Lee's building around noon most days. Little Man lives in a ground-floor apartment directly below Rosa Lee's. Patty and Ducky are in and out of his apartment every afternoon after Little Man gets home from school.

I once asked Rosa Lee why the teenage crack dealers ignore her request not to sell drugs to Patty and Ducky on credit. "Because they know Mama is going to bail her children out," she says.

There is no hint of sarcasm or irony in Rosa Lee's voice, just a simple statement of fact by someone trapped in a drug culture she helps perpetuate.

It's the kind of environment that University of Chicago sociologist William J. Wilson has studied in his work on urban neighborhoods that have become dominated by what he calls "a concentration of poverty." Wilson says it is "extremely difficult" for family members living in close quarters with drug users to come away unscathed. Rosa Lee and her family, he told me, reflect "the effects of living in neighborhoods that are overwhelmingly impoverished, with all the opportunities for illegal activities, with limited opportunities for conventional activity, so people turn to drug use and they turn to crime. The kids growing up in that household are denied mainstream patterns of behavior."

Wilson says he is "not at all" surprised by Rosa Lee's family. The pattern of their lives, he says, is "what happens when you have people who live in these kind of neighborhoods, with certain kinds of disadvantages, where they only interact with themselves. They are socio-isolated in the sense that their contacts are limited to folks like this!"

Illegal activity swirls around Rosa Lee every day. She resents having to protect her adult children from teenage drug dealers, but she always comes to their rescue. With some pride, she tells me about the time she saved Patty and Ducky from Two-Two and Little Man's wrath.

It was last Labor Day weekend. The checks had come early, on Friday and Saturday, because September 1 fell on a Sunday. Before Two-Two and Little Man could find Patty, she had cashed her $252 welfare check and spent it all in a few hours. She paid Rosa Lee the $100 that she had borrowed for crack the month before, paid off several of the other dealers who found her first, and then spent the rest on more crack.

So when Two-Two and Little Man showed up Saturday afternoon to collect $30 from her, $80 from Ducky and $150 from Patty's boyfriend Howard, Patty hid in Rosa Lee's bedroom, Ducky hid in the hall closet, and Howard climbed out the back window using tied-together sheets to reach the ground.

"I want my goddamn money," Two-Two yelled, banging his fist on Rosa Lee's metal apartment door. "Mama Rose, I don't mean no harm. If I let them go, everybody will think they can do it. Would you rather I knock on the door or do you want me to knock them on their ass?"

Rosa Lee knew Two-Two and Little Man meant business. Though she called them "young'uns," they were tougher and less patient than many of the dealers she knew in the 1970s and 1980s, when she made a living selling heroin in Northwest Washington. She didn't want to pay them out of her monthly disability check. "I didn't see any way to make it through the month if I paid all my bills and paid off their debts too," she told me.

"All of a sudden," she says, "my mind started working." She decided to become a crack seller, just for the weekend. She asked Two-Two to introduce her to a crack supplier.

"What can I make with three hundred dollars?" Rosa Lee asked the supplier, a man in his late twenties.

"You can double it," he said. Rosa Lee asked Two-Two and Little Man to wait until she sold the crack, promising that, the following day, she would pay them all the money they were owed. The pair agreed. Later that evening, Rosa Lee handed over $300 in return for thirty plastic bags of crack, each containing one twenty-dollar rock. She then sent Patty and Ducky to round up customers among the "crackheads" they knew.

As the supplier prepared the packages, Rosa Lee's fourteen-year-old granddaughter walked in. The girl understood immediately. "I don't want you to go back to jail, Grandma," she told Rosa Lee.

Buyers trooped up to Rosa Lee's apartment until 5 A.M. She sold some bags at discount and gave in to Patty's and Ducky's pleas for free samples. When it was all over, she hadn't made enough to cover her $300 outlay. She ended up paying off the debts out of her own funds.

"I could've made more if I hadn't given Ducky something now and then, and Patty something now and then," she says.

Exhausted from being awake all night, she washed up and got ready for church.

Since that weekend, Two-Two and Little Man have looked to Rosa Lee whenever Patty or Ducky can't pay up. This particular afternoon is no different. The mailman finally arrives. Rosa Lee agrees to cover the debts, the checks are cashed at a nearby liquor store, and the money changes hands.

As soon as Two-Two and Little Man leave, Patty and Ducky are off in search of more crack.

At 7:30 one cold winter morning, Rosa Lee slams the door to her apartment. She waits outside her building for a few minutes before the government-run van arrives to carry her across the city to the drug-treatment clinic.

Though there is a biting wind, she is glad to have left her crowded apartment. Inside, Patty is sleeping in Rosa Lee's double bed, which they have been sharing for weeks. Ronnie, Richard, and Ducky are asleep on makeshift beds of couch cushions and chair pillows on the living room floor. Ronnie moved in with Rosa Lee in the fall, when his youngest sister put him out of her apartment after her children discovered that money was missing from their piggy banks. It later turned out that Patty had stolen the money, but Ronnie refused to move back to his sister's apartment. He was insulted at having been suspected of stealing from his nephew and niece to pay for his heroin habit. "I'm working every day," Ronnie tells me angrily, referring to his job at a restaurant in suburban Maryland. "What do I need to go into some piggy banks for, Mr. Dash? A man can only take so much, you know what I mean?"

But Rosa Lee is not thinking about the conflicts over drugs and money that occur daily in her apartment. The van is moving steadily along the Southwest Freeway in the morning rush-hour traffic. She'll be at the clinic in a few minutes.

This is the part of her daily routine that she most looks forward to. At the clinic, she sees old friends she has known since the 1970s and 1980s, when she lived at Clifton Terrace in Northwest Washington, a three-building rent-subsidized complex near 14th and W Streets. Several of the men and women she likes, people who bought "Mexican Mud" (brown heroin from Mexico's Sierra Madre highlands) from her the 1960s, go to the clinic and then to McDonald's every morning. These are her "dope-fiend buddies," and they greet her with affection.

"How ya doing, Mama Rose?"

"Ya looking good, Mama Rose."

"Nice to see you, Mama Rose."

She likes the name, which dates from her Clifton Terrace days, and the respect that it implies. She drifts to the back of a line that stretches down the corridor toward a counter encased in Plexiglas. A sign on the Plexiglas sets the rules: "Attention . . .

Your methadone will be in three ounces of water. Please do not ask the nurse for less." Some patients believe the methadone works better if it is less diluted.

The routine is always the same. The line moves forward methodically, dozens of people from different neighborhoods and different backgrounds, all bound together by their addiction. Behind the glass, a nurse measures out the blood-red methadone into a plastic cup, places it on a revolving tray, then spins it so the patient can take the cup through the opening. The patients receive different doses, depending on their weight, how much it is thought they need to effectively curb their craving for heroin, and whether they've recently tested positive for drugs.

The nurse measures out Rosa Lee's dosage. Following the rules, Rosa Lee drinks it down as the nurse watches. The glass between them doesn't encourage conversation. The transaction over, Rosa Lee heads for the door.

As I have done on many weekday mornings, I meet her outside the clinic. When Rosa Lee sees me in the car, she tells the van driver to go on, that I'll drive her back home.

She's had the free van service since coming out of Howard University Hospital after the Dilantin overdose. Still weak and walking unsteadily with a cane, Rosa Lee asked her clinic counselor for the service but was told she would have to get on a months-long waiting list before the van could pick her up. She pointed out of the clinic's front picture window, where I was waiting for her in my car. "Do you know who that is?" she asked. The counselor knew. Rosa Lee had introduced us several months earlier, and he had seen me ferrying Rosa Lee around ever since. "You know Mr. Dash is writing about my life, right?" she continued. "Well, I need to get on that van service or I'll have to tell Mr. Dash how y'all treat an old, sick woman like me who just got out of the hospital. He'll put it all over the *Washington Post*."

Two days later, the van began picking up Rosa Lee at 7:30 A.M. Rosa Lee didn't tell me what she had done until after she had pulled it off.

"YOU WHAT?" I yell. "Rose, I asked you not to do that. I'm not going to write about them not giving you a van."

"I know it," she said. "They don't know it. Don't you know people are afraid of you?"

Since the beginning of our relationship, Rosa Lee has been gingerly exploring how she might reap some dividends from it. She's getting better at dropping my name and mentioning my interest in all aspects of her life, especially when she thinks the connection will help her get something out of whatever bureaucracy she's dealing with. She ignores my protests about using our relationship to manipulate bureaucrats, and generally tells me after she has succeeded in getting "the welfare" to do something quickly for her or in getting the manager of a public housing office to put her application on the top of the pile.

As the van drives off, Rosa Lee gets into my car and we ride the two blocks to McDonald's. She spends several hours there each day, chatting with other patients from the two nearby drug clinics and "regulars" who hang out there. Her routine is the same: She orders Cheerios or the breakfast special of pancakes, sausage, and scrambled eggs.

This particular morning, she settles on Cheerios. She tears open seven packages of sugar, dumps them in her coffee, then rips open several more and empties them onto her cereal. She can't stand to eat anything until she drinks her methadone, so this is her first food of the day.

A woman approaches. She hands Rosa Lee three dollars in a folded lump.

"More Darvon sales?" I ask.

"Yeah," Rosa Lee says.

Darvon is a prescription painkiller that some methadone patients use for a cheap high. They like the prescription tranquilizer Xanax even more, feeling they get a better "buzz" if they take it right after their methadone. Rosa Lee often has a supply of Darvon and Xanax to sell. She was prescribed both drugs after she pretended her back was injured in a bus accident last August. She has used the injury as an excuse for getting refills from several doctors. As a Medicaid patient, she pays just fifty cents for the sixty pills that come in each prescription. She resells Darvon at one dollar a pill and Xanax at two dollars.

She can't refill the prescriptions too often without drawing suspicion, so these sales don't bring in a lot of money. But they give her a certain stature with the McDonald's crowd.

Some days, she will bring in clothes that she has shoplifted to sell or give away. One time, she brought a toddler-size yellow sweat suit that her sons stole in a burglary; she gave it away to a homeless woman who was there with her three-year-old daughter. "I just felt guilty trying to sell it to her," she told me.

A few weeks after I began visiting Rosa Lee regularly, she said that several of her drug buddies at McDonald's couldn't understand why she was allowing me to write about her. "They told me, 'Stay away from reporters. They put people's business in the street.'"

I smiled and confirmed that what they've said is true. "We're nosy and intrusive. I want your permission to follow you for a long time. There will be many days when I will ask you about the same thing over and over again. You might end up cussing me out."

She laughed. "That's all right. You look like you could handle it."

Our relationship has evolved from those early days. I have tried to remain an impartial observer, but, inevitably, I have become a vital part of her life, serving variously as driver, translator, and most important, confidant, listening to her painful recriminations about her life and her children. Staying at arm's length is difficult. My refusals don't deter her from trying to get me involved.

"Mr. Dash," she says, tilting her head and softening her voice, "tell me what should I do."

"I'm not in it, Rose," I'll say.

"'I'm not in it, Rose,'" she mimics. "Why do you always say that? I need your help. I don't have anyone else to talk to."

That's why she enjoys her McDonald's visits. There, she can escape her problems for a while. One day, as she ranted about her children's drug habits, she broke down in tears about how trapped she felt.

"Mr. Dash," she said, "I don't have no friends. The only friends you know I got is up there."

"At McDonald's?"

"McDonald's. That's all. And they're not what you call friends, but that's all I got."

Most of the McDonald's crowd is a generation younger than Rosa Lee. Once in a while, though, she runs into one of her old heroin customers from the days when she waited tables at the Ko Ko Club, a nightclub that once operated at the corner of Eighth and H Streets, N.E. "That's way back," she says. "Not too many alive from those days."

"Those days" were the 1950s and 1960s. In the world that Rosa Lee knows, in the neighborhoods where she grew up, in the places where she raised her children, on the streets where she once bought and sold drugs, there are many people whose lives ended too early, cut short by too much heroin or too much alcohol or simply too much nightclub life.

One day at McDonald's, Rosa Lee pulls an old photograph out of her pocketbook. It is a Polaroid, and it shows a younger Rosa Lee, in her early thirties, dressed in a sleek black outfit, with matching pants and top. Behind her is the dance floor of the Ko Ko Club.

The photo was taken sometime in the late 1960s by a regular customer at the club. Rosa Lee had run into the man recently and he remembered the photo. He ran home to get it, and insisted that Rosa Lee keep it.

It is the only photo I have ever seen of Rosa Lee at this age; she looks smashing and vibrant. She looks as if she belongs.

She never planned to work at the club. As a teenager in the early and mid-1950s, Rosa Lee often went with her girlfriends to the Ko Ko Club to dance and drink. The club's owner noticed her and asked her if she wanted to wait tables. It was her first job. She was twenty years old, and had just given birth to Eric, her fifth child. The year was 1956.

The pay was good, and it was in cash, so she could hide it from the welfare office. She worked at night, leaving the children with baby-sitters. It was fun and exciting. There were live music and flashy customers.

One was a heroin dealer. Soon after she started working at the club, he took her aside and offered her a chance to make a little extra money: If she would sell heroin to customers that he sent her way, she could keep twenty-five dollars for every hundred dollars' worth she sold.

She concealed the heroin, which was contained in small capsules, inside her bra. The capsules sold for one dollar each, and customers usually bought three. "Friday nights was when I would sell them," recalled Rosa Lee. "Friday nights, I would sell hundreds in there. The owner never knew I was selling heroin, but he was always asking me why my tables would be full with customers when the other tables were empty. I told him, ''Cause I take care of my customers!' "

The heroin business was nothing like the crack business today. She never treated her customers the way Two-Two and Little Man now treat Patty and Ducky. She thought of herself as several cuts above jugglers, the drug-addicted dealers who sell heroin on the streets. She was a high-class dealer with high-class customers; they paid promptly and in cash.

She resisted the temptation to take a hit herself. She saw the powerful grip that heroin had on her customers, and it frightened her. Besides, she couldn't afford a heroin habit. By 1961, she had eight children to support. She took a second job at another H Street nightclub, the 821 Club, as a "shake dancer"—that is, a stripteaser. Soon, she was engaging in prostitution with club customers.

"The men would ask if they could take me home," Rosa Lee said. "I'd come right out with it. 'Yeah, you can take me home. I got eight children at home. We need some money for food!' "

She also picked up additional things by shoplifting: shoes for little Patty, pants for one of the boys. She was caught occasionally, but the judges always gave her probation and sent her home. She tearfully told them, "I've got eight children at home, Your Honor."

Rosa Lee's 1965 arrest for trying to steal the fur coat finally interrupted her lifestyle. After her release from the prison in Jessup, Maryland, in the summer of 1966, she returned to her wait-ress job at the Ko Ko Club and resumed her heroin sales. Within a few months, she had moved with all her children into a roach-infested one-bedroom apartment in Northwest Washington.

The children, especially the older ones, remember these years as a time of constant turmoil. Between 1966 and 1968, they moved four times before ending up in a sprawling public hous-ing complex in the Marshall Heights area of Southeast Washing-ton. The apartments had one thing in common: All were located in areas known for illegal drug activity.

Heroin was available to anyone who wanted it, including teenagers. In 1967, Ronnie, at age fifteen, became the first of Rosa Lee's children to try it, and he quickly became addicted. He tried hard to hide his addiction from Rosa Lee, but there was a trail of evidence: He needed money to pay for his habit, so he would sell household items or steal from Rosa Lee's purse. He skipped school often and finally just dropped out during the eighth grade.

Rosa Lee didn't connect any of this to a heroin habit. She had never paid much attention to her children's performance in school, much as Rosetta had never paid much attention to hers. Then, one day in 1969, she found empty heroin capsules and syringes in Ronnie's room.

"Are you doing it?" she asked him in a soft voice.

"Yeah," Ronnie said, ashamed. "You want me to get out?"

Rosa Lee shook her head.

Ronnie was surprised by what she said next. "She told me, just like she told me when I started smoking cigarettes, 'You got to take care of your own habits!' "

In the Marshall Heights neighborhood where Rosa Lee lived in the late 1960s, word got around that she had heroin to sell. Addicts flocked to her apartment in the housing complex on Fifty-seventh Place, S.E., a long street that ends in a cul-de-sac near the line between Prince George's County, Maryland, and the District of Columbia. Some were banging on her door before the sun rose.

"Some of them would be shaking," Rosa Lee told me. "Some said their stomachs hurt. Some said their backs hurt. And they were always begging, begging, begging. They did not have the full price. I'd sell to them at a discount because I couldn't stand the begging and the sniffling and wiping their noses. . . . I wanted them to come back. They'd pay full price when they came back that afternoon, after they had a chance to steal something or hustle up some money."

She sometimes let them go into her bedroom to inject the drug. Her youngest children often were getting ready for school, so Rosa Lee told customers to make sure the door was closed. "After a few minutes, they come out of there completely changed," she says. "They were relaxed, not worried about anything. They'd tell me how good the dope made them feel. I was curious about what dope could do for me, if I could feel good all day. . . . But I was still too scared to try it."

It wasn't long before the police also heard about Rosa Lee's business. That's when the raids began.

One night in 1969, the police battered down the door and the children woke up to find officers, their guns drawn, waving flashlights and shouting, "GET OUTTA BED! GET OUTTA BED!" Rosa Lee's youngest daughter, then eight, remembers she was so afraid that she wet her bed.

The police never found anything. Rosa Lee kept her stash at a friend's house nearby. But the raids continued, sometimes as often as once a month. The younger children had no idea why the police kept breaking down the door. But the older children knew too well what was going on. "They raided us often," Ronnie said. "We were so hot."

The police battered the door to Rosa Lee's apartment so many times that city housing officials grew weary of fixing it, and so, in August 1972, they ordered the family to move. Rosa Lee says she paid a hundred-dollar bribe to a woman in the rental office at Clifton Terrace, her name went to the top of the waiting list, and she moved into a four-bedroom apartment a few days later.

Lonely and looking for "some action" one night several

months later, Rosa Lee went into the Black Nugget nightclub at the corner of 14th and Clifton Streets, just half a block from her new apartment. Rosa Lee was thirty-six. Inside the Black Nugget she met an eighteen-year-old woman nicknamed "Lucky." Lucky approached her about a date. Rosa Lee was intrigued. "This was something new." Rosa Lee laughs. "I had never been with a woman before in my life."

At the outset, Rosa Lee hid her lesbian relationship with Lucky from her children, family, and friends. "I wasn't sure I wanted anyone to know about it." But Lucky pressured Rosa Lee to come out into the open because she wanted to move in with Rosa Lee. In early 1973, Rosa Lee relented and decided to broach the subject with her children.

She called all the children together in their living room. "I asked Bobby, Alvin, Richard, Ronnie, and Eric. I asked all of the biggest ones. All of them were there, though. 'Look. I want to talk to you about something that is very serious and I want you to think about it. I've started liking somebody very much. He makes me happy. We have fun together. Right now, I need something particular in my life. I want him to move in with us.' "

All of her children looked confused when she finished her short speech. Bobby expressed what they were thinking. "Well, Mama," he said, "why are you telling us all this? You never talked to us before" about any of the men who had periodically lived with Rosa Lee.

"The reason I'm saying this is because he's not a he," she continued. "He's a she."

The children looked at each other.

Bobby continued. "Mama, what does she look like? Is she phat [attractive]? I know you're not going to pick something that is going to shame us."

"No, Bobby," Rosa Lee assured him. "I'm not. She's very attractive. Very attractive."

Her children told her it was all right with them "if it made me happy," she says. "Bobby already understood because he was gay." Lucky moved in that evening.

After they had been together about a year, Rosa Lee walked

in on Lucky in the bathroom. A hypodermic syringe was stuck into her left arm. She was injecting Preludin, called "bam" on the street, an amphetamine-like stimulant prescribed as an appetite suppressant. Lucky told Rosa Lee that bam helped her lose weight.

Rosa Lee was not upset by Lucky's drug use. She had continued the practice of letting heroin addicts shoot up in her apartment, although she now charged three dollars. She also bought $150 "bricks" of marijuana, which she and her children would break up into 100 "nickel bags," which sold for five dollars each. "I had traffic in and out of my apartment all day long, but my sons would handle it. 'Mama, give me three bags. Give me two bags.' Bobby and Ronnie. I made a profit of three hundred fifty dollars off each brick."

Bam didn't frighten Rosa Lee the way heroin did. Lucky, after all, had been using bam for months, and Rosa Lee hadn't noticed any change in her behavior.

Rosa Lee's weight had been creeping up. She asked Lucky for a hit. "Lucky wouldn't hit me," she says.

Rosa Lee asked one of Ronnie's girlfriends if she knew anything about bam. The friend, a school crossing guard, told Rosa Lee that she used bam in the morning before she went to her post.

Every morning for the next year, the woman brought bam to Rosa Lee's apartment. She bought the drug for Rosa Lee from her father, a man nicknamed the Undertaker. In the predawn darkness, she would prepare the solution and inject Rosa Lee and herself. Lucky became aware that Rosa Lee was using bam, but she did not object and they often shot up together.

"I liked the feeling," Rosa Lee says. "I could feel it all in my stomach. That's the first thing that shrinks. Your stomach. I would go the *whole day* without eating, with a *whole* lot of energy! I would clean up the whole house. Nothing was clean enough. I'd take two or three baths. I was on top of everything. In three weeks, I lost about twenty pounds.

"So, I started getting addicted to it," she continues. "I was enjoying the feeling of it. I would give [the crossing guard] the money the night before and she'd come by with it early the next morning." The guard would inject herself and Rosa Lee before reporting to her post.

Rosa Lee always hid her drug use from her children during this period, insisting that the crossing guard leave before her youngest children got up to go to school. Later than usual one very cold morning, however, Rosa Lee and the guard were cooking up the bam in one of the apartment's bedrooms. Patty, then fifteen, was suffering from a bad winter cold. The two women thought Patty was sleeping, but the girl was surreptitiously watching them. They were not doing anything that Patty had not already seen in the hallways and drug dens of Clifton Terrace.

The crossing guard injected Rosa Lee and then herself. As Rosa Lee got ready to leave the room, Patty sat up in bed and shouted at her mother, "NO, wait a minute, Mama! Why don't you get all of it?"

Rosa Lee did not understand what Patty was talking about. "All of what?" she asked.

"She got some more in the thing, right there." Patty was pointing at the small metal cooker that sat at the foot of the bed. The crossing guard had used it to add water to the mix of crushed pills and then heated the mixture into a liquid solution to be drawn into the syringe. Rosa Lee walked over to the cooker. "Residue was all around the top like someone had pushed what they want to the side," Rosa Lee recalls. She turned to the guard and demanded, "What is this? Can this be shot?"

The woman told her it could be. Her suspicions now aroused, Rosa Lee asked another question. "Does this always be like this?"

Patty answered before the guard did. "Mama, if she did it this time, she must have practiced keeping bam from you."

Every morning, Rosa Lee was so anxious to move out into the living room, lest her children come into the bedroom and see her shooting up, that the guard would have time to hang back, following Rosa Lee to the living room minutes later. Rosa Lee now understood why. "I'd go on out [of the bedroom] not knowing that she was getting a bigger shot than me. A whole second shot."

Patty insisted that the guard cook up the residue and give it to Rosa Lee. When she injected Rosa Lee, the dose was just as strong as the first. " 'Oh, man,' " Rosa Lee said as she felt the rush of the drug. "You ain't been doing *this* to me, I know." The woman hung her head. "If you wanted some more, why didn't you tell me?" Rosa Lee asked. "You're my friend. You don't have to do that." The woman could not say anything. She cried and hugged Rosa Lee "almost like she was asking me to forgive her. I did."

There was another development that morning. After the crossing guard stopped crying, Patty demanded a hit. Rosa Lee tried to talk her out of it, but Patty insisted. Rosa Lee refused. Patty then played her trump card. "Mama, if you don't give me a hit," she said, "then I'm going to go out of here and trick." Rosa Lee was shocked. She realized that Patty was manipulating her by using a ploy that she herself would have used in the same situation. Patty had learned her lessons well. "Go 'head," Rosa Lee told the crossing guard. "Give her a hit."

Fifteen years would pass before Patty would go as long as two months without drugs.

A little more than a year after Rosa Lee consented to Patty's first hit, Lucky was convicted of forging checks and sentenced to six months in a halfway house in Northeast Washington. Toward the end of her sentence, she was allowed some time away. One Saturday afternoon, Lucky told Rosa Lee that she could not stay out the whole weekend and was due back to the halfway house that day. When she left, Rosa Lee followed her. A couple of blocks from Clifton Terrace, Rosa Lee saw Lucky rendezvous with a younger woman, whom Rosa Lee knew as "Moose." They walked off, hand-in-hand. Rosa Lee was furious. She realized that Lucky was not due back to the halfway house until Sunday.

Lucky returned to Clifton Terrace on Monday. Rosa Lee confronted her in the bedroom. "She called me a bitch and I knocked her down," she recalls. They fought. Bobby and Alvin came into the bedroom, pulled them away from each other, and told Lucky she had to leave. Lucky wanted to take her clothes, but Rosa Lee refused to let her have them.

Outside the building, Lucky stood under Rosa Lee's second-story apartment's windows and cursed her in a loud voice. The cursing drew a crowd. The larger the crowd grew, the louder Lucky cursed Rosa Lee. "She called me all kinds of old-ass bitches and everything you could think of," remembers Rosa Lee, wincing at the still-painful memory. "She called me everything but a child of God."

"Throw me my motherfucking clothes," screamed Lucky. "You ain't got to worry about me coming back."

Finally, Rosa Lee put all of Lucky's clothes in a plastic shopping bag and sent Bobby downstairs with them. Bobby walked Lucky down the street. She moved in with Moose.

The breakup left Rosa Lee crushed and deeply wounded just about a week before her thirty-ninth birthday.

The Clubhouse, a gay bar where Rosa Lee had been working for two years, gave her a party on October 8, the day after her birthday. Lucky, who routinely frequented the Clubhouse, came to the bar with Moose but left as soon as she saw Rosa Lee. Patty came to the party with a male friend. After the party was over, they took Rosa Lee home, where she told Patty she was feeling sad about the breakup with Lucky. She asked Patty to go into the courtyards in front of Clifton Terrace and buy her a bam pill from one of the street dealers. Patty's friend suggested that Rosa Lee try some heroin. Patty told Rosa Lee the heroin would make her forget all about Lucky.

After nineteen years of selling heroin, Rosa Lee finally gave in.

Patty gave Rosa Lee a hit in the same place on her left arm where she had been injecting her mother with bam, a practice she took up soon after the episode with the crossing guard. Rosa Lee says the first shot just made her sleepy. "I went into a nod but I could hear everything that was being said. We stayed up all night shooting dope. Before I knew it, I was getting high."

The pain of Lucky dumping her disappeared while she was high. "Then when I come down to earth, then I'd think about her. I didn't know Patty was into dope until this night. I thought she just used bam."

After that October night in 1975, mother and daughter became daily heroin users. Rosa Lee was never able to inject herself. If Patty or Ronnie or Bobby weren't available, she went to a Clifton Terrace oil joint and paid three dollars for someone to give her a hit.

Rosa Lee fell to the same depths as the addicts who had knocked on her door and begged for a fix: Her eyes were red and watery. Her stomach hurt when the heroin wore off. Her body quaked and shivered as it waited for the next hit.

A year later came Rosa Lee's first drug bust, not for the heroin she was taking, but for the marijuana she was selling.

The school crossing guard came to her apartment one day with a young male friend. Rosa Lee trusted the woman, and she allowed her and the young man into her bedroom, where Rosa Lee kept the marijuana. Other customers had to stand in the living room while the marijuana was retrieved from the bedroom and brought to them. The young man watched as Rosa Lee pulled two nickel bags out of her large black pocketbook.

Before dawn two days later, "BOOM!" yells Rosa Lee, clapping her hands together as she relives the shocking moment. She knew immediately what it was. She had heard the sound countless times in the past. "Jumpouts came through the door. Knocked the door down." Rosa Lee, lying in bed, saw the man who had been with the crossing guard come right into the bedroom and grab her pocketbook. He was an undercover policeman.

"NO!" Rosa Lee shouted when she recognized him.

"Yes, Mrs. Cunningham." The policeman laughed.

"I had about sixty bags," recalls Rosa Lee. She told the undercover policeman she sold marijuana in order to raise her eight children. He told her she would have to find some legal way to supplement her welfare stipend. Though she pleaded guilty to possession and was given six months' probation, she didn't stop selling marijuana.

"BOOM!" Three months later, narcotics officers crashed

through her apartment's front door again. This time Rosa Lee had about seventy bags of marijuana in her bedroom closet, but the policemen offered not to charge her if she named her supplier. She called one of her two suppliers, a Virginia man, while the officers listened to the call. That afternoon, he met her at a nearby corner in his blue pickup truck. They quickly exchanged the money and the brick.

"When he pulled away from the curb, the police officers followed right behind him," says Rosa Lee, who was amused watching the white detectives follow the white marijuana farmer south toward the 14th Street Bridge, which crosses the Potomac River into Virginia. "They didn't want him. They wanted the field. They got it. They locked him up about two, three weeks later. He didn't connect me to it. Anybody could have set him up."

About this time, Rosa Lee's youngest sister, Lawan, showed up at the apartment. Lawan was tricking with a heroin dealer for a billy and wanted to use Rosa Lee's bedroom. Rosa Lee agreed, but insisted that the drug dealer give her some heroin since they were using her apartment. He mixed cocaine with the heroin to create a speedball. Rosa Lee was skeptical. "Hell, no. I don't want this," she protested.

Lawan told Rosa Lee, "Sis, it's a bomb!"

Rosa Lee decided to try it. "It *was* a bomb," she recalled. "It was a hell of a rush. I heard bells ringing. Great God almighty! Your whole body is stimulated."

She heard her children coming home from school, so she left Lawan and the drug dealer in her bedroom. She fixed the children something to eat and returned to her bedroom. Lawan and the drug dealer "were in there fixing up more dope. I said, 'Put some 'caine on it.' I got high again."

Over the years, Rosa Lee continued to sell marijuana and operate oil joints out of various apartments in Clifton Terrace. In 1977, she added juggling along nearby 14th Street, earning a reputation as an excellent street-level heroin dealer. Between 1979 and 1983, she was arrested six times for shoplifting. Nothing motivated her to stop shoplifting or to stop dealing and using drugs.

Then on October 7, 1983, a "hit" in the neck almost killed her. To celebrate her forty-seventh birthday, she and a friend went to an oil joint on the third floor of a rundown apartment building near Howard University Hospital to shoot cocaine. The joint was run by a woman known as "One-Arm Diane." Diane was an addict who had had her left arm and right leg amputated after each limb was seriously infected through intravenous drug use. She now paid for her continuing drug abuse by working as a hitter for other addicts.

Rosa Lee had to lie down next to Diane for the woman to hit her. "The first time she hit me right." The second hit "shocked me around here," says Rosa Lee, indicating the area by rubbing her right palm across the back of her neck. "I shook my head. I thought I was going out. She hit the nerve."

Rosa Lee went home to lie down. The next morning she couldn't get out of bed. By early afternoon, she had managed to crawl to the living room couch. "You talk about pain! I had never been like that. My neck, my arm, everything was hurting me." A visiting neighbor told her that her right eye was blood-shot.

For days, Rosa Lee got worse and worse. An ambulance was called and it took her to D.C. General Hospital. The medical staff would not give her anything for her pain because of her drug addiction. She was in so much pain that she went through heroin withdrawal without realizing it. For three weeks, she kept other patients in her ward awake at night with her crying. Then the doctors at D.C. General, who never correctly diagnosed Rosa Lee's illness, discharged her.

Her arms and hands were so weak when Eric came to get her that she could not hold her winter coat. Eric demanded that the hospital staff explain why they were sending her home in such a weakened condition. Not getting a satisfactory answer, he refused to take her home and stormed out of the hospital.

The nurses on duty told Rosa Lee she had to leave. She called Ducky. He borrowed a car and came for her. On their way home,

Ducky started crying. "I looked so bad," recalls Rosa Lee. "He was driving and he had to pull over to get himself together. He said, 'Mama, I wish you would stop using drugs. You are killing yourself.'"

At home, Rosa Lee's slow decline continued. Her right hand began turning in and grew weaker. She slept sitting up in a chair. From that position, she could get to the bathroom if someone supported her while she walked. Actually, she describes her movement as more like a shuffle, dragging her feet along the floor because the effort to lift them required a strength she no longer had. Lying down in bed was out of the question. She was not able to get herself out of bed, even with help. "I would sleep, eat, and sit in the chair all day."

Finally, in mid-November, Rosa Lee's legs collapsed underneath her while she was shuffling across the living room. The neighbor who had been helping her tried to get her up, but Rosa Lee's legs were too weak. The neighbor called an ambulance. This time she was taken to Howard Hospital's emergency room. Neurosurgeon Charles Mosee examined her and determined that a neck vertebra was literally collapsing from a bacterial infection, a condition called osteomyelitis, and was putting deadly pressure on the nerves in the spinal cord. He didn't know the infection was caused by the second hit from One-Arm Diane, the hit that had left Rosa Lee in shock. He did know he had to move fast if Rosa Lee was to live. He operated immediately, and Rosa Lee would not leave the hospital for six more months.

And yet in the spring of 1984, not long after her return home, Rosa Lee asked Patty's latest boyfriend to mix up a batch of heroin for her. Patty hit her, and she was right back to what had made her so ill in the first place.

Rosa Lee is all smiles when I meet her in front of the methadone clinic one morning. Her long-awaited transfer off the welfare rolls is finally completed, and she received a letter from the Social Security Administration informing her that she will be getting her first Supplemental Security Income check in a couple of days. It is back-dated three months and will total $1,298.

Rosa Lee informs me she has told Ducky and Patty the good news, but kept the information from Richard, who has just moved back in with her after a stint in prison. I am stunned, but say nothing.

The check arrives at 1:30 P.M. on a Tuesday and Rosa Lee cashes it at a suburban Maryland liquor store. Wednesday morning, Rosa Lee tells me what happened when she went home.

Richard, Patty, and Ducky were sitting in the living room looking at her as she walked through the apartment door. Patty had told Richard about Rosa Lee's check. Rosa Lee agreed to give each of them fifty dollars and asked that they not bother her for any more money. "It was just like a child with a brand-new bike," says Rosa Lee. All three of them ran out of the apartment to buy crack.

Richard returned to beg for more money at 5 P.M. Patty came into Rosa Lee's bedroom a few minutes after Richard. And then Ducky came in. Rosa Lee gave them each twenty dollars. They left. The begging, Rosa Lee caving in, and her children returning to wake her up continued until 5 A.M.

The telling of the tale takes about two hours, with Rosa Lee acting out her role and the roles of her three children. I feel as if I have a migraine headache. When I listen to the tape of this interview a couple of days later, I can hear the anger in my voice. Rosa Lee seems unaware of it.

"There is something going on with you that I haven't yet figured out," I say.

"Tell me!" she demands.

"You set yourself up for this harassment every time!" I respond. "They had no reason to know that you were getting a check for such a large sum of money, and you told them. When you told me you had told them, I knew what was going to happen when the check arrived. You had to have known what was going to happen because you've lived through it for years and have told me about it.

"You told Patty and Ducky, the last two people on the face of the earth you should ever tell; two people who will bug and harass you at any time in the morning for your last penny so they can get a rock. Then Alvin is going to come over there selling wolf tickets and threatening to beat everyone in the house with a baseball bat if they don't stop bothering you. I don't understand it! You set yourself up to be in the middle of chaos, knowing the chaos is coming. You create the chaos. They try to trick you. They try to cheat you. You have to sleep with your money rolled up in your underwear."

Rosa Lee starts talking about her mother never giving her any money. I tell her we are talking about her relationship with her children, let us leave her mother out of this. But Rosa Lee dissembles, a skill she has finely honed. I listen as she wanders, knowing better than to interrupt her. Eventually, I bring her back to the basic question: "Why do you set yourself up to be harassed?"

"I'm glad I'm in the position to give it to them," she admits, finally. "I don't want my children to say what I say about my mom. 'Oh, I couldn't get nothing from *my* mother! I couldn't do this. I couldn't do that.' Mr. Dash, what else could I use my money for?"

Rosa Lee has $610 left from the check. She tries to get me to hold it for her. I refuse. My head is pounding when I drive Rosa Lee home. I don't envy what she faces until the remaining $610 is gone.

When I reach my home, I take an extra-strength pain reliever and sit down on the couch. I sort through why I have a headache and why I am so angry. I'm angry with Rosa Lee for setting herself up for what she then goes through. I'm angry with Richard, Patty, and Ducky for what they do to her. I decide I have no right to be angry with any of them. They are actors in their own play. I need to get off the stage and back into the audience.

After Rosa Lee and I sit down for breakfast at McDonald's the next morning, I say, "Before you get started, I feel obligated to apologize to you."

"For what?" Rosa Lee asks.

"I got a headache yesterday listening to you talk about what your children put you through," I reply. "I felt I was a little short with you because I was angry. I was angry with Patty's behavior,

Ducky's behavior, and Richard's behavior. I was also upset with you because you had set yourself up for a repeat of their behavior. I shouldn't be angry. It is not my position to be upset with you or them. I should be trying to understand why."

"That lets me know that you're really concerned about me," says Rosa Lee. "That means a lot to a woman like me, who has been used and misused. People don't give a damn about me!"

Out of the SSI check, Rosa Lee spent $142 on food. She filled her apartment's refrigerator and kitchen cabinets. Last night at home, she discovered that the large packages of frozen chicken and pork chops, and the canned fruits she loves, were missing from the freezer and the cabinets. Rosa Lee couldn't believe that the food had been eaten up so quickly. Ducky told her that Richard sold the food to buy crack.

"It doesn't make any sense, Mr. Dash," says Rosa Lee with resignation. "The way I'm living. The way we're living. And I don't know how to get out of it. I can't see my children on the street."

After her third seizure and the stern lecture from Dr. Frederick at Howard Hospital in November 1990, Rosa Lee liked to boast that she was through with dope. Despite the constant stress of her children begging her for drug money, there is no evidence that she took a single hit in all of 1991; she was doing so well that the clinic invited her to speak to a group of addicts about her experience. That's why I am startled one day in early January 1992 to notice that the back of her left hand is swollen and red. It looks like the traces of "skin-popping," a method of injecting heroin just under the skin.

Rosa Lee is in considerable pain and rubbing the back of her left hand, though she tries to keep me from seeing her do it. She is unsuccessful. "What are you looking at?" she demands, hiding her hands in the folds of her winter coat.

"I'm looking at your swollen left hand," I say.

Rosa Lee is angry with herself and angry with me. She's fallen back into drug use, and I've confronted her with it. "You know so goddamn much," she sputters, her face reflecting anger and embarrassment. "I ought to go upside your head!"

I am unmoved. "What happened?"

Rosa Lee deflates after my question. The anger and embarrassment seem to seep out of her. She is quiet for a few moments, no longer trying to hide the swollen hand. She says she wanted to tell me but was too embarrassed to bring it up. She'll tell me now.

The week after Christmas, she had been sitting in McDonald's with several of her methadone buddies. Everyone was chattering excitedly about the Christmas gifts they had received from their children. Everyone except Rosa Lee.

Most of Rosa Lee's children hadn't given her anything. She did get a card from her youngest daughter with a ten-dollar bill in it. "I couldn't say a word," Rosa Lee tells me. "I just sat there and looked, and before I knew it, I went into the bathroom and started crying."

To cheer her up, one of her friends suggested they share a billy or two of heroin. Ordinarily, Rosa Lee would have dismissed the idea. Not this time.

She wondered if it would be dangerous. "What would happen if I did some?" she asked her friend. "Would it kill me?" Her friend told her not to worry. Rosa Lee decided to risk it.

As soon as Patty heard about the plan, she was eager to join in. It would be like old times: Patty would give Rosa Lee the hit, then hit herself. Patty and the friend went looking for a neighborhood dealer called Junebug.

A short while later, Patty sat on Rosa Lee's bed and stuck the needle in the back of Rosa Lee's hand. "Mama, can you feel it?" Patty whispered.

Rosa Lee shook her head.

Patty was worried about giving Rosa Lee too much at once. She remembered Rosa Lee's first seizure, and the panic she felt as Rosa Lee's eyes rolled back in her head. "Are you ready to take it all?" Patty asked.

"If you stay here with me," Rosa Lee said.

Patty pushed the rest of the milky liquid into Rosa Lee's vein.

Rosa Lee waited for the familiar rush. But it never came. The methadone seemed to be blocking the high.

"I didn't feel anything I used to feel," she tells me.

"Why did you take a chance on dying?" I ask.

She wriggles uncomfortably in her seat. "I didn't see it that way, taking a chance on dying. I thought I might have a seizure, but I didn't think I was taking a chance on dying."

I remind her of Dr. Frederick's warning. She mutters something and averts her eyes. We spar verbally for what seems like a long time but is only ten or fifteen minutes. It becomes clear that the conversation is going nowhere. She completes my next question before I finish it.

"You really don't have a . . . ?" I begin.

"A good reason for why I took it?" she says. "No, I really don't."

FIVE

Serious Time

OVERLEAF: *Richard (left) and Bobby at the D.C. jail, 1991* (© *Lucian Perkins*—The Washington Post).

ONE SPRING MORNING, Rosa Lee and I pick up Bobby at the Northwest Washington halfway house to which he was paroled four months earlier. The three of us go out for breakfast and to review Bobby's life.

At one point, I ask Bobby, "Did you feel that because you were your mother's oldest son you should be playing the role of the male provider, the male head of household?"

With a nod, Bobby answers yes, adding "Which makes sense, don't it?" When his mother left the house to shoplift or go to work at night, he recalls, she would tell him, "Well, you're the oldest. You're going to have to be the man when I'm not here."

Bobby's eyes suddenly fill with tears. The feet of his chair scrape the floor as he pushes back from the table. What follows is an outburst of pent-up rage. Looking directly at his mother, he mentions the name of a neighborhood teenage boy Rosa Lee hired to baby-sit when Bobby was seven and had four younger brothers and a younger sister. "He raped me," Bobby declares. " 'Cause he was drunk. It hurt. Then he gave me half the money that you gave him for baby-sitting."

Rosa Lee and I look at Bobby, dumbfounded.

An awkward silence falls over us. Bobby's face is flushed with anger and pain. Rosa Lee sits with her mouth open, her eyes reflecting a sudden hurt.

"Did you know that before today?" I ask her.

Keeping her eyes on Bobby, Rosa Lee shakes her head no, as if she doesn't trust herself to speak.

"Where were you?" I ask.

"Shoplifting," she replies, turning to look at me. She has quickly put on a poker face, effectively hiding what is going on inside her.

Bobby continues. It is now a monologue. "I never told nobody. It felt like my whole mind would explode. It went on for two or three months." Each time, the teenager gave Bobby half the money Rosa Lee had paid him for baby-sitting.

Rosa Lee begins to cry, a deep, shoulder-shaking, sobbing cry. It's as if so much that she has wondered about for so many years has finally been revealed.

"Never told nobody," Bobby repeats. "He was drunk and held me down. Breathing all that alcohol smell in my face and stuff. I didn't know what he was doing. I was a little kid. I had to go to the bathroom. Blood and everything was coming out of me. I was crying. I was scared. I was shivering."

The assaults continued every time Rosa Lee hired the adolescent to look after her children. "After a month or two, I got used to it. I never enjoyed it. I enjoyed getting that *money* that Mom would give him and he'd give me half. Five dollars. Five dollars was a lot of money to a seven-year-old kid!" Bobby adds that the teenager, now a man in his fifties, works at a downtown Post Office.

"I feel hurt!" Rosa Lee cries.

Rosa Lee's decisions have not only affected her, they have had disastrous results for most of her children. To a significant extent, her six sons and two daughters had the deck stacked against them by the circumstances of their births. Rosa Lee was only fourteen when Bobby was born, and his seven siblings were fathered by five different men (some of whom were still teenagers themselves) over an eleven-year stretch.

Rosa Lee exposed all of her children to her criminal lifestyle, the underworld path she argues was her avenue to survival, and four of her six sons followed her onto the same path, with ruinous outcomes for each of them. The poor Washington neighborhoods the four boys grew up in and the academically deficient public education available to them in those communities also played significant roles in how each of them turned out. Their lives and choices provide an intricate blueprint of just how bad guidance and bad decisions so easily ensnared them in lives of drug addiction and criminal recidivism.

Just as important are the examples of Alvin and Eric, the two of Rosa Lee's sons who rejected their mother's and their brothers' lives of drugs, crime, and prison. Alvin and Eric found a different path and moved up out of poverty into conventional middle-class and working-class respectability.

Indeed, Eric's reflections on what was missing in his childhood offer a crucial clue to what went wrong in the lives of his brothers. "My mother fed and clothed us, true," Eric says. "But she was always on the go when we were children. She was always out, day and night. She was always gone!"

All of Rosa Lee's children were born at D.C. General Hospital.

Bobby was born on November 21, 1950.

Ronnie was born on May 14, 1952.

Alvin was born on April 28, 1953.

Richard was born on August 26, 1954.

Eric was born on March 11, 1956.

Patty was born on January 5, 1958.

Ducky was born on February 21, 1960.

Rosa Lee's eighth child, a daughter, was born on March 23, 1961.

Immediately after the last child was born, a physician performed a hysterectomy on Rosa Lee at her request. "The babies were coming too fast and I already had too many children," she says.

Freed from the concern about pregnancy, Rosa Lee began bringing male customers home from her night work in the summer of 1961. At the time, the family lived in a small duplex apartment in a public housing building on 53rd Street in Northeast Washington. She charged the men fifteen or twenty dollars, "according to what they wanted to do."

Ten-year-old Bobby would meet Rosa Lee at the apartment's front door. Just inside the door, Rosa Lee would turn to her customer and demand her payment on the spot. She would hand the money to Bobby. He would go upstairs and hide the money in one of the children's two bedrooms on the second floor. Rosa Lee and the customer would retire to her first-floor bedroom.

"I had to collect the money first," remembers Rosa Lee. "Those were some rough men that hung in those clubs on H Street. Some of them would try to leave without paying me."

Bobby already knew his mother shoplifted and sold heroin. "I didn't hide anything from him," says Rosa Lee. The pair shared information more like a married couple than like mother and son. Bobby kept the information away from his brothers and sisters.

When Rosa Lee started bringing men home, she told Bobby the money he was collecting was in exchange for sex. He says he accepted his mother's prostitution as just another hustle.

"What she was doing, the prostitution, I didn't see it having nothing to do with sex," recalls Bobby. "It was about making money. Some of the tricks would come back and be friendly with us kids. Buy us some toys or give us money for the movies so we would leave the house. Some of them tried to not look us in the face. I knew what was going on. My brothers and sisters didn't know."

In the fall of 1963, the electricity in Rosa Lee's apartment was cut off, since she hadn't paid the bill. Rosa Lee ran an extension cord from her mother's apartment to hers. When the public housing officials learned of this tactic, they evicted both families. Rosa Lee and Rosetta moved into a row house in another section of Northeast Washington. Between them they had seventeen children living at home.

Bobby remembers it was shortly after they moved that he came under the tutelage of older adolescents who attended Eliot

Junior High School with him and lived in his new neighborhood. He had just turned thirteen. His new friends taught him how to burglarize stores, churches, and school buildings. He recalls their motivations. "We wanted things like cars. Money. We wanted a gun. Expensive clothes. Between '63 and '67, I was breaking into everything in D.C. There was nothing I wouldn't break into."

Bobby even broke into Mount Joy Baptist Church—scene of Rosa Lee's childhood pilfering from parishioners' coat pockets—and stole some sterling silverware, silver collection plates, silver chalices, and musical equipment. He sold everything for a pittance—$100. Bobby had an added incentive. "I always shared the money I made with Mom to help feed all of us. In fact, I gave her most of the money."

Bobby was fourteen when he and three friends broke into a music shop on H Street and stole an assortment of guitars, saxophones, and trumpets.

The four thieves were trying to sneak the stolen instruments into the basement of the row house. Bobby had already called Rosa Lee to the basement to see what the boys had stolen and assess the value. "We've got some money, now!" was his happy comment to his mother when he asked her to come downstairs.

Suddenly, Rosetta came to the top of the basement stairs. She yelled. "WHO IS THAT DOWN THERE MAKING ALL THAT DAMN NOISE?" She didn't wait for a response. Bobby and Rosa Lee froze in fear when they heard her heavy footsteps coming down the stairs.

"She looked at one of the guitars," says Bobby. "One of the guitars had a price tag on it."

Rosetta told Bobby not to move. She turned to Rosa Lee and said, "Now, see! That's why your damn kids will never learn nothing. Where did they get all this shit from?"

Rosa Lee held out her hands, palms up, in an expression of ignorance. "Mama . . . "

Rosetta told Bobby, "YOU! Get this shit outta here!"

Bobby whispered to Rosa Lee, asking his mother where he should take the instruments.

Rosetta asked Bobby, "What did you say?"

Rosa Lee stepped between Bobby and her mother. "Mama," she protested, "he was asking me where he was going to put this stuff at."

"I didn't ask you a goddamn thing," said Rosetta as she back-handed Rosa Lee across her mouth.

Bobby grabbed his mother as she fell back into his arms. He had witnessed scenes like this between his grandmother and mother all his life. "Mama, how long are you going to take this?" he asked, loudly enough for his grandmother to hear.

With one powerful sweep of her arm, Rosetta brushed Rosa Lee aside. She grabbed Bobby by his shirt, took off one of her bedroom slippers, "and wore me out," he recalls. As Rosetta beat him, she berated him, too: "Stealing every goddamn thing. Bringing all this shit in my house. Your mother is no better than you. Doing the same thing your mother is doing." Bobby covered his head with his arms and cried.

Bobby and his friends moved the stolen instruments to another house. Not long afterward, Rosa Lee arranged to sell the instruments to musicians who worked at the Ko Ko Club. She gave Bobby and his three friends $200. She kept seventy-five dollars.

Ronnie's father, a heroin addict and burglar, heard about Bobby's thefts and, with Rosa Lee's approval, formed a partnership with him. "He was a perfect hustler," says Bobby. "He had jump suits. He showed me how to drive a car. Park it." He also showed Bobby how to break into houses. The pair worked together for a couple of years. While Ronnie's father worked with Bobby, he did not even contact his own son. Bobby always gave his portion of whatever money they earned to Rosa Lee. He was arrested and incarcerated on burglary convictions as a juvenile offender half a dozen times.

Rosa Lee says she did not know what to tell Bobby to get him to stop his criminal activity. Then again, she didn't feel too strongly that she should stop him. He never spent more than a couple of months in a juvenile prison. He wasn't a violent child. He didn't hurt anybody. "And he brought home money that helped feed all of us!" she adds with a note of defiance. "What good would it have done for me to get him to stop, if he would've listened to me in the first place?"

After Bobby turned sixteen in 1966, when he was in the ninth grade, he dropped out of school. He continued his house break-ins and now worked as a prostitute as well, selling sex to men and women. Several of his adult uncles came by Rosa Lee's apartment one day and beat him up, telling Bobby to get back in school or get a job because he was setting a poor example for his younger brothers and sisters. The beating did no good. Bobby did not see education as meeting his and the family's immediate needs. As a teenager, Bobby felt that all he could do was hustle sex and commit burglaries.

A year later, restless, and confused because he had begun enjoying the prostitution with his male customers so much that he was not making much money, Bobby joined the Job Corps.

The mid-1960s were restless and turbulent years for America. President Lyndon B. Johnson, as part of his war on poverty, had created the Job Corps as a vehicle for poor, undereducated youth to grab a rung on the ladder to upward mobility. The country's civil rights movement had splintered into two camps, one that continued to seek to redress the history of discrimination against African Americans through nonviolent demonstrations, and another that raised the militant banner of Black Power. There was a growing anti–Vietnam War movement that would cause President Johnson not to run for re-election in 1968.

Bobby says most of this turmoil passed him by, as it did a large percentage of the black urban poor. Joining the Job Corps, for example, was happenstance. He saw a recruiting poster in a store window. "Here is my chance to get away," he remembers thinking. Bobby tricked Rosa Lee into signing permission forms she could not read and, over her protests, left for Henderson Community College in Morganfield, Kentucky. "I knew she wouldn't have signed the papers if she knew I was going that far away," he says.

In eleven months, he earned his high school equivalency cer-tificate and received training in cooking, business management, retail sales, and basic electronic equipment repair. When he turned eighteen, Bobby returned to Washington only to find that chaos and poverty were still part of his family's daily life. Bobby decided to flee again, and in July 1969 he joined the Army.

While in the Army, he built on his Job Corps experience and enrolled in additional training as a cook at Fort Dix in New Jersey. When he reached the grade of assistant mess sergeant, he decided to sign up for duty in the war zone in South Vietnam.

"All the brothers were telling me about all the drugs they had over there and all the money that could be made," Bobby remembers. "Selling drugs, sending it home, buying a house for your mother. They said, 'Go to Vietnam! They ain't fighting over there. They are making money.' "

In a way, *making money* had been Bobby's focus ever since he was sodomized by the family baby-sitter and given a share of the fee to keep quiet. After all, it was Bobby who collected the cash when Rosa Lee brought her tricks home, who was tutored on how to be a burglar, and who sold his body to men and women. The question of his sexuality was still unresolved when he joined the Army, but eventually maturity settled the question of his preferences. "I decided I was gay and didn't worry about it anymore," he says.

Arriving at the Army base in Da Nang in 1971, Bobby had the run of one of the base's large kitchens and quickly made a Vietnamese opium connection. He tried smoking the narcotic and liked it. "It made me take my mind off Vietnam. I ain't never used drugs until I got over to Vietnam, and it was only smoking it."

To pay for the opium, he gave the Vietnamese large boxes of stolen frozen steaks. One case of steaks got him 100 vials of opium. "It was pure," he remembers. "Looked like soap powder." He was almost caught in an investigation about the missing beef, but wriggled through undetected.

Bobby's dreams of making money and buying his mother a house from wholesaling opium in the United States went nowhere. He didn't understand how to do it. Most of the drug he got his hands on, he smoked himself.

His opium use did not go unnoticed. When it was detected in

a random urine test in early 1972, Bobby was shipped home for drug detoxification at Fort Belvoir in Virginia. Rosa Lee and Rosetta visited him there. "He looked so skinny, like he didn't have any meat on him at all," remembers Rosa Lee. "Me and my mama cried when we saw him."

When he was discharged from the Fort Belvoir hospital—and the Army—Bobby was as broke as he had been when he joined up. He had no idea of what he would do for a living, and he still had a craving for opium.

Bobby didn't know that his mother was selling heroin, nor did he know that Ronnie was a heroin addict. He wanted to score, buy some opium, but had no clue about whom to ask. Finally, after he'd been home several days, he began talking to Ronnie about smoking opium in Vietnam. Ronnie offered him some heroin. Bobby was surprised that Ronnie was using heroin but accepted his offer. He emptied the tobacco from a cigarette and began refilling it with powdered Mexican Mud.

"Man, what the hell are you doing?" Ronnie remembers asking Bobby.

"That's the way we do it over there," Bobby answered.

"We don't do it like that here!" Ronnie told him.

Ronnie showed Bobby how to cook the powdered heroin in a solution of water in a metal bottle cap over a match. He drew the solution up into a syringe and injected Bobby. "I introduced him to the needle," recalls Ronnie. "I was using the needle and he was trying to smoke. So he tried it out." Bobby liked injecting heroin more than smoking opium. He was hooked again.

Bobby tried working at several jobs before returning to prostitution, this time almost exclusively with male customers. He still did not earn enough money. "Burglary paid way more," he says. At twenty-two, Bobby needed more money—for his heroin habit, the sharp clothes he liked to wear, and the teenage boys who were his lovers. "You had to give them money if they were going to be around with you," he says. "They weren't just there for the sex."

After going home with a trick he picked up on the street or in a bar or restaurant, Bobby would quickly scrutinize everything in the man's apartment. He would double back the day after their nighttime tryst and burglarize the customer's apartment. "Most of them were employed and lived alone," he says.

In the mid-1970s, Bobby was convicted in federal court of two separate burglary charges and given two consecutive sentences that ranged from two to ten years. He was first paroled in 1978 but was sent back to federal prisons six times on parole violations until the longest sentence ran out, in the spring of 1986.

In 1987, Bobby was convicted of selling heroin and was sentenced to thirty months to seven and a half years imprisonment. In 1989, he began another cycle of making parole to a halfway house, coming to live with Rosa Lee, and then purposely violating the terms of parole in order to return to prison. He acknowledges that he finds it difficult to negotiate life outside prison.

In June 1991, I interview Bobby and Richard together in the D.C. jail. Coincidentally, they had both been sent there on separate parole-violation charges. The week before our conversation, I knew that Bobby had violated parole again by leaving the halfway house he was living in for several days without permission. In addition, he had been using and selling heroin at a public housing project in Southeast Washington for two months. A mandatory urine test he took recently had been positive for opiate use, another parole violation.

With Richard sitting by impassively, Bobby tells me he refuses to take any medication for his HIV condition because he doesn't want the many men he is involved with—in prison, in the halfway houses, and on the streets of Washington—to know that he is carrying the AIDS virus. He and his partners do not use condoms, and he does not care if he infects them. His open homosexuality has led to numerous rapes in prison, and he admits to taking a fiendish pleasure in telling his rapists he is infected with AIDS after they are done.

"By not taking any medication, doesn't that amount to suicide?" I ask Bobby.

"I don't want to live," he replies.

From the time Ronnie was three years old, he thought the man his mother was dating, David Wright, was the father of all of Rosa Lee's children. "He always used to come around," remembers Ronnie. "Take us to the drive-in. I used to see him give my mother money for all of us."

Between 1955 and 1960, Wright fathered three of Rosa Lee's children—Eric, Patty, and Ducky. Wright drank heavily and worked irregularly. And he was afraid of Rosetta, who lived next-door to her daughter. He would slip in and out of Rosa Lee's apartment at night, hoping to avoid Rosetta and any welfare inspector who might pop up unexpectedly, checking to see if there was a man in the house.

"In them days, you couldn't have a man living with you 'cause the welfare would kick you off," recalls Rosa Lee. "David wanted to marry me. My mama was afraid if I married him, they'd kick me off welfare anyway. She didn't think he made enough money to take care of all of us." Rosa Lee says that her mother's opposition effectively blocked any thoughts Rosa Lee and Wright had about marrying.

Ronnie wasn't aware of the welfare connection. He was just happy to see Wright when he came over to their house. Whenever Wright showed up, there were goodies for all the children or he took them all on an excursion.

One day when Ronnie was eleven, Rosa Lee called him downstairs to the kitchen. "Your father is here," she told him, pointing to a man standing in the courtyard in front of the building. Ronnie was baffled. That wasn't David Wright! Rosa Lee offered no further explanation. She told Ronnie to go out there and speak to him.

Ronnie walked up to the man. The man asked, "Do you know who I am?"

Ronnie told him, "My mother said that you are my father." The man then told Ronnie where he had been. He said he'd been in prison, at Lorton. "He said if I ever needed anything, just tell my mother and my mother would get in touch with him, but that was a lie. I ain't seen him again until I was twenty-two years old."

The brief encounter left Ronnie hurt and confused. He never asked Rosa Lee about his father.

When he was fourteen, Ronnie worked with his mother in a Wings 'N' Things fried chicken carryout as a short-order cook. Like Bobby, Ronnie parlayed his skill at cooking into regular work at different times in his life in Washington and other places.

He was fifteen when Bobby joined the Job Corps. At this time, the family lived in a ramshackle, three-story row house in Southeast Washington, not too far from where Rosa Lee had grown up. The house rented for thirty-eight dollars a month. Ronnie was enrolled in Randall Junior High School, the same school Rosa Lee dropped out of when she was pregnant with Bobby. Ronnie was in the eighth grade, two grades behind where he should have been.

"I was shy and talked with a stammer," Ronnie remembers. He was also afraid of girls. To stop his stammering and get over his fear of girls, Ronnie drank beer and a codeine-based cough syrup, a remedy his friends had recommended. The mixture helped a bit, gave him a little buzz, but he still felt insecure and inadequate. At a party one night, his best friend, Jackie Boy, offered Ronnie a snort of powdered heroin.

Ronnie had heard of heroin. He knew one adult male relative who was a heroin addict. He didn't think much about what impact the drug might have on him. He was desperate for anything that would help him fit in, allow him to talk to girls. "I tried some," Ronnie says. "It stopped my stammering. I lost my fear of girls. I saw it as helping me. It was kind of a relief. It even made me sound better" when he and his friends did their night-time "lamppost harmonizing" of popular late-1960s rock 'n' roll songs under corner streetlights.

A year later, the family moved into the public housing apartment on 57th Place, S.E. Still in the eighth grade, Ronnie was transferred to nearby Evans Junior High School. Weeks after the move, he dropped out of school permanently. By this time, he was using heroin intravenously, and he was addicted. "One thing led to another," says Ronnie. "I knew I was strung out when I started taking things from the house" to sell to buy heroin. In between odd jobs and work as a short-order cook, stealing became an everyday way of getting the money he needed for his heroin habit. "When you're messing with drugs that is all that's on your mind," Ronnie recalls. "That was all that was on *my* mind."

By the age of sixteen, Ronnie had already drifted into a way of life that would be governed by the daily quest for the money to buy his next heroin fix. Everything else would take second place, including the women and children he loved.

Afraid of prison, Ronnie limited his crimes to car theft and petty larceny. He thought his crimes would not merit a long sentence behind bars if he were caught. He was careful to drive the stolen cars only once and then to a location where they could be stripped of everything that could be quickly sold.

A couple of years after Rosa Lee moved into the 57th Place apartment, a Cadillac-driving drug dealer nicknamed "Killer" approached her. Killer lived in the neighborhood. By this time, she had been dealing heroin for fourteen years. Killer offered her a more lucrative share—two dollars on every five-dollar bag of heroin instead of one dollar on every four one-dollar capsules of heroin—if she would switch from her current supplier and sell Killer's Mexican Mud. Rosa Lee wasn't sure. She was anxious about losing sales and money if Killer's heroin was not popular.

It had been a year since Rosa Lee confronted Ronnie about his heroin addiction, telling him to take care of his own habits. She wondered if Ronnie would know if Killer's heroin was better than that supplied by the dealer she had been working with out of the Ko Ko Club. Killer had left a sample. She asked Ronnie to try it.

Ronnie retreated to the second-floor bedroom where he lived with his heroin-addicted common-law wife and their six-month-old son. The teenage girl, whom Ronnie had introduced to heroin, was pregnant with their second child. "I just injected some of it," Ronnie remembers, "and I got a better buzz than with all of the other heroin [Rosa Lee] was selling. I told her

Killer's heroin was better. If she gave me some, I told her I'd round up her first group of customers."

Rosa Lee switched to Killer's heroin. She sold it at the Ko Ko Club and out of her apartment. In the 1970s, Mexican Mud was popular with heroin addicts all over Washington. She sold so much that it wasn't long before Washington's narcotics policemen learned of her operation and the raids on her apartment began.

On a cold December night in 1972, Ronnie was arrested for trying to steal a car in his grandmother's Northeast Washington neighborhood. He had planned to sell the car's radio. The weather was so cold the car wouldn't start, he says. "The owner showed up and put a gun in my face. He said, 'Man, that's my car. Just sit right there!' " The owner had called the police before he confronted Ronnie. Ronnie knew it was going to be a long night. He was already sick from heroin withdrawal. He was twenty years old.

His common-law wife had left him the year before and moved to Cleveland with the couple's two children. She recovered from her heroin addiction, married an orthodox Muslim, and broke most of her ties with him.

Ronnie underwent a court-ordered sixty-day period of psychological observation at the Lorton Youth Center prison and was sentenced to three years probation in May. He went right back to what he knew best, to what he had been doing for five years—using heroin, stealing cars, and working off and on as a cook.

One day in 1974, Ronnie's father showed up at Rosa Lee's Clifton Terrace apartment shortly before Ronnie came home from a cooking job. Ronnie didn't recognize him, for it had been eleven years since their meeting in the courtyard. When Rosa Lee told Ronnie the man was his father, Ronnie wasn't interested in talking to him, but at Rosa Lee's insistence, the young man shook his father's hand. They had a short conversation. Ronnie did not know until this meeting that his father was a fellow heroin addict. Could Ronnie loan him fifty dollars? That was the price of a heroin billy at the time.

Ronnie couldn't believe what he was hearing. His father, a

man whom he'd met only once before in his life, was going through heroin withdrawal and wanted Ronnie to lend him the cost of a fix. "I loaned him the money," says Ronnie. "I don't know why I loaned him the money." The small loan was never repaid.

A year passed before Ronnie saw his father again. This time his father showed up at an apartment building in Alexandria, Virginia, where Ronnie was working with an uncle, washing and waxing linoleum floors. Rosa Lee had told Ronnie's father where he could find his son.

"Here he come out there asking me, 'Do you know which apartments are vacant?' so he can break into them," recalls Ronnie. "Man, are you serious?" Ronnie asked his father. "Man, you can't come down here saying nothing like that. Man, I work here!" Ronnie told him to get away from there or he'd call the police. His father was incredulous. "Would you, man?" Ronnie says his father asked him. "I said, 'Yeah.' "

Ronnie was afraid that if his father was caught, the managers of the housing complex would find out that they were father and son. Ronnie would face a probation violation from the attempted car theft conviction and be returned to prison. "I didn't want to risk going back to jail," says Ronnie. "For what? For a man who never did nothing for me. No, sir!"

A Clifton Terrace teenager Ronnie had been dating for a couple of years graduated from Cardozo High School in 1978. She joined the Navy the following year and the couple married in early 1980. The night they married, they drove out of Washington to the wife's naval station in Newport, Rhode Island. Ronnie was hopeful that the marriage and the move would give him new direction and add purpose to his life. But he overlooked one piece of baggage he was carrying with him—his addiction.

After a couple of years in Newport, Ronnie's wife was transferred to the naval base in Norfolk, Virginia, where the couple's daughter was born in March 1984, and then to Puerto Rico, where their son was born in April 1986. Ronnie managed to get work as a cook at private restaurants in Newport and Norfolk, but his good fortune ran out in Puerto Rico. He had used heroin daily since he married but, unable to find work in Puerto Rico, Ronnie had to rely on his wife's income to pay for his habit. Initially, things worked out fine. Heroin in Puerto Rico was cheaper and stronger than heroin in Washington. For some reason—he doesn't understand why—he added drinking to the heroin use. When he drank, he often had blackouts and beat his wife, he says.

On the night of September 1, 1986, Puerto Rican narcotics detectives arrested him with a ten-dollar packet of heroin. They were surprised and disappointed by the small amount of heroin in Ronnie's possession. The detectives told Ronnie that for almost a month they had watched his car with its Virginia tags going in and out of a well-known drug area three or four times a week. They had followed him back to the naval base each time. They thought he was supplying sailors on the base.

At his trial, Ronnie told the judge he had been an addict for nineteen years, pleaded guilty to heroin possession and was sentenced to three years in an inpatient drug-treatment center. After his release from the center, Ronnie rejoined his wife and children in Charleston, South Carolina, where she had been transferred. Almost immediately, Ronnie returned to heroin and alcohol and to beating his wife. She asked him to leave.

He moved back to Washington and moved in with the same heroin-addicted relative he knew as a teenager.

Almost a year after his return, one cold, rainy 1991 winter morning at an International House of Pancakes restaurant in suburban Maryland, Rosa Lee and I bumped into Ronnie. We were just leaving after breakfast. Ronnie was sitting on a stool at the counter, near the cashier, when Rosa Lee spotted him. He was there looking for work as a cook.

"Ronnie?" a surprised Rosa Lee said. She had last seen him several years before when he came through Washington on his way to Puerto Rico, when his wife was transferred there from Rhode Island.

"Hi, Ma," Ronnie replied. Neither of them made a move to hug or kiss the other. As I looked on, it was as if I were watching two acquaintances, not mother and son.

He is a small, thin, brown-skinned man whose handsome, angular face is dominated by a thick mustache and large eyes. He looked sickly. He wore a tattered navy blue wool knit cap and a very dirty brown winter coat.

Rosa Lee fussed at him for not getting in touch with her. "I heard you've been back for a year, but you didn't see fit to call me?" she said. "You can't even call your own mother? Where are you staying?"

Ronnie told her that he first lived in Northeast Washington with the male relative. Now he was living with his aunt Lawan in Southeast Washington. Ronnie told his mother that "Chubby," as Lawan is called in the family, "is still hitting the pipe," meaning his aunt was addicted to crack.

The manager of the restaurant came out of the kitchen and told Ronnie that they had no jobs. We took Ronnie with us and dropped him off at a nearby Sizzler restaurant. He wanted to see if they were hiring. "Ronnie, you call me! Ya hear?" was the last thing Rosa Lee told him as he got out of the car in the rain. "Yeah, Ma," he replied.

Months after this meeting, Ronnie tells me that he was so hungry, broke, and tired on that rainy day that he was contemplating committing a crime so he could go to jail, be fed, and get out of the cold for the remainder of the winter. "There was so much drug traffic in Chubby's place, man, I couldn't even get any sleep. She used to come in with a trick, and wake me up on the couch, and ask me to wait outside for a while. I'd have to stand out there in the cold and smoke a cigarette or something."

He moved in with Rosa Lee not long after that chance encounter, Ronnie says, because he grew afraid of the rough characters who came in and out of Lawan's apartment. Rosa Lee tells me Ronnie is lying. "Chubby put Ronnie out," says Rosa Lee, "because she couldn't trick with him in there."

"There were times when we didn't have any shoes on our feet," remembers Rosa Lee's fourth-oldest son, Richard, about growing up on 53rd Street in Northeast Washington in the late 1950s. At such times, he and his brothers were kept home from

Richardson Elementary School. "It was never for too long, though. Mama made some kind of way to put shoes on our feet.

"You see, Mom has been through a strange situation through her life," continues Richard. "My grandmother didn't teach her some things. My mother, in fact, she mentions that to me from time to time now. Her mother taught her some things, but didn't teach her enough.

"But our survival was no problem," says Richard, smiling. "My mother knows how to survive. She got nine lives. She *never* abandoned us!"

By the age of thirteen, Richard took up the pattern set by Bobby and began burglarizing the middle-class homes surrounding the public housing complex the family lived in. He skipped school one morning and broke into a house after he had seen the owner drive off to work. The way the woman dressed and the type of car she drove told Richard there would be any number of items inside the house that he could sell quickly and profitably. What he didn't know was that there was a small dog in the house. The dog began to bark the minute Richard broke the back-door lock and came inside.

He tried to grab the dog, but the dog ran into the master bedroom and hid under the bed. The dog continued to bark, snarl, and snap at Richard's fingers when Richard tried reaching under the bed to catch him. A neighbor heard the barking and called the police. When they arrived, they found Richard hiding in a closet.

Serving a several-month sentence in a juvenile institution for the attempted burglary, Richard lifted weights during every idle moment. A bulkier, stronger Richard was sent home on parole in time for the September start of his ninth-grade school year.

Richard and Ronnie got into a tussle one evening after Richard's return. Richard grabbed a piece of chicken Ronnie was frying. Ronnie, then seventeen, was not strong enough to get the chicken leg away from his younger brother. It was the first time Richard had beaten Ronnie at anything physical.

"I laughed at him," Richard remembers, smiling at the memory. "I told him he should do some serious crime so he could do some serious time. Lift weights like I did. I told him, 'It'll make a man outta you.' "

A short time later, Richard's seventeen-year-old girlfriend gave birth to his first child.

Richard transferred into the twelfth grade at Cardozo High School when the family moved to Clifton Terrace in 1972. He attended classes for several months but dropped out to get a job. He was spending more time smoking the marijuana his mother was selling in Clifton Terrace than attending classes anyway. Besides, there was an urgent need for him to get a job.

He was eighteen years old and the father of six children by four different girls. While in the eleventh grade, he had married the teenager who had already had three of his children. Over the next three years, he got several low-paying jobs, then landed a choice position as a federal file clerk in 1975. Everyone Richard knew regarded getting a government job, federal or city, as a major accomplishment. A civil service job meant benefits and a pension. Richard felt his life was now complete. All he had to do was hold down his job until he retired.

His juvenile record as a burglar could not be counted against him. Richard was determined not to risk his job by going back to house burglaries. Like Ronnie, however, Richard had not counted on being tripped up by the one thing that he held on to from his past—drug use.

Over the next fourteen years, Richard had two scrapes with the law, but his federal employers did not find out about his arrests. In the late 1970s, police arrested Richard at an illegal dice game shooting craps. "I was winning all the money," he says. "Somebody called the police. They came from nowhere and locked everybody up."

When the police searched Richard's pockets, they found three aluminum packets of "Loveboat," the illicit hallucinogen phencyclidine. Several years later, he was arrested with $300 worth of marijuana. He pleaded guilty to both charges and was given probation each time.

In the late 1980s, however, Richard began a downward slide that he could not stop. A friend had offered him a hit of crack cocaine. Curious about the effects of cocaine, Richard sucked the smoke from the crack pipe into his lungs. "It was one of those things where I didn't think it would affect me *that* much," recalls Richard. "I had done other drugs. I said, 'Let me see what this is all about.' Yes, I was aware that it had hurt a lot of people. But I didn't think it would hurt me."

The seconds-short high led to his almost immediate addiction. "I was so strung out on the crack pipe I stopped going to work," he says. By 1989, he had so abused his sick-leave privileges that he was asked to resign or face being fired. He resigned. Several weeks later, he was caught stealing telephones inside the Washington Hospital Center and was sentenced to eighteen months in prison.

Two years earlier, Rosa Lee was herself arrested for selling heroin on 14th Street. Deputy U.S. marshals picked up Rosa Lee and about fifteen other prisoners at Superior Court for transport to the D.C. jail. On the ride to the jail in a big prisoner-transport bus, a male marshal stood next to Rosa Lee's seat. He stared down at her. She glanced up at him, wondering why he appeared interested in her. She was in the beginning stages of heroin withdrawal and in no mood for fun and games. What she really needed was a hit of dope, and he wasn't going to give her that! she told herself.

"Rosa Lee, don't you recognize me?" the man asked in a hurt tone.

She didn't recognize the voice. She looked up at his face, squinting as she always does when focusing on something or someone. "No, I don't know who you are," she told him.

The marshal said his name.

Rosa Lee sat back and stared at him. "Well, I'll be damned," said Rosa Lee, her sickness momentarily forgotten. A flood of memories came back to her. She could see it now. "The big head. The face." He had put on weight, but who wouldn't have after thirty-three years? It was Richard's father. She hadn't seen him since Richard was two months old, in October 1954.

The marshal had been a teenager then, a year or two older than Rosa Lee. He was the one who had helped her fill out the necessary forms in her successful effort to wrest control of her welfare stipend from her mother, the same boy she had been secretly seeing when she was married. When Albert Cunningham found out, he beat her so badly she left him. At that time, the teenager lived next door to her mother's house.

Rosa Lee had never told him he was Richard's father, and she decided not to tell him this night.

In December 1989, shortly after Richard was paroled for the Washington Hospital Center burglary, he and Rosa Lee were walking along H Street when Rosa Lee spotted the marshal getting on a bus. "Look quick, Richard!" she said urgently. "*That's your father.*"

Richard stared at the man. He looked at Rosa Lee and then back at the man. Until that day, Rosa Lee had always told him that Albert Cunningham was his father as well as Alvin's.

It is difficult to pin Ducky down about the details of his growing up. He is the only member of Rosa Lee's family who is not talkative. If he is not high on crack, he is often sullen or sulky. When he does feel like talking, Ducky often rambles.

Asked about a particular year in his life, Ducky often switches without warning into a period that is either years before or years after the one mentioned. Asked about a particular event in his life, Ducky's initial response is right on target for a few minutes, but then he suddenly veers off into some unconnected incident. He harbors a wide range of resentments against every member of his family, even Rosa Lee, as well as people outside his family.

When Ducky was nine years old, he wanted to be useful to his mother, but he was not yet willing to take the risks his older brothers were taking. He too wanted to bring some money into the house, and get his own money for the movies and the sweets he liked. Rosa Lee suggested that he earn some money by ferrying stolen clothing on his bicycle over to his grandmother's public housing apartment, he says. Rosetta would call people in her building to come and see the goods. "They would buy them," recalls Ducky. On average, Ducky says, he was able to bring $100 back to his mother. Rosa Lee paid him one or two dollars, "depending on how she was feeling," he says.

Ducky was twelve years old when the narcotics policemen's drug raids forced the family to move to Clifton Terrace. The move changed Ducky's routine. Instead of carrying Rosa Lee's stolen clothes over to his grandmother's apartment, he now knocked on apartment doors in Clifton Terrace to advertise and sell his mother's shoplifted merchandise. Soon, Rosa Lee had a large group of regular customers.

Ducky dropped out of the eighth grade in 1976. He was sixteen and had barely been taught to read and write. He had also started snorting powdered cocaine several months earlier. He lived with Rosa Lee, helped her sell her shoplifted clothes, and took temporary jobs as a manual laborer. In 1980, Rosa Lee arranged for him to get his own apartment in Clifton Terrace.

A year later, Ducky was hired as a security guard at a bakery. He lost the job in the early 1980s after firing his .38 caliber revolver at some kids who were stealing cakes and pies from a delivery truck. He has always felt he was unjustly dismissed. "They might have been kids, but they were stealing," he says without even a hint of irony in his voice. "I was supposed to be protecting that stuff."

A family member introduced him to the crack pipe, Ducky says, during this same period. The first time he sucked the crack vapor into his lungs, "it was like a feeling that I never experienced, so I started hitting it. I ran into a couple of girls who wanted me to experience hitting the pipe and having sex with them. Tried that, too." Since then, Ducky has associated smoking crack with having sex; he always tries to arrange to do both simultaneously. "The two go together," he says. "It's the best feeling in the world."

Shortly after Ducky's crack addiction started, a group of New York drug dealers came to Clifton Terrace. The price of crack in Washington had brought the New Yorkers to the capital. There was such a glut of crack and cocaine in New York that the prices there were depressed. The New Yorkers needed someplace to live and sell crack. Ducky rented them space in his large one-room apartment.

"They would give me my pay as far as one hundred dollars a

day, fifty dollars in cash and fifty dollars worth of crack." The New Yorkers soon learned of Ducky's desire to have sex whenever he was using crack. "Then they would put 'trick girls' on me to make me mess up my payment.

"That's something that a man smoking 'caine should never go through," continues Ducky in a wounded voice. "I went through that for almost four or five years at Clifton Terrace. Women. Making me mess up my money and the 'caine for sex."

Ducky would use up his crack with the girls and come back to the New Yorkers for more. He ended up deeply indebted to them, and they took over his apartment completely. Narcotics officers raided his apartment several times. "I went to jail a couple of times," he says. "I never squealed on anyone."

Eventually, Ducky learned how to convert powdered cocaine into the rock-like crack. He decided to go into business for himself and moved his operation into Rosa Lee's apartment in a Clifton Terrace building two doors away from his.

In the meantime, the New Yorkers felt they could do more business if they too moved out of Ducky's apartment. Patty, who had an apartment in the same building as Ducky's, invited the New Yorkers to move into her place. They made the same deal with her as they had with Ducky. One hundred dollars a day rent, half paid in cash and half in crack. Soon, Patty too was asking for more crack, and she ended up indebted to the same dealers.

Ducky was angry. He wanted Patty to kick the New Yorkers out of her apartment. They were competing with him, cutting into his profits. Patty refused unless Ducky paid her $100 a day in crack. Ducky said no. "Even if I had paid her, she would have collected the crack and still let the New Yorkers deal from her apartment," he says.

He sold crack for two months out of his mother's apartment, but eventually smoked up his profits while having sex with female customers. The last bit of cash he made was stolen in the basement of his mother's building late one night when several robbers—he suspects they were men to whom he had sold crack—yoked him around the neck and arms and took $1,500 from him. The New Yorkers were not the only ruthless criminals, Ducky learned. "Even my own D.C. boys jumped me!" he says.

That was Ducky's last venture at dealing crack. He was evicted from his apartment in August 1988 because of his drug involvement. Thereafter, he worked periodically, burglarized suburban Maryland homes on a regular basis, and smoked crack with trick girls as often as he could.

In the fall of 1990, Alvin confronted Ducky about begging Rosa Lee for money to buy crack. "I WILL BREAK YOUR FACE, DUCKY," Alvin yelled at his baby brother. Ducky made an insincere promise to stop harassing Rosa Lee for money.

"And what are you doing sleeping at the foot of Mama's bed?" Alvin asked him. "What is wrong with you, Ducky?"

Every night in this period, Ducky curled up on a small child's bed that he had salvaged from alongside a trash dumpster. Ducky had stuffed the bed at the foot of Rosa Lee's double bed. She tolerated him sleeping in her bedroom because, she said, "He doesn't have anyplace else to go."

When not living with Rosa Lee, Ducky sleeps in parks, abandoned houses or, like his brothers Bobby and Richard, revolves in and out of prison. But Ducky's convictions are small-time, always for petty property theft.

SIX

Another Way of Life

OVERLEAF: *Alvin, a Metrobus driver, on the job* (© *Lucian Perkins*—The Washington Post).

ERIC HUNG UP the telephone in his suburban Maryland apartment and cursed out loud. He couldn't decide what angered him more—that his thirty-three-year-old brother, Ducky, was badgering his mother again for money to buy crack cocaine or that his mother was calling him once more to ask him to eject Ducky from her apartment.

As Eric, then thirty-five, drove his white Jeep through the suburbs toward his mother's apartment in Washington, he steeled himself for the impending confrontation. He didn't mind getting involved. It just didn't do any good. No matter what he said, no matter what he did, nothing seemed to change.

Of Rosa Lee's eight children, only Eric and his older brother Alvin have never used drugs. They are the only ones who have never been to prison. Both have worked for most of their adult lives, and they have taken care of themselves and their families. Both are Army veterans; both have worked primarily in government jobs since leaving the military.

As adults, they have defined themselves in ways that set them apart from the rest of the family. Eric has maintained a lifelong passion for music, hosting occasional talent shows and hiring himself out as a disc jockey for local parties. Alvin and his wife saved enough money to buy a comfortable two-story red-brick bungalow in a middle-class neighborhood. He is the only one of Rosa Lee's children who owns his own home.

Both men have made it through rough passages—both had close brushes with the law, were teenage fathers, and dropped out of school—but neither one let those events knock him off the path to responsible adulthood.

Of the two, Alvin is the more relaxed. He is inclined to give cryptic answers and studiously avoids assigning blame for matters of the past. Eric, on the other hand, is so volatile and outspoken that I find myself wondering how he has escaped seriously hurting someone and ending up in jail. He is quick to assign blame and loses his temper just talking about the members of his family who have fallen into drugs and crime. Listening to both men describe their childhoods, it is amazing that they rejected the lures, avoided the pitfalls, and got around the obstacles that they faced at home and in their neighborhoods from the day they were born. Eric even sees himself in Ducky. "Ducky reminds me of myself at one time," Eric told me, "but I caught myself."

Eric and Ducky have the same father, David Wright, but that is where all similarity ends. Eric is round-faced, like their father, and stocky at 5 feet 6 inches tall, 205 pounds. He has a reputation as a fierce street fighter, a sidewalk gladiator who fights until he cannot stand. Even if Eric loses a fight, the winner does not want to tangle with him again. Ducky is shorter and slighter at 5 foot 4, 137 pounds. He has never been a fighter.

Rosa Lee's phone call on this June night was just another reminder of what Eric had worked so hard to escape. By the time he reached his mother's apartment, he was steaming. He strode into the living room and stood in front of Ducky, who was lounging on the couch after a nightlong crack binge.

"YOU'VE GOT TO GO," Eric shouted.

"This is Mama's house," Ducky said. "I ain't got to go nowhere!"

"You're going out of here!" Eric said heatedly, moving one step closer.

Ducky looked at Rosa Lee. She refused to intervene, so Ducky rose from the sofa with a resigned shrug, shoved some clothes in a plastic bag, and left.

Still smoldering, Eric turned to Rosa Lee. Recalling the scene for me later, Eric said that he felt Rosa Lee was playing the victim to win his sympathy. But he had no sympathy for her at that moment, only anger—the same anger that has burned within him since he was five years old and learned that he was wearing clothes shoplifted by his mother. He felt Rosa Lee carried the ultimate responsibility for what Ducky had become, for the years-long history of drug addiction and repeated imprisonment that has afflicted four of his brothers and both his sisters.

What followed was a scene from the drama Eric and Rosa Lee have acted out with each other without an ending for three decades.

"You never instilled any kind of values in us that were worth anything!" he raged at her.

"What do you mean, Cheetah?" she remembers shouting, using the nickname she gave Eric as a little boy because of his love for and skill at climbing trees. "I'm not a good mother?"

Eric shouted louder. "You never made it a point to see that we went to school! The things that you have taught us is that manipulating is good, if you can do it. Stealing is good, if you can do it and get away with it. Using someone is good, if you can get away with it."

But Rosa Lee gave as good as she got, shouting louder still that she had taught all her children "to survive!"

Eric stormed off. He had heard it all too many times. Survival was always his mother's last defense. Well, he didn't buy it. He had survived too—without anesthetizing himself with narcotics, resorting to drug dealing, prostitution, or stealing. He knew his mother would let Ducky back into her apartment that evening. He was bone-tired of the repeated performance. He had put Ducky out more times than he could count. Each occasion left him exhausted and furious. As he drove back home, he decided that this was the last time he would eject Ducky from his mother's apartment.

———

On a spring afternoon, not long before Eric's confrontation with
Ducky and Rosa Lee, Alvin is struggling to explain why he, like
Eric, turned out differently from his brothers and sisters.

We are sitting at his kitchen table in his Northwest Washington home. A lawn service tends the grass; an alarm system pro-
tects the house. Alvin's late-model luxury car and his customized
van sit in front of the house. He and his wife have government
jobs; Alvin drives a bus for the Washington Metropolitan Area
Transit Authority, for which he's worked since 1981. It's the kind
of stability that was missing from Alvin's childhood; Rosa Lee
moved the family nine times before he turned sixteen.

Alvin leans back in his chair, contemplating his response. His
face is small and angular, and he looks younger than his thirty-
eight years. He is self-effacing and slow to anger. When he loses
his temper—as he sometimes does when he visits Rosa Lee's
apartment and finds Patty or Ducky engaged in drug activity—
everyone knows it is best to scatter.

"It's not very complicated," he says finally. "For one, I don't
like drugs because I saw what they could do to you."

I press him to say more, but he's not given to long, introspec-
tive statements. Initially, he didn't want to be interviewed. Eric
too was ambivalent at first. Not only would my questions open
some painful and personal chapters that he and Alvin would
rather forget, but they were concerned about being associated
with the family's troubled history. As these two brothers learned
more about my efforts to understand how poverty, criminal
recidivism, and drug abuse had affected their family, they concluded that there was some value in discussing the contrast
between their lives and those of their brothers and sisters.

Over the course of several interviews, it slowly became clear
that Alvin and Eric began to set themselves apart from their family during their first years of elementary school. It was not something they coordinated. Each was unaware of the other's resolve
to get far away from the life they lived as children. Nevertheless,
both somehow came to recognize that they had real alternatives
within their reach, that they had the power to make something
of themselves if they didn't give up.

Their emotional reactions to their upbringing became motivating forces in their childhoods and carried them, albeit with some skirmishes on the edge of the law, through their adolescence into adulthood. Alvin as a young boy was struck by shame and humiliation about living on welfare. Eric responded in a different way. He felt anger and disgust about his mother's shoplifting. At critical points, they benefited from an outsider's intervention—a teacher in Alvin's case, a social worker in Eric's.

Rosa Lee can't explain why Alvin and Eric grew up to be so different from their siblings. "I didn't do anything more for them than I did for any of my other children," she says during one of our many discussions on the subject. "They always acted different, like they were shamed by it all. Even when they were little."

Alvin, in particular, showed his independence early. "There wasn't any what you call 'role model' for him to copy," she said. "His father only came around a couple of times when he was a boy, and Alvin didn't see him again until he was an adult. No, he just sort of grew up like he did all by himself."

Alvin's earliest memories go back to when Rosa Lee, Rosetta, and their children lived on the second floor of a one-bedroom apartment on Capitol Hill. Thadeous Lawrence, his great-grandfather, owned the rundown wood-frame building a block north of Mount Joy Baptist Church. "The living circumstances were crowded," he remembers. "We all slept on mattresses on the floor."

Nineteen-year-old Rosa Lee thought it was a great apartment. It was the first place she ever lived that had electricity and an indoor toilet. Winter heat was provided by a coal stove in the center of the bedroom. "The only time that stove was any good and kept us warm was when it turned red" with heat, Rosa Lee remembers. "Everybody sat around that stove in the cold weather."

A couple of months before Alvin's third birthday, city authorities condemned the house. Housing officials moved both families into a public housing project in Northeast Washington. At the time, Rosa Lee had four children and was eight months pregnant with Eric.

"I remember us moving at night," says Alvin, "some men in the family carrying the beds upstairs" in the new apartment.

His only childhood memories of his father, Albert Cunningham, come to him from his early years in that apartment. "I remember him coming by about three times," Alvin says, "picking me up and bumping my head against the ceiling" when tossing him in the air. "I remember him giving me a quarter to go to the Strand Theater."

For years afterward, Albert Cunningham did not visit at all, and Alvin would ask Rosa Lee about his father from time to time. She told the boy she did not know where he was and made it clear to Alvin she was not looking for him either. Rosa Lee's reaction did not stop Alvin from thinking about his father and wanting to see him. David Wright, Eric's father, came by often, making Alvin wonder even more where his own father was. The only news Alvin received about his father was a periodic report from an aunt who would tell him she had seen his father driving a cab in downtown Washington. Alvin was twenty years old before he saw his father again.

Alvin has held on to another powerful memory. It was a pivotal event in his life, occurring before he even entered kindergarten at Richardson Elementary School. It is a memory so searing that it still governs his behavior as an adult.

Bobby wasn't home and Ronnie, Alvin, and Richard were hungry. The only thing in the house to eat was rice, so the three boys boiled a big pot of it. Alvin decided to sweeten his rice and borrowed a cup of sugar from a neighbor. When Rosa Lee returned home, she saw the spilled sugar on the kitchen counter. She knew there was no sugar in the house and asked them where they got it. Alvin told her he had borrowed it.

Rosa Lee was furious. She made Alvin strip off all his clothes and then whipped him with a strap. As she swung the strap, she yelled, "Don't you borrow ANYTHING! Didn't I tell you not to borrow anything? Don't ever borrow anything AGAIN!"

After she finished, Rosa Lee bought a box of sugar, refilled the cup Alvin had used, and carried the sugar back to the neighbor. Alvin didn't recall his mother ever telling him that borrowing anything was against her principles, but he never forgot the lesson he learned that day.

"My mother was struggling," he says. "My mother had a lot of pride about herself. If she couldn't give it to you, then no one else would, and we'd go without. And many times we went without. She wouldn't even go to my grandmother's and ask for anything. Her *own* mother! After that, I didn't borrow or ask anyone for anything. Still don't.'"

Despite Rosa Lee's visceral opposition to borrowing, she had no difficulty accepting public assistance. Alvin's response set him apart from his mother and most of the rest of his family. Whenever Alvin heard the horn of the dark green "welfare truck," he would bolt out the back door of his mother's apartment as fast as his legs would carry him. By the time the flatbed truck pulled into the courtyard of the public housing complex for the monthly distribution of bags of food to the poorest families, Alvin was long gone.

Alvin still remembers the contents of those sealed bags: tins of canned Spam and corned beef, rice, powdered eggs, cheese, and pinto beans, along with other bulk items. Rosa Lee saw the bags of staples as a godsend in her daily struggle to feed her eight children, including the baby girl born in March 1961. Alvin saw the handouts as an embarrassment.

His brothers and uncles, who lived next-door, noticed his tendency to disappear when it came time to unload the bags—six to a family—of surplus goods. They assumed he was avoiding work. "He was embarrassed?" Eric asks. "All these years, I thought he refused to go to the truck because he was lazy!"

"Sometimes I did go," says Alvin defensively. "But it would bother me. I *hated* it!"

It annoyed Alvin that the truck's driver beeped his horn to announce his arrival at the complex where Alvin's mother and grandmother were raising families in side-by-side apartments. The beeping horn drew their neighbors' attention to who went to the truck to collect food. Alvin did not want to be seen anywhere near the welfare truck.

Alvin had a crush on a girl who lived across the courtyard; she was a year older than Alvin and a grade ahead of him in school. Both her parents had jobs, and although their salaries were so low that they qualified for public housing, they made too much to qualify for the surplus food. He was afraid the girl and her parents would shun him if they knew his family lived on welfare, something they would certainly learn if they saw him carrying the bags into his home.

Alvin didn't understand why the family needed to take the free food. His mother was working every night, waiting tables and dancing at the nightclubs on H Street. In the mornings, as he and his brothers were leaving the apartment for school, Rosa Lee often left too, on her way downtown. She came back in the late afternoon with shopping bags full of clothes for the family. "We had the best of shoes," he remembers. "Foot-Joys. She picked expensive things for us. On Sunday or Easter, we looked real nice. Extra nice. I remember people coming and looking at some of the merchandise she would bring home in big bags. She'd have bags full of clothes. It never dawned on me that she was shoplifting."

It was in the third grade that Alvin learned about drugs. Rosa Lee let one of her teenage brothers give weekend-night parties in her house while she was working at the nightclubs. "There'd be maybe thirty or forty people in the house," remembers Alvin. "Lights down low. Me, Ronnie, and Richard, we'd come downstairs and watch the dancing through the stair rails. I remember seeing guys in the corner smoking marijuana. They were puffing it differently than you would smoke a cigarette. They would hold the smoke in their lungs. We didn't call it marijuana. We'd say, 'They're smoking that stuff again.' "

Rosa Lee didn't know what to make of her third-born son. Even as a toddler, he had behaved differently from his older brothers. He would follow her around the apartment, observing everything she did. If she stopped to do something, he sat nearby and watched. Some of Rosa Lee's friends noticed his quiet behavior; Alvin overheard them telling Rosa Lee that he would grow up to be a "good person." He liked the sound of that.

He didn't like the things he overheard at school. Some of his better-off classmates at Richardson Elementary made fun of the poor children from "the 'jects"—the public project where Alvin's family lived.

Alvin managed to escape much of this "Jone'in'," or brutal teasing. Maybe it was because he didn't respond to the taunts; maybe it was because he befriended some of the boys who lived in the middle-class private homes along nearby East Capitol Street. Whatever the reason, the things he saw and heard while visiting his new friends opened his eyes to a new way of life.

His friends' parents interpreted Alvin's quiet, introverted demeanor as good manners and made him feel welcome. During his many visits, he took a close look at the well-kept furniture at his friends' homes, comparing it with the worn secondhand furniture at his own. Each of his friends had a bedroom and a bed all to himself; he had always shared a bed with two of his brothers.

Alvin made other comparisons. His friends' parents were teachers, secretaries, Post Office clerks; his mother left her children at night and went off to wait tables at nightclubs. When he was invited to share meals at his friends' homes, they sat at a dining-room table set with flatware; his family's meals were haphazard at best, whatever Bobby fried or boiled and set down before them in front of the television with a bowl and spoon.

"I started picking up on these things," he remembers. "I knew I wanted to live the way I was seeing them live. I was too young then to understand how to get there. As I got older, though, I began picking up on how to get it more and more."

Eric has never had Alvin's quiet temperament, not even as a little boy. "I was a bad-ass child," he says. "You couldn't make me do nothing!"

He says this with the conviction of a man who knows himself and the forces that shaped him. "I was so bad because I was missing my mother," recalls Eric. "My mother was *never* home." Ten-year-old Bobby would make Eric and the other younger children take turns washing the dirty dishes, making the beds, sit quietly watching television, and go to bed at assigned hours. "My mother really didn't stay home that much."

We are seated at Eric's new dining-room table in his suburban Maryland apartment. The table's shiny black top gives the room a sleek, modern look. Eric leans forward as he speaks, making sure the tape recorder catches his words. "I remember my mother saying I wasn't going to be NOTHING!" he thunders.

He is unaware of how often he raises his voice when he talks about Rosa Lee. He is so consumed with anger at his mother, I sometimes have to point out to him that he is shouting. "My mother makes me feel like I owe her something, and I don't think I owe her anything!" he says. He focuses mostly on her mistakes: he's too angry to see any of the obstacles she faced, any suffering that she may have endured because of her own upbringing.

"Sometimes, I really feel bad about what went on," says Eric. "I think I could have been a lot further than what I am now in life, if she had paid a lot more attention to us. Our education. Only three of us can really read. Bobby, Alvin, and Richard. That's one thing I stay mad about!"

Evictions forced Rosa Lee and her mother to move their families in 1961 and 1962, and Eric attended two schools in the first and second grades. He fell behind; some days, he didn't go to school at all.

First, the family moved in the fall of 1961 to a two-story row house at Ninth and F streets, NE. It was rat infested but cheap, a house two poor women with seventeen children between them could afford to rent. The principal at nearby Goding Elementary School looked out his office window and spotted Rosa Lee's and Rosetta's children playing in the street one day during school hours. The women hadn't enrolled them yet. The principal came out onto the sidewalk and yelled at the children to come over to him. "He asked us," Eric remembers, " 'Where do you live? Where are you suppose to be?' " Eric and Alvin remember they all pointed to the front door of the house they lived in.

The principal knocked on their door and told both mothers, "It's not permitted to let your kids run around without being in school." The children were registered the next day. Eric was assigned to first grade and Alvin to fourth.

Six months later, their new landlord evicted them. "He told us he would never have rented the house to us in the first place if he had known we had so many kids," recalls Rosa Lee. She and her mother rented another row house several blocks away at 11th and C streets, N.E. Eric and Alvin were transferred to Lovejoy Elementary School.

Upon arriving at Lovejoy, Eric told one of his teachers that he was having trouble learning to read. He remembers the teacher telling him, "Don't worry, you'll get it in the next grade." Rosa Lee, unable to read herself, wasn't much help. On many days, she wasn't even home when Eric and the other children returned from school.

Eric often found himself the target of taunts at school. Rosa Lee was selling some of her shoplifted goods in the neighborhood to the parents of Eric's classmates. Word got around. "Your mama steals!" he remembers some of his new classmates yelling. Eric couldn't shrug off the teasing as easily as Alvin. "I fought quite a bit," he says. "I fought boys, girls. It didn't matter. If they were too big, I'd throw bricks at them."

Worst of all, he suspected the taunts were true. "My mother would leave the house empty-handed in the morning and come back with four shopping bags of anything you can name. Clothing. Appliances. Curtains." Eric even overheard the adults who came to their house talking about his mother. "I think it was intentional when they said those things in front of me," he says today. "Same ones who were buying things were the ones doing the talking. They said things like, 'Rosa Lee. Get her to get anything I want, you know. Come around here with all that stolen stuff.' From the beginning, it embarrassed me."

One day, he remembers saying to Rosa Lee, "People say that you're stealing stuff."

Rosa Lee didn't deny it.

"Why do you do that?" he asked.

"So you can eat!" his mother said.

"But Ma, we're eating every day!" he said.

Rosa Lee said the welfare check was too little to feed and clothe all eight of them, but that didn't satisfy Eric. "I just never understood why she had to do that, but I think I was really

affected the older I got," he says now. "I really started feeling
and knowing the meaning of embarrassment."

By this time, Alvin also knew about his mother's stealing. "I
heard my uncles and other family members talking about it," he
remembers. Unlike Eric, he accepted it without complaint. He
harbored no anger toward Rosa Lee and loved her as she was.
Sometimes at night, he'd wake up in the crowded bed he shared
with his brothers wondering if his mother was all right in those
rough nightclubs she worked in.

One night, he worked himself up worrying about her and
decided to go see how she was doing. Eleven-year-old Alvin
slipped out of the house and walked the mile to where his
mother was shake dancing at the 821 Club on H Street. There
was no adult at the door to stop him, so he walked into the
nightclub. Rosa Lee was going through her dance routine. During one of her turns, she saw her son standing near one of the
tables. "I couldn't believe it," remembers Rosa Lee. "There was
my Alvin standing in the middle of the room. No one saw him.
Everyone was watching me!"

"She stopped," Alvin remembers, left the stage, and hustled
him off into the dressing room. She made him wait there while
she went out and finished her number. Then she took him home.

"She laughed," Alvin says, as she walked him home. "She
told me that I could not come down to her job like that. I told
her I was worried about her, so I came looking for her. She told
me not to do it again."

Almost a year later, in October 1965, Rosa Lee was arrested for
trying to steal the fur coat at the suburban Maryland department
store. The period while she was in prison and Rosetta cared for
her children was not easy for any of them. Rosa Lee's children
ached for their mother's return. They waited for ten months.

Rosa Lee's older children felt Rosetta treated them differently
than her own children. Alvin says he noticed the differences in
treatment but was not bothered by it. Eric still resents it.

"I loved my grandmother," says Alvin. "Here she was watching eight kids who were not hers. I knew my mother had got

caught stealing. That was thrown at you all the time" by his grandmother and her children. Alvin did not like the comments, but remained quiet. "Grandma was a fairly big woman. Big hands. Quick to hit you. Strike out at you. If she couldn't do it, she had kids that would back her up. Her sons would come from nowhere. So there was nothing you could do. You couldn't say what you didn't like or disapproved of."

Eric felt Rosetta resented taking care of him and his siblings. "I hated my grandmother," he says. "It makes me sad when I talk about my grandmother. I wouldn't ask her for food because she called us 'greedy, always begging.' When my mother went to jail, she pushed all of us in a little bedroom. She'd keep our door shut. We weren't allowed in the front room."

Her attitude toward Rosa Lee's children conveyed a message, says Eric: " 'You're not my kids. You're my daughter's kids. Y'all bad kids. Goddamn Rosa Lee's kids. Bad-ass kids.' I never could understand what did we do that was so wrong to make our grandmother treat us like that."

Rosetta "pushed her kids to go to school and made sure they had clean clothes to go to school in," recalls Eric. "Her kids were pampered. But we used to go to school dressed any kind of way." If Rosa Lee's children protested about the clothes Rosetta dressed them in, "she'd hit you. Hard enough to make you want to move."

Eric was in the second month of the fifth grade when Rosa Lee was arrested. He could not stomach his schoolmates' taunts about the wrinkled and dirty clothes his grandmother dressed him in, and so he began skipping school. He doesn't know how many months he missed, but "it was a lot," he says.

Many evenings, he sat out in front of the house "looking up and down the street, wondering when my mother was coming home," he remembers. "I'd sit out there until dark."

In late July, Rosetta told Rosa Lee's children that their mother was coming home, "but she didn't tell us what time," recalls Eric. The eight of them waited in front of the house all day. In the early evening twilight, Eric was the first to see Rosa Lee "half a block away," he remembers. "Boy, we took off running down

Eleventh Street." Rosa Lee laughed and smiled as all of her children crashed into her.

The following afternoon, Rosa Lee took her children to nearby Lincoln Park so she could talk to them. The oldest among them, starting with Bobby and ending with Eric, complained about the way their grandmother had treated them. Rosa Lee told them not to worry; she planned to move them all as soon as she could get an apartment. She began the series of moves that took the family to five apartments over the next two years.

All of the apartments they lived in were cheap and heavily infested with cockroaches. They shared one apartment, really a combination oil joint and trick pad upstairs from an infamous nightclub called the Blue Angel, with drug addicts and prostitutes. Rosa Lee worked in the Blue Angel at night while her children, in the apartment's back room, listened to the sounds of heroin addicts, prostitutes, and their tricks coming in and out of the apartment's front room.

It was while the family lived over the Blue Angel that Eric first became aware that his mother was a prostitute. "I didn't like it," he says, his voice rising in anger. "I made it known I didn't like it by the way I acted. BAD! She would always say, 'I got to have a friend. I got to get money to feed y'all.'" When he came home from school each day, Eric would look around to see whether there were men in the house. If there were, then he'd leave and wait outside until the men left.

The children were often up late at night and too tired to concentrate at school during the day. They would barely settle into one school before they were switched to another. There was no stability, just chaos and turmoil.

"Every school I went to, I was put on the front row," remembers Eric. After a while it dawned on him that the teachers put him up front so they could watch him. His reputation as a bad boy followed him from school to school.

Whatever school Eric attended, he would pray that the teacher would not call on him to read what was written on the blackboard. Eric could not read it. "Don't call on me," he silently prayed. "I don't want to be embarrassed."

For those times he was called on, Eric developed a strategy to hide his illiteracy. "I always shaded it off by saying something smart and getting into trouble," he remembers. Many times he was sent to the principal's office. "I was the baddest child in the school. I thought it was an accomplishment. That was the label I used to get by the fact that I could not read. I always kept it to myself. I never would talk about it. Never would ask for help. No one knew, not even my mother."

He could not hide his illiteracy from his teachers. "They knew," he says. "They didn't try to do anything about it. They were transferring me to higher grades because of my age. You could see it in my grades. I was always failing everything. It was like they didn't care. I could sit there in class and go to sleep. They wouldn't bother me. When they passed out papers, I got no papers."

Finally, in 1968, the family settled into the two-story apartment on 57th Place, S.E. Alvin enrolled at Evans Junior High School, where he met a teacher who saw something in Alvin—and who set out to help Alvin see it too.

Gartrell Franklin remembers the exact date that he met Alvin—November 1, 1968, Franklin's first day as a history teacher in Washington's public schools. Both were newcomers to Evans Junior High School, an imposing red-brick building on East Capitol Street. Franklin was twenty-three, fresh from Howard University and bursting with energy and idealism. Alvin was fifteen, an eighth-grade transfer.

Alvin wasn't Franklin's best student that first year, but the young teacher was drawn to him. "He seemed more mature than children his age," Franklin recalled as we talked about Alvin at Franklin's suburban Maryland home. He and Alvin have been friends now for twenty-five years. "He would ask you things after class. Students didn't normally do that."

Just as the eight-year-old Alvin studied the differences between his life and that of his middle-class friends, now the teenage Alvin soaked up the guidance and friendship of Gartrell Franklin. His conversations with Franklin revolved around black history and the black consciousness movement of the 1960s. Franklin organized an after-school Black History Awareness group; Alvin joined and brought along three of his friends.

It was an exciting and difficult time to be young and black in America. Six months earlier, Martin Luther King, Jr., had been assassinated. His death sparked civil disorders in many major cities, including Washington. Stores were looted, buildings burned, people killed. Though Alvin hadn't participated in any looting, he had seen the goods his mother and siblings had brought back to the house from H Street.

Only a month before King's death, a presidential commission headed by Illinois governor Otto Kerner had issued its findings on similar disturbances the previous summer in Newark, Detroit, and other cities. The commission's conclusion was stark. "Our nation is moving toward two societies, one black, one white—separate and unequal," its report stated. "Discrimination and segregation have long permeated much of American life; they now threaten the future of every American."

In this atmosphere, Franklin preached against drugs and pushed Alvin and his friends to make something of themselves. Alvin remembers Franklin saying over and over: "Get that education. You need that education!" Franklin was the first person in his life to emphasize the importance of education, Alvin says.

Alvin and his friends regarded Franklin as more than just a teacher. "He said all the things that a father, if he were there, would say and do," Alvin says. None of the boys had much, if any, contact with their fathers.

The boys wanted to know everything they could about every black leader, living or dead, in America. They talked about the Black Panthers, Malcolm X and the Nation of Islam, and King's Poor People's Campaign. They hung on Franklin's every word.

Alvin listened to Franklin because he was educated and forceful. "He always carried paperwork around with him," remembers Alvin. "He looked like a professor. Upright! Strong!"

Then, on a spring night in 1969, Alvin put his future in jeopardy. Bobby was home after a year in the Job Corps and was a couple of months away from joining the Army. He invited Alvin along on a burglary of a school: for reasons he can no longer fathom, Alvin went. Alvin waited outside while Bobby and another boy broke into the school through a bathroom window. In the still night air, he heard the wail of a police siren. Someone had spotted them. Bobby and his friend emerged from the building, empty-handed, and they all ran.

Alvin eluded the police by hiding in the bushes of a nearby back yard, where he found himself face-to-face with a startled German shepherd. Even in his terror, he was angry at himself. He hadn't stolen anything. He hadn't even gone into the building. Yet here he was, fleeing the police. "I knew I would have been charged if the police would have caught us," Alvin said. "From then on, I knew I had to make a drastic change in my life to stay away from this atmosphere."

A short time later, Bobby approached Alvin about joining him in another burglary. Alvin declined in such a forceful manner Bobby knew that Alvin would never go with him again. Bobby was disappointed. "He was my little brother," Bobby says. "I wanted him to follow me. But I knew he wasn't into crime the way I was. He wasn't into it at all." Bobby joined the Army in July.

A year after the school burglary attempt, sixteen-year-old Alvin became the father of a baby girl while in the ninth grade at Evans Junior High School. The mother was a sixteen-year-old cheerleader at Eastern High School.

This was also the period when narcotics officers began to regularly raid the family's 57th Place apartment. Alvin did not know his mother was selling heroin. "I remember the house used to get raided many times," he says. "It was degrading. They'd make you drop your pants and spread your buttocks" to see if Rosa Lee's children had hidden drugs in their body cavities. "All these things they'd do to you looking for drugs. That upset me. I was humiliated! *Really, really, really,* it affected me."

After each raid, Alvin asked Rosa Lee whether she was dealing drugs. She told him no, but he had noticed that the drug dealer called Killer was always at his house playing in the crap games his mother ran. "I didn't believe her," says Alvin, "but I never saw Killer pass or give her any drugs. He probably did it when I wasn't there."

"I didn't tell Alvin or Eric about the drug dealing," remembers Rosa Lee. "Alvin would have gotten mad with me, and with Bobby gone, he was really the son I relied on at that time. Eric would have said something nasty to Killer or my customers. Try to start a fight with one of them. Messed up my business."

Alvin was anxious to get away. "All hell broke loose after we moved to 57th Place," he says. But he couldn't leave yet. He was just entering the tenth grade at Spingarn High School in the fall of 1970.

Then Alvin got into a hallway fight at Spingarn with another student and was suspended. He tried night school but found the teachers there "were not serious or committed to the students," so he dropped out again and worked as a construction laborer.

Being a father "helped me to grow up quicker," recalls Alvin. "You know, buying the baby things my daughter needed. Looking after her."

Weeks after his eighteenth birthday, Alvin joined the Army. He earned a high school equivalency certificate at Fort Sam Houston, Texas, returned to Washington the next year to marry the mother of his then two-year-old daughter, and took his family with him when he was shipped to an Army base in Okinawa.

The 1968–69 school year also marked a turning point for twelve-year-old Eric. Until then, Eric had found school an exercise in frustration and anxiety. But that September he transferred to Shadd Elementary, where he met sixth-grade teacher Hank Wilson. "He worked with you all the way to the point that you could understand what he was teaching," Eric recalls.

Eric confided in Wilson that he had trouble with reading and spelling. Wilson gave Eric special exercises to create sentences using words Eric knew. When Eric accomplished the task, Wilson took him out for pizza as a reward.

Wilson told Eric that the exercises demonstrated that he had an aptitude for learning. No other teacher had ever said that. "I felt great about myself," Eric says, his voice still reflecting his excitement twenty-five years later. "I even went to school! I'd get up early and go to school!"

Eric's sudden enthusiasm for school ended when he graduated from Shadd and entered the seventh grade at Evans Junior High. No teacher encouraged him or worked with him as Wilson had the year before. He remembers being placed in an ungraded class with unruly, slower learners. He stopped going to school, and Rosa Lee didn't intervene.

About this time, a social worker named Nancy McAllister walked into his life. She came to Rosa Lee's apartment one morning to check on fifteen-year-old Richard, who had just returned home after spending the summer in a juvenile detention home for burglarizing the house where he encountered the barking dog that hid under the bed.

As a frequent visitor to Washington's poorest neighborhoods, McAllister wasn't surprised to find several of Rosa Lee's children at home during school hours. "For three or four families on that street at that time, school was not a priority," McAllister told me. "The children knew that their parents wouldn't bother them too much if they didn't get up."

McAllister asked Eric why he wasn't in school." He came out with some flimsy excuse," she recalls.

Then Rosa Lee chimed in. "They won't listen to me. I try to get them up. Maybe you could do something."

McAllister did not believe Rosa Lee's protestations. She sent Eric back to Evans that afternoon.

Eric latched onto McAllister as a mentor, frequently dropping by her office at Shadd, his former elementary school. She gave him books; he eventually told her that he had trouble reading them. She arranged for him to be tested and found the results significant: They showed that Eric had no apparent learning disabilities. "There was nothing wrong with Eric," McAllister said. "He just had never been taught to read."

She persuaded him to accept tutoring on Saturdays. Over the next eighteen months, she drove him to the tutor's house. Gradually his reading improved, although it never became easy for him. Still, McAllister was pleased.

It wasn't McAllister's job to keep up with Eric. She did that on her own. She saw something in him—a strength of character —that she wanted to preserve. "He was determined that he was not going to be like his brothers and sisters," McAllister says Eric had told her. But she was fighting against forces outside her control.

One force was sexual activity. In the spring of 1970, Eric learned that he was about to become a father. He was fourteen and the mother was thirteen—the same age as Rosa Lee when she got pregnant with Bobby. As soon as the pregnant girl's mother told him, he went to Rosa Lee. "My mother had no problem with it," Eric says. "Alvin had already gotten someone pregnant."

Eric's son was born in December, ten months after Alvin's daughter. "My mother really, really helped me out," recalls Eric, who was still attending Evans Junior High. "She shoplifted baby clothes. She helped me out with Pampers and milk." The following fall, Eric dropped out of the eighth grade and went to work at Wings 'N' Things with Rosa Lee and Ronnie.

McAllister implored Eric to stay in school, but she says Eric felt he was a grownup because he had a son to support. "He didn't want to be around the children at Evans Junior High," she recalls. "He really felt they were still kids."

The mother of Eric's son also dropped out of school. They dated for about two years and then broke up. "I caught her with another guy," says Eric bluntly.

When he wasn't working at the chicken carryout, Eric passed the time by hanging out on 57th Place. Three adult female prostitutes who lived near Rosa Lee's apartment offered him a deal: Would Eric like to work for them, procuring customers? Eric agreed.

"I used to set them up with old guys," he says, his voice conveying a tone of wonderment at his own behavior. "I didn't fully understand what I was doing. They liked me because they said I did not treat them badly."

After several weeks, he bragged to McAllister about what he had been doing. He was not prepared for the blistering lecture that followed. He doesn't remember her exact words, but he remembers how humiliated he felt. "She just said, '*What* do you think you're doing!'" He stopped working for the prostitutes soon after.

Eric and McAllister have stayed in touch. Eric credits her and Hank Wilson with steering him away from a life of crime. "I was on my way" to jail, he said. "They showed me a better way of living. They showed me the positive side of life. I already had the negative. They showed me what was possible if I just cared about myself."

On a cool October afternoon, Alvin and I are talking at his house, reflecting on all that has happened to his family since he returned from the Army two decades ago. He and Eric went into the Army separately after their eighteenth birthdays, served two-year stints, and came back to Washington to find the family in the grip of drug addiction. There wasn't much they could do about their family's drug life so they concentrated on establishing futures for themselves.

Shortly after he returned to Washington at the end of 1972, Alvin enrolled in Washington's Federal City College as a part-time undergraduate student and worked as a mail clerk in the Veterans Administration. He took a training position with the Fairfax County Fire Department in Virginia for a year and in 1981 accepted the full-time job driving a Metrobus. In the meantime, he and his first wife divorced, and Alvin remarried in 1984.

"I didn't let drugs grab me," says Alvin softly about his success. "They were there. My friends were using drugs. I'd see them shoot needles into their arms. Heroin. Cocaine. See, I was around it. I've seen them wrap a belt around their arms and pump the veins up. I saw it. I ignored it. I couldn't see myself doing it. My friends respected me. They would say, 'He don't do it!'"

He is pleased that Rosa Lee, after years of heroin use, has enrolled in the methadone program and is trying, with some success, to stick to it. Like Eric, he is tired of Rosa Lee's calls for help, tired of rushing over to her apartment to act as referee in a game that never ends, tired of holding money for her so that

Ducky or Patty or Richard won't be able to get their hands on it.

Alvin recently told Rosa Lee, "Don't call me about the kids!" He has told Rosa Lee he is no longer going to run over to her apartment and threaten his siblings and put them out. He's done that many times and Rosa Lee always lets them back in. "I was putting out a lot of energy doing that and nothing was changing at all," he says, a rare hint of anger slipping into his voice.

"I accept that she is always going to have me to fall back on to do things for her," Alvin told me, but if she wants her drug-abusing children put out of her apartment she is going to have to do it. As for Rosa Lee herself, Alvin says, "I've accepted my mother's way of living."

Before Eric joined the Army in 1974, he tried hard to make it as a singer and bandleader, but the nightclub stints and stage shows never brought in enough income. After he returned, a brief marriage ended in divorce and Eric, like Bobby before him, joined the Job Corps to get out of Washington. For a year, he took reading lessons and received training as a painter, plasterer, and dry wall hanger. He also fell in love in the Job Corps and when he returned to Washington in 1977, his girlfriend came with him. They had a son in October 1978.

Eric and his girlfriend began having problems when their son was a year old. Distraught, the woman turned to Rosa Lee for solace. Rosa Lee was high when the woman came to see her. She didn't know what to tell the woman, and she didn't want the woman's pain to cause her to lose her high. She had no control over Eric and didn't want to get in the middle of the couple's problems. So she suggested to her grandson's mother that she try a snort of heroin. "It'll help you forget all the pain, darling," she remembers telling the woman. It was exactly the same suggestion Patty had made to Rosa Lee four years earlier when Rosa Lee was mourning the breakup with Lucky. The result was the same as well. The woman became an addict and a prostitute. Eric has never forgiven his mother for that. "She would do things that made me turn totally away from her," he tells me.

For several years, Eric tried again to make a living as a singer and bandleader, but it didn't work out. He now had custody of his son, and it was unnerving to be bouncing from one job to another. Eventually Eric landed a contract as a street sweeper with Washington's Public Works Department. He worked his way up, earning several promotions and pay raises; he learned to operate heavy equipment and secured a good job at the city's Blue Plains Sewage Treatment Plant. In 1992, he was laid off because of Washington's financial woes, but he was rehired two years later. He has since moved to a job with the federal government's National Park Service.

Alvin and Eric say they are not sure why they turned out so different from the rest of their family. They clearly remember their childhood reactions—shame and humiliation for Alvin and anger and disgust for Eric—to their circumstances and their mother's stealing. They also do not know why they, rather than any of the other six siblings, responded in the way they did.

Both feel that their early rejection of a life that required accepting welfare and making ends meet through stealing served them well until they entered their adolescence. They were then fortunate to connect with two very decent people, Franklin and McAllister. Without the instructions both adult mentors gave them, they feel they would have been without direction. "I can tell you we weren't given any kind of direction at home," recalls Eric. "At least not the right kind of direction."

Both men remain committed to helping their family members whenever necessary, but they are emotionally worn down and wary after being called on so many times to rescue not only Rosa Lee and their brothers and sisters, but their nieces and nephews as well. Still, Alvin says, "I'll do what I can."

There is a story that Eric tells to show how divergent the path that he, like Alvin, followed was from the one taken by the rest of the family. It is set in 1982, when Eric worked briefly as a D.C. correctional officer.

Getting the job made him feel good. Not only had he established himself as a law-abiding citizen; he was now being entrusted with the responsibility of guarding those who had taken the path he had avoided. "I felt great," he said. "I was in the government!"

He was assigned to one of the Lorton prisons, but he often picked up additional money by taking an overtime shift at the understaffed D.C. jail. One night, he saw Rosa Lee. She was locked up on a shoplifting charge.

She spotted Eric in his navy blue uniform and shouted excitedly to the other prisoners.

"That's my son!" she said in a voice filled with pride, as Eric stood by, embarrassed. "That's my son!"

SEVEN

A Daughter Watches
and Learns

OVERLEAF: *Rosa Lee and Patty tussle playfully* (© *Lucian Perkins*—The Washington Post).

PATTY IS SITTING UP in her mother's bed, dressed in her mother's white nightgown, and surrounded by her mother's belongings. At thirty-four, she is very much Rosa Lee's little girl. Rosa Lee bustles around the bedroom, straightening this and dusting that, although the room is as clean as ever.

Patty's feeling much better today than she did yesterday, when she ran out of money and went into heroin withdrawal. Yesterday was a day to forget, a day of sweating, abdominal cramps, watery eyes, and a runny nose. When Patty awoke this mild June morning, she was ready to face the world again. Later on, she hopes, her friend Steve Priester will give her money that she can use to buy drugs.

Priester is lounging in a chair, listening as I interview Patty. He is one of Patty's three "boyfriends," as she calls them. They've known each other for about nine months, ever since he moved into an apartment on the ground floor of the building where Rosa Lee and Patty live. When Priester's roommate kicked him out in December, Patty invited him to stay with her for several weeks in Rosa Lee's one-bedroom apartment.

Patty knows little about him, except that he is fifty-seven and comes from West Virginia. He periodically receives a check from relatives there, a small sum of money that he is eager to spend on her. In some ways, their relationship is simple enough: She sleeps with him, he gives her money.

But Priester wants more than sex. He tells Rosa Lee that he loves her daughter and that he intends to break Patty of her drug habit. His declarations seem odd because he knows that his money ends up financing Patty's drug use. Still, his concern for her seems genuine.

More than once, Rosa Lee has complained to Patty about her prostitution. She can't understand why Patty, who is HIV positive, makes no attempt to protect herself or anyone else. Whenever she's been drinking, she's told everyone in their neighborhood that she is carrying the AIDS virus. She's discussed her infection openly around her three boyfriends. They apparently accept that having unprotected sex with Patty exposes them to infection.

When Rosa Lee engaged in prostitution, before anyone ever heard of AIDS, she did it, she says, primarily to feed her children, not her drug habit. There is a difference, she says. Now it kills her to see her daughter travel this road.

"Patty makes me so shamed," Rosa Lee tells me one day. "I tell her, 'When you go outside, Patty, don't you feel those people talking about you? Don't you feel it?'"

And what does Patty say? I ask.

Rosa Lee's lower lip trembles, as it always does when she is upset. "She says, 'Mama, don't get mad at me. Ain't that the way you did it?'"

"You're going to have to take off that damn jacket and tie before we go in there," Rosa Lee said as I parked my car outside the three tan-brick buildings that make up Clifton Terrace.

That was fine with me. It was the last Sunday in May 1988, a hot, humid afternoon, and my shirt was already soaked. We had come to Clifton Terrace to look for Patty. Rosa Lee had offered to introduce her to me.

I had known Rosa Lee for five months at this point and it was only two weeks since her release from the D.C. jail, where we had met and she had agreed to let me spend time with her.

Rosa Lee wasn't sure of Patty's whereabouts. She had heard through the prison grapevine that Patty had turned over her first-floor Clifton Terrace apartment to several New York crack dealers, who were using it as a base of operation. It was a twenty-four-hour-a-day operation, so Patty could not stay in her apartment. She slept wherever she could find a bed.

Rosa Lee hoped that Ducky, who lived on the fifth floor of one of the Clifton Terrace buildings, could tell us where Patty was staying. The last time Rosa Lee had seen Ducky, he had been working for the same New York dealers.

Ducky answered our knock. His slight frame was swimming in a badly wrinkled, pin-striped three-piece suit. The suit was light green. The collar of his tan shirt was open and darkly soiled. The sag in his shoulders, the weary look in his eyes, the way he moved, all made it hard to believe that he was twenty-eight years old.

He listened warily as Rosa Lee explained that I was interested in writing about the family. He said he had just returned from church. "I'm very religious," he said. "I've been born again." As he talked about his renewed commitment to Christ, Rosa Lee shook her head as a warning to me not to believe him.

Finally, I interrupted. "Your mother has told me that you cook powdered cocaine into crack for New York City dealers operating out of your sister Patty's apartment in this building and that you have been addicted to crack for some time now."

Ducky literally jumped in his chair when I began talking. After I finished, he shot his mother a questioning, alarmed look.

"I told him everything, Ducky," Rosa Lee said, "so you can stop all that 'born again' shit."

Ducky's religious cloak fell away. He said that he and the New Yorkers had split. Now he was trying to sell crack on his own.

Rosa Lee asked if he knew where Patty was staying.

"Pussycat's," he said.

Rosa Lee scowled. Pussycat ran an oil joint in an apartment one floor below. Pussycat charged three dollars for entry. She also rented "works"—a hypodermic needle and tourniquet—for three dollars.

I asked Pussycat's real name. "I don't know her real name," Rosa Lee said brusquely. "I wish you'd stop asking me about last names and real names. People don't want you to know that. You might be setting them up to be arrested by the police or something."

Rosa Lee rapped hard on Pussycat's door. Someone opened it a crack. "Hello, Mama Rose," a man's voice said.

The door swung open. When the man saw me, he quickly began to close it. Rosa Lee stopped the door with the palm of her left hand. "He's with me, Bernard," she said with quiet authority.

Bernard stood aside. Behind him, two women lay on stained sheetless mattresses on the living room floor, their bodies limp. We had found Patty and Pussycat.

It was so hot it was hard to breathe.

"You can go into the back!" Rosa Lee commanded Bernard.

Rosa Lee bent over Patty, who wore black slacks, a red shirt, and no shoes. "Wake up, Patty, wake up," Rosa Lee said, slapping her face. "I want you to meet someone." Each time Rosa Lee slapped her, Patty's eyelids opened for a few seconds.

"This isn't going to work," Rosa Lee said. "You'll have to meet Patty another day."

Two months later, I finally talked with Patty. I met her at the D.C. jail, where she was being held on a drug charge. Narcotics officers had raided her Clifton Terrace apartment seven months earlier. The New York drug dealers who rented her apartment were not there and did not return after the raid, but the policemen found twenty-four packets of crack and $300 in a bureau drawer. A warrant was issued for Patty's arrest on charges of running an illegal establishment. After months of searching, the policemen finally found Patty inside Pussycat's oil joint at the end of June. By this time, a second group of New York drug dealers was working out of Patty's apartment. Patty pleaded guilty to cocaine possession.

Jail meant a forced withdrawal from heroin for Patty, so I didn't know what to expect when we sat down to talk in her cell.

She'd been in jail for a month, the longest period she had been without drugs since she was sixteen. But she seemed to be bearing up well. She had gained weight and looked nothing like the emaciated woman I had seen on that mattress.

I know Patty is Rosa Lee's favorite among the eight children, and I mention to her that Bobby had told me that she is the best at manipulating their mother. Patty agrees and laughs.

"I can manipulate her like she do me," she adds. "I'm just like her. Anything my mother did, I did it. The way she walks, I can walk. The way she talks, I can talk. I just wanted to be like my mother all my life."

Patty has had even less education than her brothers, having gone no farther than the fourth grade. She dropped out at age fourteen when she was pregnant with her son, Junior.

The teenage father of her son had wanted to marry her, but Patty wasn't interested in having a husband. A husband would tie her down, put demands on her. But giving birth to a baby changed her status in her eyes. "Ever since I had a little baby, I was a grown woman," she brags. Two pregnancies with two different men followed Junior's birth. She aborted both because she did not want any more children. One was enough for her to say she was an adult.

As the interview progressed, Patty spoke rapidly, looking down at the chewed fingernails of her right hand, just as her mother does when describing some painful or embarrassing incident. I was not prepared for her candor: Within the first hour she told me that a thirteen-year-old male relative had raped her when she was eight. He threatened to hurt her if she told anyone. The assaults continued and the relationship eventually became consensual. It ended when Patty was twenty-two.

I later confirmed her account with the relative, who agreed to discuss it as long as he was not identified. He denied threatening Patty and defended his behavior, saying Patty would often climb into the bed he shared with two other male relatives. When I pointed out the age difference between the two of them, he grudgingly acknowledged, "Yeah, I guess you could say it was rape. I hadn't really looked at it like that."

When Patty was a teenager, Alvin found out about the relative's behavior and beat him up, Alvin later told me.

The first rape happened in January 1966, while Rosa Lee was incarcerated in the Jessup, Maryland, prison. When Rosa Lee was released in July, Patty tried to tell her about it, but she didn't know how. Looking back, Patty says she believes her mother should have known something was wrong, should have wondered why the teenage boy was hanging around her so much. "I feel like she could have done something to stop it."

By the time Patty was born in January 1958, Rosa Lee already had five children, all boys. Rosa Lee named her Donna, but no one has ever called her that. When she was little, she was known as "Papoose," because Rosa Lee thought the shape of her eyes resembled those of a Native American baby. Over time, Papoose became Patty.

When she was young, Patty had long, straight hair that Rosa Lee liked to twist into a single braid down her back. She had her mother's dark skin and her father's round, cherubic face. Otherwise, David Wright didn't have much of a role in her life; when he died in the mid-1970s, Patty didn't even consider attending his funeral.

In the succession of cramped row houses and apartments where Rosa Lee and the children lived during the 1960s, the boys shared mattresses. Patty often slept in her mother's room by herself, since Rosa Lee was working nights at the Ko Ko Club and the 821 Club. When Rosa Lee was shake dancing at the 821 Club, she would practice her routine in front of a mirror in her bedroom. Patty was the only one of her children who was allowed to watch.

Patty was three years old when Rosa Lee began bringing home some of the customers. Rosa Lee thought nothing of having sex with Patty in the room, even in the same bed. As Patty grew older, her mother's nighttime trysts would awaken her. "I would look over and Patty would be sitting up in the bed, wide awake, watching us," remembers Rosa Lee. Patty slept in the bed with Rosa Lee until she was ten years old.

Several months before Rosa Lee was first sent to prison, she caught seven-year-old Patty instructing an older neighborhood boy in sexual intercourse in an upstairs bedroom of the row house Rosa Lee shared with her mother and their seventeen children. Rosa Lee was shocked. She chased the boy out of the house, then sat down to talk to Patty. She wanted to know from whom Patty had learned about sex. Rosa Lee assumed one of her own younger brothers had taught Patty about sex or even initiated her into sexual activity. But that was not the case.

"Patty looked me dead in the face," Rosa Lee recalls, "and said, 'You, Mama.'" Patty recounted in detail lying in bed at night watching Rosa Lee with boyfriends and with tricks. "I had nothing more to say," adds Rosa Lee. "I realized it was my fault. She was just doing what she had seen me do and wanted to imitate me. She's been like that all her life."

Rosa Lee argues she was working as a prostitute so that she and her children could *survive*. "You keep talking about prostitution," she tells me heatedly one day. "I saw it as survival."

In 1969, when Patty was eleven, one of her mother's customers made an unusual request: He asked Rosa Lee if he could have sex with Patty.

There's no way to recapture exactly what went through Rosa Lee's mind as she considered this request. It is not something that she wanted to remember or talk about. After Patty told me about it, I waited almost three years before broaching the subject with Rosa Lee. When I did, she angrily denied that it ever happened and accused Patty of lying. She was sure that if I asked Patty again in her presence, Patty would admit that it was a lie. But I knew Rosa Lee well enough to tell that she was lying and that Patty had told me the truth.

Five months after Rosa Lee's denial, the three of us were spending the day together. We were eating lunch in a downtown restaurant when I gingerly brought up the issue of Rosa Lee prostituting Patty.

Rosa Lee turned to Patty and waited in silence for her daughter to answer.

Patty looked her mother in the eye. "The big fat man," said Patty, and then named him.

Rosa Lee began questioning Patty, as if getting more facts might help jog her memory. "How old was you, Patty?" and "Was I on drugs then?" and "Did he approach me, or did he approach you?"

"He approached you about it," Patty said calmly. "He'd give you the money. Give you about forty and I would get ten dollars of it. That's all I would get. 'Cause I was a little girl. You asked me about it, and I said, 'Yeah, I want to help you.' Remember that? You were feeding everybody and doing it all on your own."

Rosa Lee turned to me. There was pain in her eyes. "Okay," she said. "I just feel so shamed."

Piece by agonizing piece, the story came out. Patty said her mother asked her to have sex with the man, who was then in his mid-forties. Patty agreed. Rosa Lee told the man it would cost forty dollars—twice as much as she had been charging him. The man drove Patty to his home in suburban Maryland. When Patty returned, she put two twenty dollar bills in Rosa Lee's hand.

"Boy, my mind was gone," Rosa Lee says. The man came back to have sex with Patty three or four times. After each time, Rosa Lee asked Patty, "Did he hurt you?" Sometimes Patty would tell her yes, but she continued to have sex with the man on a regular basis.

One morning Patty woke up in severe abdominal pain. She couldn't stand up straight and couldn't walk, she remembers. An ambulance was called and took her to D.C. General Hospital. She had gonorrhea. She was kept at the hospital for a short period to make sure the infection cleared up.

Rosa Lee decided to use Patty's illness to get more money from the man. She told him that Patty had been taken to the hospital because of complications caused by a pregnancy. Hospital officials were upset because Patty was so young, Rosa Lee told him, and they wanted to know the name and age of the father. The man pleaded with Rosa Lee not to give the officials his name.

Rosa Lee told Patty about her scam and asked Patty to tell the man, when he came to see her in the hospital, that she wanted to abort her pregnancy and needed money to have it done outside the hospital. "When he came, I couldn't stand to look at the *dog!*" remembers Patty. "I hated him!" But she did what Rosa Lee had asked.

"I ain't never seen a man so scared in my life," says Rosa Lee. "He sure didn't want anybody to know that he was having a baby by a baby." He gave Rosa Lee $240 to get Patty an abortion.

There were other men after that, perhaps as many as a dozen. One was a thirty-three-year-old relative. The men offered to pay much more than Rosa Lee's usual rate, $100 or more, amounts that made Patty's head swim. Patty said her mother always asked her if she was willing. Patty never turned her mother down. "I went with the tricks for my mother," she says. "I had a body like I was fourteen. The men was hurting me so bad I could have died. But I seen how hard it was for her to take care of all of us. I love my mother, so I would do it all over again. But I was getting very hurt. . . . At times I wanted to hate her, but I couldn't see myself doing that 'cause my mother's too sweet for that."

The interview has been draining for all three of us. Rosa Lee is hanging her head, unable to look at me or Patty. Patty is relieved, she says, that this part of her story is out and that I am planning to write about it. She wants people to understand why she is the way she is, as she puts it.

"Is this part of the bond between you and Patty?" I ask Rosa Lee, verbally prodding her to lift her head. "Part of the very close relationship that you two share? You don't have that kind of relationship with your other daughter or with any of your sons."

"Yeah," replies Rosa Lee. "We can do things together and I don't hear about it any more from Patty. We all have did things to make money. Trick people out of money."

"I'm curious about why you lied to me when I asked you about it," I say.

Rosa Lee drops her head again, slightly muffling her voice. "I don't know," she says. "I didn't know if I should have went that far."

"Why are you staring at your ring?" I continue. "Look at me!"

Patty laughs. She is enjoying her mother's unease.

Raising her head, Rosa Lee cuts an angry look at Patty. "Me and my daughter," she says in an even voice, "we have been through so much together. And some things I'm very ashamed of, you know. And the things that she had did for us. 'Cause she was attractive and I wasn't. She did things that other girls wouldn't do, like have sex with grown men."

As a fourth grader at Shadd Elementary School in the fall of 1969, Patty stood out for all the wrong reasons. At eleven, she was two years older than most of her classmates.

She had spent three years in the third grade and had never been taught to read. Her attendance was spotty. She was headed for trouble, and her teachers didn't know what to do about it.

The other children teased Patty because she couldn't read. "I hated school," she recalls. "The boys would tease me when I wouldn't do nothing with them. Girls used to do it all the time in front of boys who might like me." They'd say, "She can't even read. Spell cat! Spell I!"

Nancy McAllister—the social worker who had had such an impact on Eric's life—tried to intervene with Patty, making frequent visits to Rosa Lee's apartment in the late mornings, well after school had started. Rosa Lee was always at home and McAllister did not even suspect that she was selling heroin. "But I knew something was going on," she recalls.

McAllister often found Patty at home as well. Rosa Lee would tell her that Patty was sick, but McAllister didn't believe it. She suspected instead that Patty had been staying up late at night. "I'd see her just laying around in bed," she said. "I would get her to go to school."

But what concerned McAllister most was the way Patty dressed on Fridays. "I remember being so amazed at this girl," McAllister said. "She used to come to my office in a wig that reached her waist. She always wore tight, short skirts. At eleven, she was very shapely. Fridays were when most of the men got paid. Those who had jobs."

McAllister asked Patty why she dressed the way she did.

"Oh, this is my evening to do my thing," McAllister remembers Patty saying.

"What thing?" McAllister asked.

"Oh, you know" was all Patty would say.

"Patty never really came out and told me," McAllister continues. "She was really beyond her years. The kinds of things that she would talk to adults about were not kid things." McAllister suspected something was wrong, but she had no conclusive evidence that she could report to authorities. Besides, Patty wasn't the only student whose home life seemed troubled. "The teachers probably had ten or twelve other kids with the same kind of background. It was just overwhelming."

Change the name and go back twenty years, and it's hard to tell the difference between Patty's school record and Rosa Lee's. Both fell behind at an early age. Both began skipping school regularly. Neither one had a parent who believed education was important. Neither one learned to read by the time she dropped out.

There's one more parallel: Rosa Lee was fourteen when she gave birth to Bobby, her first child. Patty was fourteen when Junior was born. And like her mother, that's also when she dropped out of school.

Patty learned about drugs much the same way she learned about sex. By watching.

She was about eleven years old. She had noticed that Ronnie, seventeen, and his girlfriend would lock themselves in his room in the afternoon. Patty wondered what they were doing. She figured she could find out by hiding in their bedroom closet.

"That girl used to hide in my closet," Ronnie remembers. "She used to find out where I'd hide my money and steal it." Patty says she spent the money she stole from Ronnie on doll babies, candy, and ice cream.

After several thefts, Ronnie began checking the closet every time he came into his bedroom. One afternoon, however, Ronnie and his girlfriend didn't bother to check. Anxious to get their fix, they hurried into the bedroom, took out a bag of white powder, cooked it into a liquid, and filled a hypodermic needle. Patty had a clear view through the slightly open closet door. "I watched Ronnie put the needle in his arm," she says.

After Ronnie pushed the liquid into his vein, she watched her brother's worried frown change to a look of pleasure. She stepped from the closet. Neither Ronnie nor his girlfriend showed any reaction until she told Ronnie she wanted to try it. "You better not," he said, "but then again, if you're going to try it, let me hit you first."

Ronnie refused to inject her that day. But, Patty told me, "I knew then, 'Well, I'm gonna try that one day.'"

That day came in late 1973, just a few weeks before Patty's sixteenth birthday. It was the day Patty witnessed her mother and the school crossing guard doing bam and exposed the crossing guard for holding some back. Patty had demanded a hit and Rosa Lee had given in.

As Rosa Lee tells me about this critical moment, she looks pained. She says she did too much "dirty living," that if she hadn't used drugs, her children wouldn't have either. But at the time, she felt as if she had no choice, that she had no way to stop Patty from traveling the same road she had.

A year later, Patty graduated to heroin. A year after that, so did Rosa Lee. By 1976, they were both heavy heroin users. "Our getting high together and even tricking together wasn't like mother and daughter," remembers Rosa Lee. "It was like two sisters."

By the time Patty was sixteen, Junior was two years old. She paid for her heroin with her welfare check, working as a hitter, stealing, pulling any scam she could think of, and "whoring, selling my body," she says. "I didn't like it, but I didn't like me or my mother to suffer." When she went tricking on 14th Street, N.W., Rosa Lee often went along, Patty says, "to watch my back and make sure I didn't get caught up with anything crazy."

Three years later, she had her own apartment in Clifton Terrace, which she shared with a man named Joe Billy, whom she considered her common-law husband. Joe Billy was a 14th Street juggler who kept a little money on him and supplied Patty with all the heroin she needed. She stopped working as a prostitute.

In 1983, the Superior Court's family division took ten-year-old Junior away from Patty because it considered him a "child in need of supervision." Two years later, Joe Billy was arrested on a heroin charge, went into withdrawal in the D.C. jail, suffered a stroke, and died. Patty, without a welfare check or a man in her life, went back into the street. This time she worked as a drug dealer as well as a prostitute.

"I was never as good as my mother dealing," says Patty. "I don't have the patience for it." Soon after she started juggling on the street, she used up $850 worth of heroin belonging to a dealer she was supposed to be working for. "He was looking for me to kill me," she recalls. "He got his girls to jump me. Put a gun in my face. I hid out 'til my mother came home. She paid it off for me. Not all at once. Little by little."

"Patty thinks she's as good as I am at manipulating," says Rosa Lee, laughing. The three of us are sitting around her living room talking about a scheme Patty had tried to pull off to get money out of Rosa Lee a couple of nights before. "She's watched me manipulating and surviving for so long she comes up with scams that she's seen *me* pull! She thinks I've forgotten them."

Patty's latest scam unfolded on a bitterly cold night in mid-February, but cold weather—or any type of bad weather, for that matter—does not stop Patty in her daily quest for drugs. Patty was broke, it was 1:30 in the morning, and the checks that arrive on the first of the month were still two weeks away from delivery. Because of that, Patty could not get credit for heroin or crack from the local dealers. She suspected her mother had some money, probably hidden in her underpants, where Patty couldn't get to it. She enlisted one of her regular tricks to help her in a plan to get money from her mother. Patty entered the apartment with the man, walked quietly past Richard, asleep on the couch, and slipped with the man into her mother's bedroom.

Rosa Lee was sound asleep. Patty punched her several times

on the arm to wake her. "Mama," Patty said. "Mama. Wake up! I got to talk to you."

Rosa Lee was tired. She knew Patty had awakened her to talk her out of money for drugs. "Patty, please don't ask me for no money," she whined. "Please don't ask, because I don't have it."

Patty told Rosa Lee that the man with her had let her smoke crack in his apartment, that the man fell asleep and left two billies lying on a coffee table. Patty said she injected both of them. "I knew I could pay for them," Patty told her mother.

"You mean, you knew I could pay for them," shouted an angry Rosa Lee, "but I'm not giving you a goddamn cent!"

Rosa Lee reached over the side of her bed and pulled her large black pocketbook up onto her lap. Patty had not thought of looking in there because her mother *never* left money in her pocketbook when she went to bed. Rosa Lee opened the pocketbook and dramatically pulled out a bill. She was already out-acting her daughter. "You see what I got here?" said Rosa Lee. "I got exactly ten dollars."

Patty had seen this dramatic gesture since she was a child. She knew not to believe her mother. She was now convinced that her mother had more money than the ten-dollar bill. Indeed, Rosa Lee had another two hundred dollars in twenty-dollar bills rolled into a tight knot in a stocking and pushed into the top of her underpants. She kept the bed covers up over her stomach so Patty could not see it.

"Get out of my face, Patty!" yelled Rosa Lee.

Her yelling had awakened Richard. He came into the bedroom. He asked what the man was doing in Rosa Lee's bedroom. No one answered Richard, but Rosa Lee said to Patty's friend, "Well, mister, I don't know what happened, but you're not getting any money from me."

Patty began begging Rosa Lee, saying the man would hurt her if Rosa Lee didn't give her forty dollars for the two billies. "I don't give a damn, Patty" was Rosa Lee's only response.

By now, Richard too had figured out Patty's scam and told the man he had to leave. The man, who had seated himself on a chair in Rosa Lee's room, got up and walked out of the apartment without a word of complaint.

Patty looks a little sheepish and Rosa Lee chortles as she concludes the story.

"Ain't no man going to put two billies down in front of a dope addict and fall asleep!" Rosa Lee laughs. "Mr. Dash, even you know better than that!"

Months later, Rosa Lee is telling me in front of Patty how embarrassed she is that Patty is prostituting herself with a lot of the boys and men in their community, and most of them are not using condoms.

"If they think they caught the virus from Patty," says Rosa Lee, "they might come in here and shoot all of us. I can't get her to stop, Mr. Dash, or at least make them wear a condom."

"Is that true?" I ask Patty. "Most of the men don't wear condoms?"

"That's true," Patty stutters, "but it's not my fault. They don't like to wear them. Most of them know I got the virus anyway. If they don't know, they know that I'm a drug addict and a prostitute. Who else is going to have the virus, but *me!* It ain't no secret who gets the virus." All three of her boyfriends, "Howard, Steve, and Anthony, know I have it."

"I'm selling sex for money for drugs," she continues. "I don't care if they use a condom or not. Just pay me my money! It's up to them to use a condom."

"Do they ever express any fear about catching the virus?" I ask.

"No, and I don't bring it up," replies Patty. "What am I going to bring it up for?"

It is a July morning in 1992 and Rosa Lee has Patty on her mind.

We are having breakfast at McDonald's. Rosa Lee is upset: Her latest urine sample at the drug-treatment clinic was "dirty"—the second time she has tested positive for heroin this year. One more strike and she will be required to appear before a team of counselors, who could decide to suspend her from the program.

"Mr. Dash," she says, "I can't go back to the way I used to be."

For more than a year, her urine samples had been clean; she had such a good record that a market developed for her urine among the other methadone patients. In the bathroom, someone would whisper, "Rosa Lee, you clean?" and hand over a dollar or two. The clinic didn't monitor the bathrooms closely, so the risk of getting caught was low. Then, for some reason, she began to slip. Over a six-month period, she used heroin six times. Every time, Patty was involved. Six times is not the same as a daily habit, but it's still not good enough.

Patty is part of the problem, Rosa Lee tells me. If only Patty weren't addicted to heroin, if only Patty didn't bring heroin into her apartment, if only she could get Patty into methadone treatment—if only she could do something about Patty, then she wouldn't be facing the risk of getting thrown out of the program.

She tells me she plans to take Patty to the methadone clinic the next Monday and enroll her. Monday comes and goes without Patty enrolling, and I hear nothing more about it.

In August, Rosa Lee is arrested for shoplifting several expensive scarves from the downtown branch of Hecht's. The day after spending a night in jail, she calls to tell me about the incident. She needed money, she says, to pay off one of Patty's drug debts. The dealer had threatened to hurt Patty.

Rosa Lee is planning to plead guilty. I remind her that the last time she appeared in court, in 1991, the commissioner warned her that another shoplifting charge would land her in jail for a long time. "Why do you have to remind me of that?" an irritated Rosa Lee asks me. "You're like the goddamn voice of doom. 'You know they're going to give you a lot of time, Rose,' " she says, mimicking me. "How do you know so goddamn much, anyway? Did God go on vacation and put you in charge?"

"OK, OK," I plead with her. "I'm sorry I mentioned it."

At her trial in September, she tells Commissioner John W. King that she is guilty. King listens intently as her criminal record is outlined—a total of thirteen convictions for shoplifting and drug-related charges—and then pronounces sentence: two years probation.

Rosa Lee decides to celebrate. On the way back to her apartment, we pick up a pizza. Lucian Perkins, a *Washington Post* photographer who has been working with me since the beginning of the project, arrives.

Patty is happy to hear the good news. As we eat, I notice a flurry of activity. There's a knock at the door. It's Junebug, the drug dealer who lives on the first floor. He and Rosa Lee talk quietly and he leaves. I assume that Patty has persuaded Rosa Lee to buy her a bag of heroin. Sure enough, Patty brings out a metal bottle cap, mixes some powdered heroin with water in the cap, and heats it with a match. She injects herself in her abdomen.

Patty motions to Rosa Lee to lie down. To my surprise, she does. Using the same needle, Patty injects her mother in the leg. Rosa Lee's eyes flutter for a brief second, and our eyes meet.

Patty has allowed Lucian to photograph her before while injecting heroin, but this is the first time that he has seen Rosa Lee do it. Over my left shoulder, I can hear the whir and click of his camera. When we leave, neither Patty nor Rosa Lee says anything about what has happened, and neither do I.

When I return from a few days of vacation, there is an urgent message on my office voice mail from Rosa Lee. I call her. As soon as she hears my voice, she interrupts. "I want to apologize. I know you didn't like what you saw, and I wanted you to know I'm sorry. Very sorry!"

"You don't have to apologize to me," I tell her.

"You can try that on someone else, buddy," she says. "I saw your face when Patty hit me. You were in front of me. I saw your eyes! I'll never let you see me take another hit!"

I hadn't realized that I had shown any reaction, even though it was difficult for me to watch. Nor was I prepared for her apology. After all, she had told me about other slips. Why did it matter so much if I saw it rather than heard about it?

But it did matter. To Rosa Lee, it mattered a great deal.

Over the next several months, the slip-ups stopped. She began badgering Patty once more about having unprotected sex with Priester and other men. She talked about moving again—this time to a senior citizens' housing complex—to get away from the drug traffic in her apartment.

Rosa-Lee had tried to cut ties with Patty before, without much success. This time, she told me, would be different: She would make arrangements for Patty to take over her apartment; Patty would pay the sixty-four dollars rent out of her welfare check.

I ask Rosa Lee what she would do if Patty spent the money on drugs and lost the apartment.

"Mr. Dash, that's her business," she said. "I don't care."

EIGHT

The Third Generation

OVERLEAF: *Junior stands in front of the Washington Highlands apartment complex where he occasionally sold crack* (© *Lucian Perkins*—The Washington Post).

Rosa Lee sensed that something was wrong as soon as she stepped off the Metrobus and started to walk up Fourth Street, S.E. On most sunny afternoons, the drug market outside her apartment building is in full swing. But on this Saturday in June 1991, the crack dealers who usually congregate on the parking lot and sidewalks were nowhere to be seen.

Squinting in the midday sun, Rosa Lee scanned the street. To her surprise, she spotted two of her grandsons, ages eleven and twelve, standing at the entrance to the parking lot. One was looking up Fourth Street, the other down. Across the street, in a cluster of teenagers, stood Patty's son, eighteen-year-old Junior. Rosa Lee knew her grandson occasionally sold crack, but she didn't know why his young cousins were hanging around the street's drug market.

"What are you doing?" she demanded to know.

"I've got Junior's back," the younger boy told her.

"What do you mean, 'You got Junior's back'?" Rosa Lee sputtered, but her question was rhetorical. She knew exactly what her grandson meant. He was acting as a lookout for Junior. But before the youngster could explain, Junior sprinted across the street.

"Grandma," Junior said. "They ain't doing nothing. All they

doing is earning a few dollars." Junior was trying to calm his grandmother, but Rosa Lee knew better.

"Yeah, and earning a little time in jail," Rosa Lee said. Rosa Lee thought the two younger boys were watching out for police patrols. The truth was that they were not concerned about the police at all.

Later, when I interviewed Junior, I found that his behavior that day was a striking example of the dangerous tests of manhood that occur on the streets of some Washington neighborhoods and take the lives of so many young black men.

Junior said he paid the boys ten dollars each to watch out for a neighborhood drug dealer who had been selling crack to Patty. Junior believed the dealer was planning to kill him to settle a grudge. He told his cousins to warn him if they saw the dealer's white car.

In the parking lot in front of Rosa Lee's building the previous day, Junior had "stepped to" the dealer—that is, challenged him. "It was a beef about my mom, at first," Junior told me. "My mom owed him money and never paid him. My mom wasn't ever going to pay him. So he said he was going to hurt her. He had been calling Grandma's apartment saying he was going to do something to everybody up in there if my mom didn't pay him his money. I said, 'Hey, if I catch you, I'm going to have to hurt you.' "

Rather than hide, Junior decided to bring the confrontation to a head. He had to be on the street or lose face. He borrowed two guns from a childhood friend and hid them in bushes nearby; at the first sign of the dealer's white car, Junior would retrieve either the .44 with the extended clip or the Tec-9, whichever was closer.

Word of the possible shoot-out had spread through the Washington Highlands neighborhood, clearing the street of all but the fearless, the foolish, and the unsuspecting. But the dealer never showed up; he later decided to let Patty's debt go.

Rosa Lee didn't know any of this when she confronted her three grandsons. She knew only that the drug culture had worked its way into a third generation of her family.

————

Unlike his mother and grandmother, Junior has never used drugs. "The people who use leave their minds on the street," he tells me one day several months after the face-off with the drug dealer. "I'm not going for that."

As a young boy living in the Clifton Terrace housing complex, Junior gradually became aware that the men and women streaming into his grandmother's apartment were there to buy drugs. He saw how heroin destroyed his mother and hurt his grandmother. Drugs were a fact of life at Clifton Terrace, and he decided at an early age that he wanted no part of it. "I wasn't interested in drugs at all," he says. "When I heard about pot and all that, I wasn't with that. . . . I wasn't with all that smoking and getting high."

He says this matter-of-factly, as if we are talking about yesterday's weather. It is our third interview, but I have yet to break through Junior's mask. He lets people see only as much of himself as he wants them to. If someone shouts at him, he rarely shouts back. His doelike eyes remain blank, his voice stays level, his facial expression reveals nothing.

He smiles, though, when I challenge his reputed ability as an excellent boxer and an above-average basketball player. "I don't beat up on old men," he says, offering instead to take me one-on-one in basketball "any time and any place."

Junior's demeanor resembles that of the teenage "enforcers" who come by Rosa Lee's apartment the first of every month to demand that Patty and Ducky pay their crack debts. It is the demeanor that the psychologist Richard G. Majors calls "cool pose," a coping response black males adopt when the combination of racial discrimination and social status denies them access to conventional mainstream middle-class life.

Majors, a researcher at the Urban Institute in Washington, D.C., has studied the attitudes of black teenage boys in poor urban communities. "Many poor black males have this unfulfilled sense of self," says Majors, who spent his early childhood living on welfare and, thereafter, grew up in his maternal grandmother's black, working-class household, living on the edge of poverty in Ithaca, New York. "They become obsessed with this

need to be tough and they can't turn it off. They're on stage all
the time."

The need to protect this image of toughness accounts for the
higher rates of homicide, accidents, self-destructive behavior, and
incarceration for black males across urban America, says
Majors. Among African American males, he adds, cool pose is
pervasive among the underclass, prevalent among the lower and
working classes, and even exists in modified form within the
middle class.

"But among the black underclass, the emotionlessness is noth-
ing more than the notion of masculinity," Majors continues.
"These youths are obsessed with issues of pride and dignity.
Never lose your cool, even when you are fighting. All they have
is this cool. Cool is like building a fortress around yourself."
Majors's last statement resonated with me when I thought of
Junior; he lives within his own fortress, something professionals
who worked with him as a young boy had also noticed.

During the 1990 Christmas holidays, Junior's uncle Ducky
learned the hard way not to disrespect him. Ducky used to smack
Junior around when his nephew was a little boy, but since then
Junior had picked up a considerable arsenal of boxing skills during several years of boxing competition in the Hill, a tough Pittsburgh neighborhood. Junior had been living there in a group
home for juvenile delinquents.

Ducky asked Junior for a loan of a couple of dollars. The holiday spirit made Junior feel generous, so he pulled out a fat roll
of bills, money he had made selling crack. He had intended to
give his uncle three or four singles, but Ducky tried to snatch the
roll from Junior's hand.

Ducky had barely pulled back his arm when Junior's fists
began to fly into Ducky's face. Junior was no longer the child
Ducky used to push around. Ducky tried to fight back, but he
was no match for his nephew's speed and strength. Junior pum-
meled Ducky until he had to be pulled away. As his fists flew, his
face remained impassive.

Afterward, Junior picked up the fallen money roll from the
floor without comment. He showed no sign of anger or satisfac-

tion. Ducky may have been family, but trying to take money out of Junior's hand was blatant disrespect. Even as a child, Junior had adopted a code of living which dictated that he could not let anyone hurt, threaten, or disrespect him, not even someone in his family.

Rosa Lee had seen the fight from start to finish. She hadn't known her grandson could fight as well as he did, and despite the circumstances, she felt some pride in his ability. "Junior was whipping Ducky bad, like he owned him," Rosa Lee recalls, "but the thing that I could not get over was Junior's face. It never changed. He didn't look like he was fighting at all! If Patty hadn't been there, I don't know who would have stopped Junior."

I suggest that she, as Junior's grandmother, could have stopped the beating by jumping between her grandson and son.

"Who?" replies Rosa Lee, giving me her you-must-be-crazy look. "Not me. Junior's fists were moving too fast. I might've got hit. Ducky had no business trying to grab that boy's money. I bet Ducky won't try that again."

The following fall, I try to assess how extensively Junior has become involved in dealing crack. He tells me that he is working occasionally as an enforcer and a bodyguard for some of the neighborhood's top dealers, and that he stopped selling crack himself at the end of the summer at the request of his fifteen-year-old girlfriend. "She felt it might take me away from her," he says. "I was making money. I was making over $600 a night."

Bragging about how much money you make is part of the bravado typical of teenage crack dealers. Actually, Junior probably made much less, but he likes to give the impression that he has money to burn. His lifestyle—which includes a sparse, inexpensive wardrobe of jeans and T-shirts, and sleeping on Rosa Lee's bedroom or living room floor every night—doesn't suggest he has lots of money.

Earlier in the week, I had suggested that we go together to see *Boyz N the Hood,* the John Singleton movie about three boys growing up in South Central Los Angeles. Doughboy, played by the rap star Ice Cube, deals in drugs and sees no future for himself; Doughboy's brother, Ricky, has a chance at a football schol-

arship if poor grades and test scores don't get in his way; Tre has
the brightest prospects, thanks to a strict father who has raised
him with strong values. An argument over a girl and turf ends
with a gang of boys hunting down Ricky and killing him in a
drive-by shooting.

Junior seemed interested in my offer, but before we could
make plans to go, he saw the movie on his own. He tells me he
liked the movie because it was real. It reminded him of Clifton
Terrace and Washington Highlands, the two neighborhoods he
knows best. He has seen "guys bumping you just to get some
attention" and then pulling out a gun.

He also says he identifies more with Doughboy than with Tre.
Doughboy wouldn't back down from a fight; Tre did.

"I grew up like that," he tells me. "Tre didn't. Ice Cube was
like me."

Junior was born on October 21, 1972, when Patty was fourteen.
By the time he was two, his mother was using heroin. Some days,
she says, she was so high that she has a hard time remembering
how she performed even the simplest task—changing his diaper,
feeding him, getting him ready for bed. Junior remembers that
during the early years of his life his father visited him only spo-
radically, but that these visits tapered off and then stopped
altogether.

One of Junior's earliest memories is of the police breaking
down the door of Rosa Lee's apartment looking for drugs. He
was two months shy of his fourth birthday. "I just remember
them knocking on the door," Junior says. "We all woke up. They
hollered, 'Open the door or we're going to chop it down!' "

He remembers the sounds more than the sight: ax on wood,
then shoes, then the shouts of the officers. Standing in the hallway watching the door splinter, he was not afraid. He looked up
at his mother, grandmother, and uncles. Their faces showed no
fear. He did not know that they had all been through this many
times before. "I was wondering what was going on," recalls
Junior. "I didn't know Grandma was selling drugs."

As the policemen poured through the jagged opening, his

mother yelled at them. "Why'd y'all break down the door?" Patty shouted. "You didn't give anybody a chance to open it." One of the police officers cursed at Patty, but Junior does not remember what he said. Rosa Lee responded by loudly cursing the policeman who had cursed Patty. "Grandma started going off," says Junior. The officers then quickly handcuffed Rosa Lee's hands behind her back and hustled her toward the demolished door.

That is the image that stays with Junior: his grandmother, her hands cuffed behind her back, being led out of the darkened apartment shouting at her children over her shoulder.

"Don't worry, I'll be all right," Rosa Lee remembers yelling to her children and grandson. "I'll be all right." This was the morning that police found sixty nickel bags of marijuana in Rosa Lee's apartment after the undercover policeman with her crossing-guard friend had witnessed a drug purchase. She received six months' probation for this, her first drug arrest.

The year between the ages of four and five was a pivotal point in Junior's life. Not long after the drug raid, he was hospitalized for several weeks for what he remembers today was a kidney problem. Patty says nothing was wrong with Junior's kidneys. Junior's penis was swollen and he could not pass his urine, she says, but, uncharacteristically, she declines to specify what happened to her son. Whatever occurred, from that point on Junior formed a protective shell around himself and attacked with a purposeful fury anyone he thought was trying to hurt him. He also developed a cruel streak.

Shortly after his return from the hospital, Patty whipped him for a transgression she doesn't remember. After she had gone to sleep, Junior took revenge on Patty's cat. She was awakened by her cat "making all kinds of noise," she says. She ran to the kitchen. "He put my cat's tail in the fire on the stove, and burned his tail off. I hit Junior so hard with my fist, he ran out the damn door."

When Junior entered elementary school, the teachers found him hard to handle. "Junior had a problem with my brothers always beating on him," Patty says, arguing that this contributed to Junior's childhood belligerency. "That's six boys beating on him. So he took it out on the kids at school." Patty says she was summoned to school several times during Junior's first-grade year because he was threatening classmates with a knife and demanding they pay him a dollar apiece. "Junior had the whole class afraid of him," she recalls. "Each child brought him a dollar a day. When a little girl did not bring Junior the dollar, Junior pushed the little girl off the sliding board and busted her head! That was scary for me then."

Junior says that most of his anger grew out of being displaced as the most important person in Patty's life when she began seeing and then living with Joe Billy, the man she considered her common-law husband until he died in 1985.

The way Junior sees it, life was sweet until Joe Billy came around.

"It probably was," agrees Patty. "Junior was getting everything he wanted. He used to be the only little boy with twenty dollars at the age of three. I used to give Junior money like it was going out of style. I didn't want him to want for anything like my mother didn't want us to want for anything."

After Joe Billy came to live with them, Junior says, his home life fell apart. The telephone was cut off when the bill went unpaid. Patty fell behind in the rent. There was never any food in the house. Junior didn't realize it, but Patty was often high when he asked her for something to eat. Annoyed that his requests interfered with her high, Patty gave Junior money to buy hamburgers and candy. When Junior could not find his mother, he went to his grandmother's apartment and asked Rosa Lee to feed him. There was always food in his grandmother's apartment and she always fed him.

Patty adds that Joe Billy made her stop giving Junior money and letting her son have his way. "When I'd tell him to go to bed, Junior would sneak out and I wouldn't do nothing," Patty says. "Joe Billy would whip his butt!"

Junior blamed Joe Billy for his mother's heroin addiction, although he knows now that Patty had her first hit three years before she ever met Joe Billy. "Back then, she was in heroin, but not *in it* in it!" insists Junior. "But when he came, he made her addicted like deep. She was not like that before he came. He brought my mom down. That's why I hated him."

Junior became aware that his mother was a heroin addict when he was in first grade. He had grown up knowing what a heroin addict was. He had seen men and women in the hallways of Clifton Terrace nodding with half-closed eyes from the effects of the drug, saliva dripping from their mouths. The sight had always disgusted him, and he wondered what adults saw in a substance that left them so out of control. Having never seen his mother nod or drool with half-closed eyes, the possibility that she could be a heroin user never occurred to him.

Then one afternoon after school, Junior saw Joe Billy walking around the intersection of 14th and W streets, N.W., yelling out the name of the brand of heroin he was selling. Junior knew enough to understand that Joe Billy must be an addict as well. Joe Billy did not see him, and Junior backed up the street toward Clifton Terrace. He resented Joe Billy and now saw this revelation as an opportunity to make his mother angry with Joe Billy. He was going to tell her!

That night, Junior walked past the open door of Patty and Joe Billy's bedroom and saw two needles on the dresser. His mother and Joe Billy were hunched over a bright light, the only light in the room. He stopped to stare. They looked up, saw him, and shut the door. He went to bed angry. He now knew that his mother, too, was an addict.

Junior felt he had something to prove at school. Part of it was the name he carried, Rocky Lee Brown, Jr. "Just having the name of Rocky," he says, "in school people wanted to fight me just to fight me. I didn't want to back down from anybody. If you back down, you're a punk all your life. I got suspended too much for fighting."

He remembers losing one fight to an older boy. When Patty found out, Junior says, she told him that if he didn't whip the boy, she would whip Junior. "So after that, I whipped him real bad."

When Junior was eight, the principal saw him showing off a hunting knife he had brought to school. She called the police. Junior was locked up in the D.C. Receiving Home for children for several days.

"They did not want him in their school," Patty remembers. "They wouldn't even report to me when Junior did not go to school."

Junior was rapidly getting out of hand. Neighbors excitedly banged on Patty's apartment door one weekend afternoon. They told her Junior was in the small grocery store at 14th and Clifton streets passing out twenty-dollar bills to anyone who wanted money. The news frightened Patty. She thought Junior had gotten hold of her rent money. A panicky Patty raced to the store. Other adults had collected the money Junior gave out, and they handed it to her. Junior ran.

"It was a good thing he ran," Patty remembers. "He made me blow my high. I might have killed him."

Junior had not been passing out Patty's rent money, she discovered when she returned to the apartment. From the top of her bedroom dresser, Junior had stolen the money Joe Billy had made selling heroin the night before. A policeman brought Junior home late that night. "I let Joe Billy beat his butt for that," says Patty. "He shouldn't have been doing that."

Between the ages of eight and nine, Junior began regularly burglarizing homes with his two best friends, "Bam-Bam" and Keith. Both boys were several years older than Junior. On one occasion, the trio broke into a neighborhood halfway house for paroled convicts. They jimmied open a locked bureau drawer in the house's office and stole envelopes filled with cash.

"I gave my mom about $500 from that break-in," he remembers. "I don't remember how much we got, but I had a lot of money." He told Patty that he picked up the money after he saw a drug dealer drop it. He knew his mother did not believe him.

"He did share his money with me," Patty says. "He gave me several hundred dollars the first time and a lot of money many times after that. He always lied about where he got his money. I would look at him like he had really bumped his head. He knew I knew better than the lies he told."

By age nine, Junior had a reputation at Clifton Terrace. He hung out with a gang, known as the Clifton Crew, composed of older boys who also lived in the housing complex—teenagers who had dropped out of school and already spent time in juvenile institutions. They groomed him to be just like them. Junior did anything they required of him. He wanted to be part of the Clifton Crew, and it didn't take long before they accepted him. The way that Junior looked up to these older boys was not unusual.

"Sixty percent of black boys come from fatherless homes," says Richard Majors. "Most of them are being raised by their peers in these underclass communities."

The older boys liked him, Junior says, because "I was vicious back then. I'd take you out in a minute, whether you were grown or not. 'Cause growing up around Clifton, you grew up like that. Everybody was wild around there!"

Junior now had access to guns. "I don't know from where Junior got his guns," says Patty. "Those boys around Clifton got guns like that," she adds, snapping her fingers. "Junior used to bring me guns and bags full of money." Patty sold all the guns when money was short.

With Junior's acceptance into the Clifton Crew, Patty's relationship with him began to change. He would try to fight back when she whipped him, although he was protective of her. When Junior heard that a man had tried to rape Patty in a Clifton Terrace stairwell, he tried to stab the man in the back with a large knife. The man was sitting out in the courtyard one evening, and Junior slipped up behind him. "He turned and saw me," says Junior. "I was going to poke him up, but he jetted [ran]. I couldn't catch him."

Patty saw Junior chasing the man. "A grown man," recalls Patty, still amazed at the memory. "Chasing him with a butcher knife." The man yelled at Patty that she had better come and get Junior before he hurt Junior. Patty later explained to Junior that he had been given erroneous information. Junior didn't believe her. He thought she was just telling him that so he'd leave the man alone, but he let the matter drop.

On another occasion, as Patty and Junior were walking together into their building, a man Patty knew told Junior he was going to beat him because he was so bad. Patty says Junior pulled a knife out of his pants pocket and told the man, "I'll put this knife up your ass, too!" From that day forth, the man never said anything to him besides hello.

Occasionally, Junior would do something that really angered Patty, and she would use her fists to let him know. "Junior mostly had his way, but when I did hit him, I was mostly high," she tells me one day. "I would whale on his ass with my fists!"

To fend off her beatings, he threatened to use his knife on her. He now says his threats were justified. "She was trying to hurt me!" he says. "She was using her fists. I remember she blacked my eye. That was child abuse, what she was doing. . . . That's my mom and everything, but I wasn't going to let her hurt me."

Patty became afraid of her son, fearful that if she whipped him, he would stab her in the back or cut her when she was sleeping. "Junior was a scheming little rascal," she says. "He would sneak up on you and do things to you. He'd burn your house down. He would do something evil like that."

By the fall of 1982, when Junior was ten, Patty had lost all control over him. He continued to commit burglaries with some of his teenage friends; he shared some of his take with Patty, and she used the money to support her heroin habit. Joe Billy also became wary of Junior; each gave the other a wide berth when they were in the apartment.

Junior was arrested six times between October 1982 and the summer of 1983, mostly for committing robberies while wielding a knife. Each time, the court released him into his mother's custody.

The breaking point with the city's juvenile criminal justice system came after a robbery late one night in June 1983. Junior held up an undercover police officer at knifepoint and stole the money the detective was using to make a drug buy outside a

Clifton Terrace building. The officer later told Junior's uncle Eric that he had seriously considered blowing "Junior's head off," but thought better of it, says Patty. The officer was being watched by other plainclothes detectives. They came directly to Patty's apartment. Joe Billy showed the policemen where Junior was hiding under the couch.

Suddenly, the outside world became intensely interested in Patty, Junior, and their life at Clifton Terrace.

One social worker concluded that Patty was afraid of Junior and rarely attempted to discipline him; another social worker said that the twenty-five-year-old Patty seemed to treat Junior more like a brother and did not take his delinquency seriously. Their relationship was not unlike Rosa Lee's relationships with Patty and Bobby. Junior skipped school about half the time, missing eighty-seven days of the 1982–83 school year.

In July, a family court judge ordered Patty to arrange for psychiatric counseling for Junior. He warned her that she faced the possibility of Junior being taken away from her and put into an institution. Patty told the judge she would get counseling for her son, but she did not.

Back at home, Rosa Lee tried to frighten Junior in front of Patty, telling him that if the court put him in a prison for children, other boys would probably sodomize him because he was so small. "Junior didn't pay me a bit of mind," remembers Rosa Lee. "He acted like he wasn't scared at all."

"He was very protective about hiding his feelings," echoes Patty.

In August, Junior and Bam-Bam were caught burglarizing the halfway house for convicts that they had broken into before. Junior was taken into custody. A child-neglect hearing was set for September.

When a friend read and explained to Patty and Rosa Lee the notice of the neglect hearing, Rosa Lee warned her daughter that the court was about to take Junior away from her. "But what am I doing wrong, Mama?" Patty asked, crying.

"You're not raising him, Patty," Rosa Lee said.

"Tell me what to do, Mama," Patty responded.

"If you don't know what to do, Patty, it's too late for me to tell you," Rosa Lee said, adding, "but remember, when you lose Junior, you'll lose your welfare check."

The night before the neglect hearing, Rosa Lee, Patty, and Bobby shot up $160 worth of heroin. In the morning, Rosa Lee and Patty were broke. They went to D.C. Superior Court without their morning billy and began experiencing withdrawal on the bus taking them downtown. By the time they entered the courtroom, both women were sick.

Rosa Lee and Patty took seats in the back of the courtroom waiting for Junior's case to be called. Patty began dry heaving and making loud gasping sounds. The judge looked up and everyone in the court turned to look at them. Rosa Lee was mortified.

Rosa Lee elbowed Patty in her side. "Stop it, Patty!" she said in a harsh whisper. "Everybody is looking at us. The judge is looking at us!"

Patty says she didn't realize that social workers had reported her heroin addiction to the judge before the hearing. When the clerk called Junior's name, he mentioned that the hearing was not only about alleged lack of parental supervision but about drug addiction. As Patty and Rosa Lee walked to the tables in front of the judge, Patty thought to herself, "He said drugs. Junior doesn't use drugs. They must be talking about me!"

Moments after Junior was brought in, the judge asked Patty whether she was addicted to drugs. "I didn't lie to him," she remembers. "Why lie about it? I couldn't handle myself, much less a son that was running around crazy!"

Junior was in his cool pose mode and nothing the judge said could shake him out of it. The judge told Junior if he put him into an institution, "you're not going to like it," Patty remembers. In reply, Junior said something smart-mouthed to the judge. The judge winced.

Finally, the judge asked them all to stand. Patty stood, flanked on the right by her mother, and on the left by Patty's court-appointed lawyer. To the left of his mother's lawyer stood Junior, with his attorney on his left.

The judge asked Patty if there was anything else she wanted to say before he took her ten-year-old son away. "There is nothing else I can do, Your Honor," Patty replied. "I can't control him. Go ahead and take him."

The judge turned to Junior and told him he was taking him out of his mother's custody. Junior rolled his eyes at the judge, as he had been doing throughout the hearing. "Are you crazy?" Patty whispered to her son. She was sick and frightened, and she suddenly realized her son had no grip on reality at all. "The judge was getting very angry," she reports.

The judge again explained to Junior that he was being taken away from Patty. Junior rolled his eyes once more. The judge told the U.S. marshal to take Junior away. Patty and Rosa Lee turned to leave. Junior moved to join them. He thought he was leaving with his mother.

When the marshal grabbed him by both shoulders, Junior realized for the first time what had happened. "He looked at the marshal, and then he looked at me and started crying," says Patty. "Mommy, don't let them take me!" he screamed. "Mommy, don't let them take me! I'll be good." Patty began to cry. Rosa Lee began to cry.

Junior remembers the scene vividly. "I went off," he told me. "Started cussing, throwing chairs." Junior began kicking the marshal and screaming. A second marshal came running. "It took both marshals to hold Junior," Patty says. "He was going wild. I went towards him, and then Mama grabbed me. I was screaming and crying, too! He didn't think it was going to happen. He thought he was going to get away with it again."

He turned toward Rosa Lee. "Grandma! Grandma!"

Rosa Lee held her open hands out to him in a gesture of helplessness. "I told you! I told you!" Rosa Lee cried.

The marshals lifted Junior, one clutching him around the chest and the other holding his legs.

Junior screamed obscenities. Years of anger about his mother and her relationship with Joe Billy spilled out like venom: "YOU LET THAT FUCKING MAN IN OUR HOUSE! YOU PUT THAT FUCKING DRUG DEALER AHEAD OF ME! HE

MESSED UP EVERYTHING! FUCK Y'ALL! FUCK ALL OF
Y'ALL! I'M GOING TO GET Y'ALL!"

Rosa Lee and Patty, both depressed and sick, walked slowly out
of the court building and west two blocks to the downtown
Hecht's. Inside the department store, Rosa Lee shoplifted earrings
and wallets while Patty acted as lookout. When Rosa Lee had filled
her large pocketbook, mother and daughter caught another bus.

At the intersection of 14th and W streets, N.W., Rosa Lee was
able to quickly sell the stolen items. They bought two billies of
heroin but were so sick by this time that they didn't bother to
walk the four blocks home.

Instead, they went into an alley behind an abandoned house
on W Street. Addicts had been using the spot all through the
summer as an outdoor oil joint. "There were chairs, bushes, and
stuff so no one could see you from the street," remembers Patty.
"You can do it all right there. I skin-popped it to get over my illness. Then I hit Mama."

Patty's welfare check stopped coming several months later.

For the next seven years, the government was Junior's parent and
the juvenile system was his home. It was left up to Junior to stay
in touch with Patty; she rarely made an effort to find out where
he was.

His first stop was the D.C. Receiving Home, where officials
quickly concluded that he needed a highly structured program to
help him overcome his severe educational deficiencies and emotional difficulties. He made progress during his two years there,
then was sent to a foster home in Virginia. Within a few weeks,
however, he was arrested on theft charges with two older boys.
He was convicted in April 1985, the same month Joe Billy was
arrested and died.

Five months later, Junior was shipped off to the juvenile
group home in Pittsburgh. A few months after arriving there,
Junior ran away. He made his way back to Washington and
showed up at Patty's Clifton Terrace apartment. After five days,
Patty notified the city's human services agency. Her thirteen-
year-old son was shipped back to the home.

Twice over the next year, he came to Washington for approved visits. Both times he ended up in trouble. He was caught in a stolen car. He ran away from the counselor who was supposed to escort him on the return trip to Pittsburgh. He was arrested by police for possession of a handgun.

By the summer of 1987, the juvenile authorities had decided that Junior needed more discipline if he was ever going to straighten himself out. They sent him to Vision Quest, a program in rural Pennsylvania for teenage delinquents who have washed out of more conventional group homes. "We take the toughest of the tough," says Michael Noyes, a Vision Quest spokesman.

Developed in the 1970s when pressure began building to do more than just warehouse delinquents in decaying urban facili- ties, Vision Quest symbolizes the evolution of society's thinking about juvenile crime. The program seeks to take troubled youths out of their urban environments and teach them a new set of val- ues in the wilderness. The teenagers learn to "master any envi- ronment," Noyes told me—and thus, the theory goes, build a sense of self-sufficiency and self-esteem that will turn their lives around.

The different quests are modeled after Native American rites of passage, Noyes said, and are structured "to provide the opportunity for the kids to reflect on past" behaviors and future goals.

Junior had a difficult time adjusting to the strict discipline and limits. He went on ten-day hikes with no eating during the day, then spent a year on a horse-drawn wagon train quest to Florida and back, a 4,000-mile round trip with seventy-five other teenagers. The trek itself is arduous, and the counselors impose a work ethic that matches. The youths work with ani- mals, prepare meals, set up and break camp, all in an effort to foster a sense of cooperation and self-discipline.

"You chop wood," Junior says. "You stay in teepees. Then you go on a quest. A quest is if you want to starve yourself for three days, you can. Hiking to meet you destiny. After the quest, you go on the train. You clean the wagon. You clean the horses. And you move, move, move. . . . When it gets cold one place you move somewhere where it is hot. In that period of time, you're suppose to change in all that time. Then you're out."

As far as he's concerned, the counselors and wagon masters had nothing but contempt for black kids like himself. "There's a lot of prejudice there," he says. "They used the word *nigger*. A lot of them are from Georgia, and a lot of them are from Tennessee."

He says tobacco-chewing counselors would get so close to him that they would spray brown spittle on his face as they yelled at him. He got into a fight with a wagon master who had choked him and left marks on his neck.

Is this a fair description of what he experienced? There's no way to know. Vision Quest officials don't think so. This much is certain: Junior completed quests but changed little. He went back to the Pittsburgh home in 1989 and immediately landed in trouble. He and several friends from the home stole a car, went joyriding, and were caught. Junior spent the next nine to ten months in the home's "lockup," its most restrictive living quarters.

In July 1990, when he was seventeen, the home's officials decided he had been there long enough. "They gave me a bus ticket back to D.C.," Junior says.

Junior and I are still getting to know each other when I hear that two police officers came to Rosa Lee's apartment complex with a warrant for his arrest. They found him in a hallway with a twelve-year-old cousin, handcuffed him, and took him to the D.C. jail.

Two weeks later, in February 1992, I am interviewing him in a small conference room at the jail. He is wearing an orange jumpsuit, the standard garb for a new prisoner awaiting trial. There's an irony to the scene: this is where, in 1988, I first interviewed his grandmother and then his mother.

Junior doesn't want to say much about the case. I know from court records that he is charged with attacking Deon Cheeks, eighteen, in November at Clifton Terrace. According to the records, Junior surprised Cheeks in a corridor about 11:30 P.M., stabbed him, and fled with $100 Cheeks had in his pocket.

Junior says he doesn't have any idea why he's been charged. He says he wasn't anywhere near Clifton Terrace or Northwest Washington that night. He remembers spending the evening at Rosa Lee's Washington Highlands apartment.

He says he knows Cheeks—the two grew up together at Clifton Terrace in the 1970s. He says the police might be confused because he and Cheeks had a fistfight not long before the night in question.

Junior is upset because no one in his family has come to bail him out. "I don't like this," he tells me. "I have never been locked down. I've just been in group homes and Vision Quest. This is the first time I've ever been in a secure jail."

His bail had been set at $1,000, which, according to court rules, meant that he or a family member had to post only $100— 10 percent—for him to be released. No one, not even Patty, will do it. His anger is particularly directed at his mother and her heroin and crack habit. If she wasn't so addicted to that "little nasty stuff, she could have got me out of here," he tells me.

But Junior has learned not to rely on his mother for money. And if she doesn't pay her debts to an impatient crack dealer, there's no reason to expect that she is going to come up with $100 for Junior's bail. When he was selling crack on Fourth Street, S.E., his mother was the only person to whom he would not sell crack on credit. Instead, he'd give her a few dollars and walk away.

His lawyer tried to get the court to reduce his bail. But Judge Cheryl Long looked at Junior's juvenile record and decided that Junior was "likely to flee" before trial.

"The defendant does not appear to be a stable member of the community," Long wrote. "He is nineteen years old, has virtually no record of employment, and has lived intermittently with his mother and his aunt, and with other undisclosed persons prior to his residence with his aunt. This is an extremely nomadic existence for a person of his age."

Moreover, Judge Long continued, in a statement to an official with a pretrial services agency Junior said that he had been employed as a salesperson for a week before his arrest. When the official contacted Patty, she said that Junior "is completely unemployed," the judge said. "If the defendant will blatantly tell falsehoods at a time that is critical to his own release, he is quick to be dishonest, and he is not to be trusted."

Prosecutors held Junior's case for grand jury action, which meant it would be months before he would stand trial. While he was waiting, he was transferred from the crowded jail to the Modular Facility at Lorton.

He made collect calls to Rosa Lee, pleading for help; he made so many calls that she stopped accepting them.

One day she hands me a letter from Junior and asks me to read it to her. The letter, which is missing capital letters and commas in crucial spots, is evidence of his writing skills. One test he has been administered indicates that he reads at about a fourth-grade level. According to a prisoner study, this is typical for the average Lorton inmate, who, like Junior, falls between the ages of eighteen and twenty-four.

"Hi how is the family?" Junior has written in neat and legible script. "fine I hope. Me I am thinking like this. When I come out I will do good with some 'Help.' I mean I will do better with Help!!

"my mom I hope she give up coke so she can get her own apartment. you stop the coke from taking your life and you feel good. my mom needs that feeling. . . . I will make my mom see the light because here make me see it."

Then he returns to his own plight. "I hope God see to forgive me for the thing I did. . . . Love you all. God will help the ones who need Him. He will help the ones who love him so I will try and help me."

Junior's concern about his mother is still evident when I see him at the prison a few months later. It is early August, and Rosa Lee and I have come to spend a few hours with Junior—and with Bobby, who is also locked up there.

Rosa Lee embraces Bobby and reaches out to touch Junior's shoulder. Mother and son hold each other tenderly for a long time. Bobby's thin arms rest on Rosa Lee's broad back, a stark reminder of his battle with pneumonia in June. "I had one foot in the grave," Bobby murmurs to Rosa Lee. Doctors feared that Bobby may have full-blown AIDS.

Bobby and Junior listen quietly as Rosa Lee complains about Patty's crack use and her prostitution. Neither says anything, but when Rosa Lee begins to make excuses for Patty's behavior, Bobby explodes. "I don't want to hear it," he tells her.

"I'm just letting you know how far it's gone, Bobby," she snaps.

She turns to Junior. "I'm just letting you know how far it's gone, Junior. I'm sorry, but I have to tell the truth."

Bobby is worried that Patty's luck is going to run out, that one day she won't pay off a debt and someone—Patty or Rosa Lee or Junior—is going to get hurt. "Let Patty start dealing with her problem," Bobby says, agitated.

Junior jumps in. "When I get out of here, I wish to put my mom in a program. The one where you are locked down. You can't get out."

Junior wants to have his mother committed to a psychiatric hospital. I point out that the courts can't force people into this kind of treatment unless they are a clear danger to themselves or society. Junior won't give up. He cites Patty's staged suicide attempts as proof that she's a danger to herself. "She just needs someone to pull her in," Junior says. "That's the only thing that's going to help my mom now."

After months of saying he knew nothing about the stabbing of Deon Cheeks, Junior pleaded guilty to the attack. On June 7, 1993, the case of *United States v. Rocky Lee Brown* is called for sentencing at D.C. Superior Court. Rosa Lee and I take a seat near the front of the courtroom. Two of Rosa Lee's grandchildren, a sixteen-year-old girl and a thirteen-year-old boy, sit near us. Both teenagers have skipped school to come to court today.

"Mr. Brown, do you have anything to say before I pass sentence?" Judge John H. Bayly asks Junior.

"Yes, I do, Your Honor," Junior begins. "I want to say I'm sorry, you know, for what I have done. . . . I'm asking you to, you know, give me a chance so that I show that I am sorry for what I have done, Your Honor."

Bayly says nothing in response. No lecture about the lure of the streets, no threats about what he might do if Junior comes back to his court on another charge. Bayly sentences Junior to two to six years in prison, but suspends it because Junior has been locked up for sixteen months awaiting trial. Then Bayly gets tough: He puts Junior on probation for three years, orders him to work 200 hours of community service, requires that he seek a job, and fines him $500.

"Does he have the five hundred dollars to pay today?" Bayly asks Junior's lawyer, Fred Sullivan.

"No, Your Honor, actually he's been on a $1,000 bond since February of '92, unable to pay that bond, so it is going to take him a while to accumulate that kind of money."

Bayly backs off a little. "Well, I'll make the five hundred due by the third of June of 1994 in its entirety."

The prosecutor in the case, G. Michael Lennon, takes note of Junior's troubled background in telling the judge that Junior must be held accountable for his actions. "No one could fail to recognize the problems that he had as a child and as a teenager," Lennon says, "but what's troubling is all the intervention so far appears to have very little positive effect. And I think that some of the responsibility for that has to be Mr. Brown's."

Later, I ask Junior what he thought of Lennon's remarks.

Junior replies in a voice edged with anger. "He's saying they gave me a lot of help but that I ain't respond to none of it. I say they didn't give me no help."

In May 1994, eleven months after his release, Junior was arrested driving a stolen car. Police officers ran his name through their crime computer and found an outstanding warrant, issued in February, for his arrest on charges of armed kidnapping. Junior was returned to Lorton. A Superior Court grand jury later indicted Junior on the February charge, adding armed robbery, assault with a dangerous weapon, mayhem while armed, and possession of a firearm during a crime of violence.

NINE

Coming Full Circle

OVERLEAF: *Rosa Lee leads the congregation in song at the Chapel Hill Baptist Church in Rich Square, North Carolina, June 1993* (© *Keith Jenkins*—The Washington Post).

It is early evening on Saturday, December 5, 1992. I call Rosa Lee's room at Greater Southeast Community Hospital, where she's recuperating from double pneumonia. The last time we talked, she was resting comfortably after a scary night in the emergency room. But this is her eleventh hospitalization in the last four years, and her doctors are worried that her HIV condition has developed into AIDS.

I am unprepared for what she has to tell me.

"Patty's been arrested for murder," she says.

I laugh in disbelief. Patty arrested for murder? She's never been arrested for anything even remotely violent. All her criminal convictions have been for minor charges relating to prostitution and drugs.

"I'm serious, Mr. Dash," says Rosa Lee, her voice dry and raspy. "She set up Mr. Steve to be robbed by some crack boys, and they killed him. Patty called me from the homicide squad last night. She was crying. She said she didn't know they would kill Mr. Steve."

"Mr. Steve" was Rosa Lee's name for Patty's boyfriend Steve Priester. Rosa Lee told me that Patty had admitted to participating in robbing Priester, though not in his murder. The police had her confession on videotape. Even if Patty had no role in the murder itself, she could expect a substantial jail term.

In the past, whenever something went wrong in her family, Rosa Lee always fell back on the same litany: I did the best I could. I did what I had to. I survived.

Not this time. After Patty's phone call from police headquarters, Rosa Lee didn't know what to do. Ordinarily, she would have called someone for help or consolation. During the years I have been interviewing her about the family, she has called me dozens of times, seeking advice, information, or just a shoulder to cry on. But after a sleepless night, she still had called no one— not even Alvin or Eric, the only two of her children upon whom she can truly rely.

On the night when her favorite child was accused of first-degree murder, Rosa Lee chose to be alone.

That same weekend, police filed a warrant in court that more fully described the events surrounding the murder of Steve Priester.

"On Friday, December 4, 1992, at about 2 P.M.," the warrant began, "officers at the Metropolitan Police Department were called to an apartment at 425 Atlantic Street, S.E., for a complaint of a burglary. When police entered the apartment, they discovered the lifeless body of the victim, Steven Priester, handcuffed and gagged, inside the closet of the apartment. . . . He had suffered a bullet wound to the head."

According to the warrant, police had arrested two suspects and were looking for others. By questioning Priester's neighbors, police learned about his relationship with Patty and that she was the last person seen with him before his death.

Ten days later, in Judge Cheryl Long's sofltly lit courtroom, the videotaped image of Patty Cunningham appears on a television monitor. The screen is positioned to give the judge the best view; she has to decide whether the videotape provides enough evidence to hold Patty for trial.

Patty is watching too, from the defendant's table.

On the videotape, Patty is sitting at a desk. She is wearing red slacks and a red blouse. A white scarf is tied around her head. The date and time flicker briefly, then disappear: "December 4, 1992, 10:10 P.M."

A detective, Vivian Washington, asks Patty if she understands why her answers are being videotaped. Normally, a suspect is interviewed without a camera present and then is asked to review a typed transcript for accuracy and sign it.

"I can't read," Patty tells Washington.

As the videotape rolls, it is clear that Patty already has told her story to the police and is repeating it for the camera. She speaks rapidly and stammers repeatedly. Her account is confusing, but it provides the basic outline of how she became mixed up in the robbery scheme.

She and Priester were at Rosa Lee's apartment on Thursday night, December 3, when someone knocked on the door about 10 P.M. It was Turk, a sixteen-year-old who lived in the building next door.

Motioning Patty out into the hallway to talk, Turk said two friends were thinking about robbing Priester when he left the apartment building. They had seen Priester around the complex and knew that he spent a lot of money on Patty. Did Patty know if Priester had any money on him right now?

Patty said she went outside, where she met Turk's friends—a "tall, dark-skinned dude" and a "short, brown-skinned woman with a mole on her cheek." If Patty knew their names, she didn't use them on the videotape. She told them that Priester didn't have any money on him. A plan was hatched to rob Priester at his apartment, where presumably he kept some cash. It would be Patty's job to let the robbers in.

Patty tells Detective Washington that she agreed to the scheme but only because the "tall dude" had threatened to hurt her if she didn't.

About 11 P.M., she says, she walked Priester to his apartment a few blocks away. Minutes later, there was a knock at the door. It was Turk, his two friends, and another man. Patty let them in. "The tall dude gave me twenty-two dollars for opening the door," Patty says on the videotape.

And what was Priester's reaction when she saw the four come into his apartment and Patty leaving?

"He just looked at me," Patty tells Washington. Patty immediately bought twenty dollars' worth of crack from a neighborhood dealer and went home to smoke it.

On New Year's Day, about two weeks after Judge Long ordered that Patty be held for trial, Rosa Lee moved out of the Washington Highlands apartment where she and Patty had been living. She financed her move with money from Patty's $258 January welfare check, which arrived at the end of December, and sent Patty a money order for $100, money that was put into Patty's jailhouse account. Washington's welfare agency was unaware that Patty was in jail, so the checks continued to come for months after her arrest. A relative of Rosa Lee's charged her twenty-five dollars a month for receiving Patty's checks at her apartment.

Rosa Lee had been planning the move for several months, since long before Patty's arrest, but her new apartment wasn't ready until now. Rosa Lee was happy to leave; the old apartment held too many painful reminders of the deterioration of her family. It had seemed chaotic when Patty was there; now it just seemed empty.

Her new place is a one-bedroom unit in the senior citizen's wing of a public housing building on North Capitol Street, N.W.; she had applied for it after one particularly bad weekend of fending off Patty and Ducky's requests for money to buy drugs. She qualified not because of her age—she was only fifty-six at the time she applied—but because she is considered medically disabled due to her HIV-positive status.

Rosa Lee considers the move a fresh beginning in a new place in the new year. Because Patty is not with her, heroin is no longer coming into her apartment, so Rosa Lee is no longer tempted to use it. Her drug use is limited to the methadone she takes every morning.

The new apartment still smells of fresh paint when I arrive for my first visit. We sit in Rosa Lee's bedroom because Richard is sleeping on the living room couch; he recently got out of jail, and Rosa Lee has let him stay with her.

Her bedroom television is on, as usual. It is Inauguration Day. On the screen, crowds are gathering at the Capitol to see Bill Clinton take the oath of office. Rosa Lee pays no attention. She has no interest in politics or government. She has never voted. "It's not going to make one bit of difference in my life," she once told me. "White people are going to treat us like they want to anyway." In her mind, white people have all the power, and they don't care about blacks. "I wouldn't go *two* blocks to vote," she says. "I have seen too much and hasn't nothing changed. The only thing that's changed is we don't have to ride in the back of the bus."

There is almost no connection between Rosa Lee's world and the world of Washington's policymakers and politicians. One day soon after the November election, I mentioned Clinton during a conversation with Rosa Lee; she didn't know his name or that an election had been held.

"Where's he from?" she asks about Clinton.

"Arkansas," I respond.

"Mr. Dash, you are lying" is Rosa Lee's first response. "You mean to tell me they elected someone from down there? That's the South, isn't it? I know we're in trouble now. Elect a *southern* white man president. That's terrible!"

I explain at length that Clinton is not the type of southerner she is thinking about.

Rosa Lee listens patiently. After my last point, she says, "You can believe *all* that shit you just said, if you want to. I *know* white people haven't changed that much!"

On the television, Clinton is finally making his way to the platform for the swearing-in. Rosa Lee is showing me some of Patty's letters from jail. The letters are in someone else's handwriting.

Rosa Lee's lower lip is trembling. "She didn't kill him! She was drunk. I know Patty when she gets drunk. She's just like a little child. I don't think I ever let her grow up. She was my first daughter, and I kept her kind of under me."

Tears run down Rosa Lee's face in unbroken streams, soaking her white blouse.

"She wouldn't hurt Steve," she wails. "That man took care of her so good. I mean they robbed him. . . . I wish I'd been home instead of in the hospital. I would have made Mr. Steve stay there. He listened to me quite well. He wouldn't have gone home with Patty as drunk as she was.

"Patty sounds like a child in her letters," Rosa Lee continues. "All she talks about is coming home! When I was in jail, I didn't write that stuff about coming home. I just said, 'I hope y'all are all right. I'll see you when I get out. Bring me a few dollars if you can.' " But Patty doesn't seem to grasp the enormity of her crime, Rosa Lee says. "It's almost like she doesn't realize what she did," she says.

Rosa Lee cries louder. "I wish she would stop writing me those kind of letters and let me know that she can adjust to what she did!" she cries. "I don't want to hear about she wishes she could come home and she's sorry about this and sorry about that. All that kind of stuff. Stop writing me those crazy letters!"

It would be months before we would know how the court viewed Patty's involvement in Priester's death. I try to divert Rosa Lee's attention. "Here comes your president," I say, pointing to the television.

"I'm not thinking about that man!" she replies.

The ceremony begins. "I do solemnly swear . . . "

Rosa Lee listens to Clinton repeat the oath, then gets up heavily from her bed and goes to the bathroom to wash her face.

It's late February, and I've been probing Rosa Lee's memory all week for any family history she might have picked up directly or inadvertently. She is happy for the diversion, anything that will take her mind off Patty. I'm reviewing with Rosa Lee how her grandfather Thadeous Lawrence's bootlegging probably helped her family survive when they were sharecropping in the 1920s and 1930s on the farms around Rich Square, North Carolina.

Rosa Lee suddenly interrupts with a question that is out of the context of our conversation, but emanates from a memory that

has just come back to her. "Why did the white men have priority at any little young woman they wanted then?" she asks me.
"They could have any little black girl they wanted. Why?"

"How do you know that?" I respond.

"My grandmama told me," she says. "My aunt Teeny told
me."

In the mid-1970s, after she became a heroin addict, Rosa Lee
made many trips to her grandmother Lugenia's house on 17th
Street in Northeast Washington. Lugenia lived there with her
youngest daughter, Jean Lawrence "Teeny" Wiggins, and her
only son, Joseph Lawrence. Lugenia's oldest daughter, Ozetta,
had died in 1950. Thadeous Lawrence had died in 1961. Lugenia, who died in 1985 at the age of eighty-eight, outlived all her
children.

During one visit on a weekend afternoon, at Teeny's urging,
Lugenia told Rosa Lee how black girls from sharecropping families were raped by white overseers, the bosses, on the Bishop and
Powell Plantation and other farms, the places where their forebears had worked and lived since the end of slavery.

"The bosses of the lot, these white men who worked for the
plantation owners," continues Rosa Lee, recounting the stories
her grandmother and aunt told her, "you could tell when they
wanted something. They all would come out there. Come out
there in the field while everybody was working. And they're
looking at the young girls. Her mouth. Teeth. Arms. You know,
like they're looking at a horse. Feeling her breasts and everything. The white men would get to whispering."

The boss would say to a girl's mother, "I want that young'un
right there. Has she ever been touched?"

"And the mothers let them men do that?" Rosa Lee asked her
grandmother.

"What the hell do you think they could do?" Lugenia
answered. "Couldn't do nothing!"

The mothers would get added benefits for the family, such as
a reduction in work or additional food rations. "Extra bread.
Extra rice. Extra stuff," Lugenia told Rosa Lee.

The overseers preferred light-skinned black girls, the children of previous rapes, but dark-skinned girls did not escape. "Grand-mama said a lot of times they had to hide Mama," recalls Rosa Lee. Rosetta was dark-brown skinned with a voluptuous shape that developed early. "They would come down there to the field she was working in, and they'd take a good look at her."

Rosetta did not escape the rapes. "Your mama was put to auction so many times," Lugenia told Rosa Lee. "They just kept wanting your mother." The overseers would assign the girls they wanted sexually to work in isolated parts of the farm, away from their families. The girls would try to get out of the work detail. "It never worked," Lugenia said. "Those men always got them."

"And Grandmama, and you really let them do it?" Rosa Lee asked again.

"I keep telling you there was nothing that could be done!" an angered Lugenia replied.

Teeny had been adding to the conversation now and then, urging her mother not to leave anything out. She now inter-rupted her mother. "Mama, why are you pinching off? Tell Rosa Lee everything what was going on down there in those sticks. It was not as easy as everybody thinks."

Lugenia looked at her daughter and then turned back to Rosa Lee. The same had happened to her, Lugenia continued, with two white overseers when she was fourteen. Years later, two of Lugenia's three daughters, Rosetta and Teeny, were raped. The overseers didn't bother Ozetta "because she was so fat," Lugenia said.

What about the children who were conceived? Rosa Lee asked.

"The children didn't matter," said Lugenia. In most cases, the children were left with their mothers, but not in all cases. Once a girl was pregnant, she was generally never bothered again. "They only wanted virgins," Lugenia told Rosa Lee. "They felt they'd catch diseases if they fooled with any girl that wasn't a virgin."

"Your mother never mentioned any of this to you?" I ask Rosa Lee.

"No," she says. "It was almost like she was hiding it from me."

On March 12, the grand jury indictments in the Steve Priester murder case are read to Patty and her teenage codefendant, Demetrius "Turk" Hanna, in Judge Long's courtroom. Patty and Turk, standing next to each other wearing jail-issued blue jumpsuits, look down at the defense table as the judge's clerk reads the long list of identical criminal charges against them.

Rosa Lee, Junior, and I are sitting in the third row of spectator seats.

Rosa Lee smiles at Patty until the clerk begins to read. The charges come as a shock to Rosa Lee. A look of fear and worry replaces her smile. This is a lot worse than she had imagined. She doesn't understand it.

Patty and Turk are each charged with ten criminal violations: conspiracy, four counts of first-degree murder, three counts of armed robbery, one count of possession of a firearm during a crime of violence, and carrying a pistol without a license.

Tears sprout from Rosa Lee's eyes as U.S. marshals lead Patty and Turk from the courtroom. She dabs at her eyes with a crumpled tissue as we push through the double set of swinging courtroom doors. In the hallway, she staggers as she walks, complaining of weakness and nausea. It is as if Rosa Lee has been indicted instead of Patty. She is confused and frightened by the seriousness of the charges Patty faces. She knows that conviction on any of the murder or armed robbery charges can mean many years in prison.

"Where did all those charges come from?" she shouts as we step into the courtyard in front of Superior Court. "The prosecutors act like they think Patty was there when Steve was killed. She wasn't there!"

"Rose," I reply quietly, "you don't have to shout at me. I'm not the person who has to be convinced that Patty was not there."

Junior's face reflects no emotion, and he remains silent as we walk slowly to my parked car with Rosa Lee between us.

"I know, I know, Mr. Dash!" she wails, the tears beginning to stream down her face. "But what are they doing? They're trying to give Patty a lot of time, and she didn't shoot that man."

Rosa Lee has told Patty's court-appointed lawyer, Leroy Nesbitt, the type of relationship she and her daughter had with Priester. "Mr. Steve used to come and feed us," she says she's told Nesbitt. "I stopped calling him 'Mr. White Man,' because he was so nice, and started calling him Mr. Steve. I've seen him take care of Patty like a baby. Cooked for her. Washed dishes for her. Gave her baths. Put clothes on her. Mr. Steve loved my daughter."

Rosa Lee told Nesbitt that the entire ugly episode grew out of Patty's desire for money to buy crack. "You know how a crack-head is," she said. "When someone offers them a piece of crack, they'll sell their soul, practically."

The next day, Russell L. Jenkins, twenty-seven, and his pregnant girlfriend, Valerie D. Osborne, twenty-eight, are arrested in their Washington Highlands apartment—three blocks from Priester's—and charged in Priester's murder. Six weeks later, the fifth suspect, Maurice A. Morris, twenty-eight, is arrested and jailed.

The news of the arrests brings Rosa Lee some relief. "Good! Now we can get this case ended," she says. "I want Patty to get her time so I can know when we can be together again. I need her with me in case I have more seizures. I want her with me again before we're both dead from the AIDS virus. I don't know how much time we've got."

Rosa Lee can see my excitement. It is April, and I have just returned from a trip to Rich Square. Through census records at the library in Jackson, the county seat for Northampton County, I was able to trace her ancestors back to the turn of the century. In the courthouse, I found the 1916 marriage record for Thadeous Lawrence and Lugenia Whitaker.

A look at the birth records revealed some new information about the family.

Three days after Rosetta's thirteenth birthday, on April 20, 1930, she had given birth to a baby girl she named Geneva. Ben, who in the records is named Earl Wright, Jr., after his father, was born a full two years later, on June 21, 1932, the year the Lawrences and the Wrights would leave Northampton County forever.

"I always thought Ben was my mother's first born," a surprised Rosa Lee tells me. "Where is this sister of mine? Did you find her, too? How old would she be? She would be about sixty-three? I'd like to meet her."

No, I hadn't located her sister, I manage to convey in between the rapid-fire questions, but I did meet two of her cousins.

"How'd you find them?" she asks, each question following the last before I can finish responding to the first. "I don't know none of the people down there. Ben's the only one who knows them. How am I related to them? My mother or my father?"

I explain that I tracked down the relatives through marginal notations in the 1910 and 1920 censuses, indicating that the black Lawrences lived and worked on the Roanoke River farms south of Rich Square.

Driving along rural Chapel Hill Road south of Rich Square, I had stopped and talked to a middle-aged black man burning leaves in his front yard. I asked him if he knew of the Lawrences. He didn't, but he directed me to his ninety-eight-year-old grandmother, who lived in the house next-door. The elderly woman had known all the Lawrences and told me where I could find Hilda Lawrence Tann, the daughter of Thadeous Lawrence's nephew Albert. Hilda, in turn, introduced me to Daisy Evans Debreaux, a first cousin of Lugenia's who grew up with her and her siblings.

"I had a long talk with both of them," I tell Rosa Lee. "They both asked that you come down there to see them, spend some time with them."

"How am I gonna get way down there in them sticks?" she replies.

"I'll take you," I say.

Rosa Lee has never shown much interest in her family's history. When I met her, all she knew was that her family came from somewhere in North Carolina. Patty's imprisonment, however, makes her eager to do something besides sit around and worry. The case seems to drag on and on. Patty is willing to plead guilty to lesser charges and testify against the others, but negotiations with the prosecutor are on hold for reasons that Rosa Lee doesn't understand.

For weeks now, Patty has been calling her collect from the D.C. jail nearly every night. "Mr. Dash, Patty will kill herself," Rosa Lee says. "I know 'cause she feels as though she ain't got no reason to live. She says, 'Mama, you're all I got. Mama, don't leave me.' That's why I don't like to read her letters. They are hurting letters. I feel so sorry for her."

Before we can go on a trip, Rosa Lee finds she has some business to attend to. In early May, she learns from Richard that her long-estranged husband has been murdered. Checking with Capitol Cab, the company from which sixty-one-year-old Albert Cunningham had recently retired after years of employment, Rosa Lee learns that he has indeed died and was buried at the Quantico National Cemetery on April 30.

Superior Court records show that on the morning of April 20, Albert Cunningham was beaten to death with a hammer in his Northeast Washington apartment by thirty-five-year-old Pamela B. Hudgens, an HIV-positive addict with whom he had a "quasi-sexual relationship." Hudgens, who was on welfare, and her husband had moved into Albert Cunningham's building about six months before the murder.

Over a period of months, Hudgens had engaged in "heavy petting," without intercourse, with Albert Cunningham in exchange for money. On the day of the murder, during a petting session, Albert Cunningham expressed dissatisfaction about spending too much money and not having intercourse. "With his pants down and erect penis exposed, he grabbed Ms. Hudgens and slammed her to the ground. Ms. Hudgens got up, grabbed a nearby hammer," with which, the D.C. Medical Examiner's Office determined after an autopsy, Albert Cunningham was hit on the head thirteen or fourteen times.

Hudgens pleaded guilty to second degree murder. Prosecuting attorney Wyneva Johnson argued for a stiff sentence, telling the court at Hudgens's sentencing that the woman left Albert Cunningham "on the floor moaning" and made no attempt to get him medical attention. "There was blood everywhere in the apartment. As he was laying in the apartment in need of help, still alive, she could have sought some care for him and did not," Johnson said. Hudgens was sentenced to fifteen years to life in prison.

Rosa Lee has a vicarious interest in these facts, but underlying Albert Cunningham's death she sees an opportunity to enhance her income.

"I should be getting widow's benefits from the Army or Social Security or both," she tells me a few days after she called the taxi company. When she met twenty-year-old Albert Cunningham in 1952, he had just retired from the Army on medical disability after injuring his right hand. He had worked most of his life, so he had to have made a considerable contribution to Social Security, she says. She had already talked to benefits officials. They told her to bring a copy of their marriage certificate and provide proof that they have never been divorced.

"You two separated in 1953, and now you're going to try to get widow's benefits?" I ask, the disbelief clear in my voice. I knew that she had barely seen the man in four decades. "They're not going to go for that."

"Yeah?" responds Rosa Lee, frowning as if there is something wrong with me. "What's wrong with that? *I'm* his widow! He never divorced me. I don't remember signing no papers. He never gave me and Alvin a *dime!* Now maybe I can get something back after all these years."

This effort, too, was a welcome distraction from Patty's plight.

Rosa Lee retrieved a copy of the November 8, 1952, marriage certificate. She and Albert Cunningham had married about 6 P.M. in the home of her minister, the Reverend Raymond M. Randall, next door to Mount Joy Baptist Church. Court records showed that Albert and Rosa Lee had never been divorced. Rosa Lee spent several months filling out forms and arguing over the telephone with Army and Social Security benefits officials, managing to get around every bureaucratic obstacle thrown in her path.

Rosa Lee received a $2,000 check from the Army and, by August, $255 in monthly widow's benefits from Social Security. Her monthly disability check was reduced from $447 to $258, but both checks raised her total monthly income to $513.

It is early June, and Rosa Lee and I are rolling south along Interstate 95 through Virginia. The methadone clinic has given Rosa Lee a small, tan-colored metal box, with lock and key, containing enough of the drug for a four-day trip. As we cruise along, Rosa Lee is reminiscing about the two weeks she spent in Rich Square during the summer of 1944, before she turned eight, the only other time she has been there.

She is fixated on the lack of indoor plumbing. The two-room shack where she stayed didn't even have an outhouse. During the day, people walked into the nearby woods to relieve themselves, always watching out for snakes. At night, the family used a tin slop jar. Every morning, the slop jar was emptied into a freshly dug hole. "It smelled!" recalls Rosa Lee with an upturned nose and a shudder.

The shack resembled the typical dwellings that white landowners built throughout the South for black sharecroppers. These dwellings were abandoned in large numbers in the 1950s, when farm machinery was replacing human labor and the sharecropping system faded away. There was a front door on the shack, Rosa Lee remembers, but no front window. In the center of the main room was a wood-burning stove. The shack's wooden planks were the only barriers to the outdoors; there was no insulation. Rosa Lee could feel the wind when it blew through the spaces between the planks. She damn sure didn't want to be down here in the winter, she thought.

The house had three windows, one on each side and one at the rear. Rosa Lee remembers rubbing dust and moisture from the thick, yellow plastic panes in the windows so she could see outside. Glass kerosene lamps provided light at night. There were crates and boxes to sit on, but not one chair. A hand pump outside supplied water.

Rosa Lee recalls asking her mother, "Mama, how did y'all *live* down here?"

Rosetta Wright looked at her with a pained expression and turned away.

We reach Rich Square in the early afternoon. As I turn into Hilda and Bud Tann's driveway, Rosa Lee stares in amazement at the large, modern tan-brick house where her cousin lives. "Big Bud," as everyone calls him, answers our knock. Hilda welcomes Rosa Lee with a warm hug.

Hilda, sixty-three, is a large woman with a light-brown complexion and an infectious high-pitched laugh. Arthritis has locked her left hip and knee, requiring her to lean heavily on a cane or a walker, "depending on how I'm feeling," she says.

She has prepared a big dinner, and Rosa Lee and I help ourselves to chicken and dumplings and collard greens. After the meal, Hilda and Rosa Lee settle into the overstuffed couches in the living room. I sink down in the upholstered high-back chair to listen.

Hilda tells Rosa Lee that one of the couches belonged to Lugenia. In the late fall of 1985, just weeks before she died, Lugenia came back to Rich Square after fifty years in Washington and stayed with Hilda for a few weeks.

Rosa Lee and Hilda swap tales of the family, and Rosa Lee begins to open up about her life of crime and drug addiction. I know that Rosa Lee is nervous about revealing too much, fearing rejection. But Hilda already knows some of Rosa Lee's history from other family members.

"You needn't worry about it now, Rosa Lee," Hilda assures her. "That's all behind you now."

"Yes, you're right," Rosa Lee says in a quiet voice. "Praise the Lord!"

They talk until the shadows darken the living room. The only light is from the television. I say goodnight and leave for my motel. Rosa Lee is so busy talking that she hardly notices.

The next morning, we pick up ninety-year-old Daisy Debreaux at her white-and-green wood-frame house and go off in search of the land that Rosa Lee's mother, grandmother, and grandfather once farmed. Daisy lived on the plantation with her husband for seventeen years, until 1949, and hasn't been back there for forty-four years.

Daisy is a thin, brown-skinned woman with a head of thick, white hair. She speaks in a deliberate cadence, barely parting her lips when she smiles. When something strikes her as funny, she lets loose with a deep, body-shaking chuckle.

We turn east onto the dirt-and-gravel Benthall Cook Road and head toward Bull Neck Swamp, a fertile piece of land on the north bank of the Roanoke River in the center of the Bishop and Powell Plantation. When we come through a break in the thick forest, Daisy sucks in her breath in surprise.

Where she and generations of Lawrences and Whitakers once lived among acres of trees is now cleared land. "There used to be dozens of houses on both sides along here," Daisy says, pointing a thin finger at the fields where the young tobacco and cotton plants still hug the ground. The spring just past was an especially wet one, and the crops were planted later than usual.

Indeed, when I was here in April and tried to get onto the plantation along Heart Swamp Road, I was forced to turn around halfway because Bridgers Stream had risen, submerging by a couple of feet the bridge that spans it. I had wanted to see the area in Bull Neck Swamp where Rosa Lee's grandfather had probably hidden his moonshine still.

A couple of miles farther and we reach a clearing where stand all the components of a modern farm: a large white-and-green farmhouse, a two-story office, hangar-sized garages for huge farming machinery, two tall gray-metal silos. No matter which way we look, there is almost no visible evidence here of the life that Daisy once knew. Beyond the farm equipment is a pond where Daisy used to fish and caught some "right nice fish." The pond is the only thing familiar.

As we walk through the cotton fields, Rosa Lee is overcome by emotion. A forgotten memory reemerges: Every day of her two-week stay that summer of 1944, Rosa Lee's mother woke her before dawn and took her to the cotton fields. They picked cotton for three hours—Rosa Lee on her knees—before break-fast, returned to the fields for several hours before lunch, and then again in the afternoon.

After a few days of this regimen, arms aching and knees sore,

Rosa Lee remembers asking her mother, "Mama, why do I have to pick cotton?"

"That's what I brought you down here for," Rosetta told her. "To show you what we have to go through in life to take care of you and feed you."

After touring the plantation, we return to Daisy's house on rural highway 258, a couple of miles southwest of Rich Square. The day is pleasant, and Daisy leaves the front door open. A screen door keeps out the flies. We settle in her living room to talk about what life was like when Daisy and Lugenia were girls.

Rosa Lee starts the conversation by asking about Lugenia. Daisy warms to the subject immediately. "Everybody called her 'Chicken.'" Daisy laughs. "I don't know why they called her Chicken, but that was what we called her." Daisy and Lugenia attended school together near Rich Square. "We fought together. Each other. She was mean and I was mean," she says, chuckling.

Daisy's father worked on the Bishop and Powell Plantation. Her mother did "day's work" on the local farms and domestic work in white people's homes. At age fourteen, Daisy began farm work for thirty-five cents a day. "We chopped [weeded] cotton, peanuts, corn," she recalls. "Picked cotton, shucked peas, stacked peas on poles."

She takes us through her marriage to Miles Debreaux at age twenty. Four children, two of whom lived to adulthood. "Now more grandchildren and great-grandchildren than I can count." She laughs.

The Lawrences, she tells us, lived on the Bishop and Powell Plantation at least a generation before her birth, in 1902, which would put them there a decade or so after the Civil War ended. In that case, they were probably the descendants of the slaves who worked on the property before Emancipation.

Rosa Lee informs Daisy that I've discovered in the county birth records that her mother gave birth to a girl two years before her brother Ben was born. "I sure would like to know what happened to her and if she's still living," Rosa Lee tells

Daisy. "I didn't know 'til now that I had an older sister. Do you know anything about her? Where she's living now?"

As Rosa Lee talks, Daisy's smile suddenly drops from her face. She looks down at Rosa Lee, who has made herself comfortable sitting on the rug at Daisy's feet. When Rosa Lee finishes speaking, Daisy looks up and out her front door at the highway. She sits absolutely still and says nothing.

We wait several long, awkward moments before I suggest to Rosa Lee that we move on to another topic. Rosa Lee asks Daisy whether she knew that her grandfather Thadeous was a moonshiner.

The smile returns to Daisy's face. "Sure did," she says. "The moonshine was good along in that time, old bootleg whiskey. I drank it. Liked it, too. They had a still in the woods. The sheriff's deputies would break it up and they'd plant them another one somewhere. It was white whiskey." Daisy laughs.

After a few minutes, Rosa Lee tries to steer Daisy back into a conversation about her missing sister. Daisy's response is the same. Her face freezes with a serious expression; she looks out the front door and says nothing.

Saturday morning we gather at Hilda's house on our way to interview a retired Northampton County prosecutor who, I've been told, knows a lot of the history of the plantations around Rich Square. We're going to meet him at his antiques shop in Woodland, a village five miles northeast of Rich Square.

In Hilda's back yard before we leave, Rosa Lee begins questioning Hilda about her mother. Hilda tells us about Rosetta, calling her by her nickname, "Hootie." Rosetta used to come to Rich Square often before her death in 1979, Hilda says, bringing down secondhand clothes from Washington for the struggling black families around Rich Square. Laughing, as she often does, Hilda says Rosetta told her "she owned twenty-two children," meaning that's how many she gave birth to.

Rosa Lee tells Hilda that she "owns nine children," including among her children the son of a heroin addict that Rosa Lee informally adopted as an infant and raised until his mid-teens.

On the drive to Woodland, I tease Rosa Lee about claiming she gave birth to nine children. She gives an embarrassed smile. "Down here, having a lot of children for a woman was very important," she says. "It meant you were all woman! I used to hear my family talk about it when I was child."

"Is that why you had eight children?" I ask.

"I don't know," she pauses, as if considering it for the first time. "It might have been, but I don't remember thinking it, at the time."

We arrive a little late for our appointment with William H. S. "Bill" Burgwyn, Jr., and he fusses at me for our tardiness before telling me his family goes back to some of the first white settlers in Northampton County, and that he has a prominent relative who was a Confederate colonel in the Civil War. Rosa Lee listens with half an ear, seeming more interested in poking around the shop.

Burgwyn and I settle down to talk about the Depression, how it affected Joe Purvis, the man who rented the Bishop and Powell Plantation, and what if anything he might know about the Lawrences and the Whitakers. Burgwyn, now in his mid-seventies, was a teenager at the time, and has an encyclopedic memory of what the prices were for the main cash crops—cotton and peanuts—in Northampton County and how the prices plunged when the Depression hit. "Everybody around here was just losing their land right and left," he remembers. "The banks were fore-closing and then the banks went broke. You could make a good crop as you wanted, but you couldn't sell it for anything."

This is the period when cotton dropped from $500 to $25 dollars a bale. Peanuts sold for three to five cents a pound in the 1920s. By 1930, a pound was selling for three-quarters of one cent.

"Joe Purvis left here during the Depression and moved to Maryland," recalls Burgwyn. "He lived the rest of his days up there."

About the black sharecroppers who worked under Purvis on the Bishop and Powell Plantation, Burgwyn did not remember Lugenia's family, the Whitakers, but he knew of the Lawrences through Thadeous's older brother, Charlie. Charlie Lawrence was Hilda's grandfather.

"Charlie Lawrence killed a white overseer named Herman Chapel on the Bishop and Powell Plantation when I was a little boy," says Burgwyn. "It was over a black woman." Burgwyn says the details in his memory are sketchy, but the shooting of Chapel by Charlie Lawrence is something people in and around Rich Square still remember and talk about as if it happened in recent years.

Later, eighty-seven-year-old Samuel Glenn Baugham, without so much as a pause to think about it, tells me the killing occurred on April 14, 1922. Baugham, the local amateur historian who knew Thadeous Lawrence as well as Herman Chapel and Charlie Lawrence, says, "They were fighting over Liza Bishop," who, he adds, already had three children by Joe Purvis. "Both men had been drinking or it never would have happened." Charlie Lawrence claimed self-defense. He had just come from squirrel hunting with a shotgun and, during a heated verbal exchange, Chapel reached for the pistol in his belt. Charlie Lawrence shot Chapel in his stomach and Chapel died sitting on a rock trying to hold his entrails in.

Burgwyn's father was Charlie Lawrence's defense attorney, Baugham remembers. Charlie Lawrence was convicted of second-degree murder and sentenced to twenty years in prison. "Charlie died in prison," says Baugham. "I don't think he lived seven, eight years after it happened."

I'm fascinated by these details of Southern race relations in the 1920s. A black woman with three children by the white man who is renting the Bishop and Powell Plantation sparks a fight between a white overseer and a black sharecropper. This is not the material you find in a history book.

But after mentioning the incident to me, Burgwyn suddenly raises his bushy eyebrows and his voice. "Let me ask you a question," he says. "You know I was a district attorney for twenty-three years and that's why I got a suspicious mind."

"Just like a reporter," I respond. "Reporters are suspicious people, too."

"That's right." Burgwyn laughs. Then, sternly, he asks, "You're not doing this to stir up any racial thing?"

"Here?" I ask, stunned by a question that brings to mind southerners' complaints about northern civil rights workers coming into the South to agitate for equal rights in the 1960s.

"Yeah," Burgwyn answers, his eyes locking onto mine.

"No." I laugh. "Not at all."

Rosa Lee is suddenly nervous about the turn my conversation with Burgwyn has taken. He and I remain relaxed with each other, but she wants to change the subject. She interrupts to ask Burgwyn if he sells secondhand clothes. He points to a bag with women's clothes. If Rosa Lee wants any of them, he'll talk to her about the price.

Burgwyn turns back to me, saying, "The reason I'm saying that to you, Mr. Dash, is that we have a great relationship in this area. We have black commissioners. Both our representatives in Raleigh are black. We're not unhappy with that. We're not miserable about that. They are all friends of mine."

Rosa Lee is anxiously walking around the shop in a hurry to leave, so I cut the conversation short, after assuring Burgwyn again that causing racial strife is not the reason for my interest in the Lawrences and the Whitakers. Outside, Rosa Lee complains to me about "getting the white people stirred up around here." When I laugh at her concern, she becomes upset.

There is the sharp edge of a hysterical note in her voice, something I have never before heard from this tough woman, something that tells me she is genuinely frightened. "I'm serious," she says, open fear reflected in her eyes. "You don't know these white people down here. They could kill us and no one would know what happened."

I'm surprised by Rosa Lee's fear. Then I recall she told me earlier that when she had gone into Rich Square in the back of a pickup truck with her mother one day during her 1944 visit, white people stared and pointed at them. "They looked at us like we were dogs!" she told me. Rosa Lee became frightened then and begged her mother to hurry with her shopping so they could get back to the farm.

Looking at her now, I think that she and Burgwyn are caught in the same racial time warp governed by mistrust and fear. I assure Rosa Lee I will try not to aggravate any more white people while we're in Northampton County. She looks relieved.

The day before our trip to Woodland, I had found a sharecropper's shack one mile north of the village that resembled the one Rosa Lee described staying in in 1944. We went to see it after we left Burgwyn's shop.

"Yeah, that's close," says Rosa Lee as we stand outside the weathered building. "Except this porch is bigger than the one on the other house."

For some reason, seeing the house jogged Rosa Lee's memory of how her mother remained stuck in the patterns of life on the Bishop and Powell Plantation when she was living in Washington. "My mother used water over and over again before pouring it out," she tells me as we lean on the shack's rickety porch.

On bath nights in Washington, Rosetta would gather all her children in a bedroom on the second floor of the wood-frame row house. She'd tell the children to strip. Rosa Lee was always the first one she ordered into the heated tub of water. "She would bathe and scrub me," remembers Rosa Lee. After rinsing off the soap, Rosetta would tell Rosa Lee to get out and dry herself while telling one of Rosa Lee's brothers to get into the tub. Rosa Lee would then pass the towel to the brother who was getting out of the tub. At the end of the washing, "if the water wasn't too dirty, she might use it to scrub the wooden floor," she says.

Rosa Lee remembers Thadeous Lawrence sitting and talking to his daughter one evening while she bathed Rosa Lee and the other children in the usual manner. He asked Rosetta why she used the water over and over again for each child. "To save water," Rosetta told her father. "You never can tell when that pump in the back yard will give out."

The same evening, Thadeous also asked her why she bathed Rosa Lee in front of her brothers.

"What's the difference?" Rosetta responded. "These are her brothers."

To wash dishes, Rosetta would heat three pans of water on her wood-burning stove. One pan to wash, one pan to rinse, and one pan for the dishes to sit in. After the dishes were finished, all of the dirty water was poured into a large bucket. Rosetta then told Rosa Lee to wash the colored clothes with it. "It seemed like she just valued water so much!" Rosa Lee says.

On Sunday morning, we attend services at Chapel Hill Baptist Church, founded the year after the Civil War ended. The original white, wood-frame building was replaced with a red brick one in 1973. Though Rosa Lee's grandparents and mother attended Branches Chapel Baptist Church, one mile west, four generations of Rosa Lee's living relatives are active members of the Chapel Hill church today.

Near the end of the two-hour service, the Reverend Franklin D. Williams, Sr., invites Rosa Lee to say something to the 125 or so worshippers. He had heard about her visit from one of her relatives. Rosa Lee beams. All eyes are on her as she walks quickly to the front. She is wearing a pink, two-piece suit with a wine-colored blouse and a string of white pearls. Her red shoes match her long red fingernails. She is the best-dressed woman here today.

She tells them she was a young child when she was last in Rich Square. Until this return trip, she had not understood the difficulties her grandparents and parents faced when they share-cropped on the nearby plantation. She had looked back over her own life, she tells them, and is not proud of much of what she has done. "When you change the way you've been all your life, anything is possible," she says. "I thank God for giving me another chance in life."

Rosa Lee shuts her eyes, pushes her palms together, and belts out the opening verse of "Search Me, Lord," a gospel song she learned as a child at Mount Joy Baptist Church.

Oh, search me, Lord!
Oh, search me, Lord!
Turn the light from heaven on my soul

If you find anything that shouldn't be
Take it out and strengthen me.

Older members join in. Reverend Williams rushes to the piano and begins to play. Even the small children, who moments before squirmed with impatience, sit transfixed. The entire congregation sways in the pews.

I sit in wonder at the power of Rosa Lee Cunningham. She steps in front of people who have never seen her before and inspires them to sing this song of redemption. I can't help but think that if circumstances had been different, if she hadn't faced so many obstacles in her life, her drive and her charisma might have caused her to create a different life for herself, her children, and grandchildren.

I want to be right.
I want to be saved.
I want to be whole.

The investigation of Steve Priester's slaying takes a turn in Patty's favor in October. The prosecutor, Heidi Pasichow, accepts Patty's statement that her role in the robbery was to open the door for Turk and the other three. If Patty will agree to testify against the others, Pasichow will drop the first-degree murder charges against Patty.

As plea bargains go, it's not a bad deal. Patty still faces a substantial prison term, but at least she doesn't have a life sentence hanging over her head. On October 22, in Judge Long's courtroom, Patty pleads guilty to first-degree burglary and conspiracy to commit robbery. She won't be sentenced, however, until she is finished testifying. If all the defendants go to trial, that could take months.

The delay is excruciating for Rosa Lee. Whenever she sees me, she badgers me for details of the case. She knows I am monitoring every twist and turn of the other four defendants' hearings. She thinks of little else. Then, in mid-December, a late-night telephone call gives her something else to worry about.

It is 11:45 P.M. and she has just fallen asleep. The caller is the security guard in the lobby of her apartment building. A Robert Cunningham is here, the guard says. Do you want him to come up?

Rosa Lee is confused. Bobby is supposed to be in jail. What's he doing here?

A few minutes later, she opens the door and draws back in disbelief. Standing in the hallway, dressed in a prison-issue blue cotton jumpsuit and a thin windbreaker, is a shrunken version of her eldest son. His breathing is labored and heavy. He tells her that he has just walked from the jail, a distance of three miles. He has been given a medical parole because he is dying of AIDS. His weight has dropped from 160 pounds to less than 100.

Two days later, Bobby collapses on Rosa Lee's bathroom floor. Rosa Lee can't lift him. She calls 911, and soon her tiny apartment is filled with paramedics and equipment. They take Bobby to Howard University Hospital, where he deteriorates quickly. When he dies on January 18, 1994, he weighs 72 pounds.

Bobby is the first of Rosa Lee's children to die, and she has no money to give him a funeral. Because she is poor and Bobby has no estate, the city's Department of Human Services agrees to pay for the funeral and, later, the cremation.

Rosa Lee is standing near a lavender-colored coffin when I arrive at Frazier's Funeral Home on Rhode Island Avenue, N.W. The casket lid is closed. "I didn't want anyone to see the way he looked when he died," she whispers.

I take a seat in the second row, next to one of Bobby's cousins. Eric comes into the parlor. He looks around the room, sees Rosa Lee in the first row, then decides to sit next to me. He has never resolved his anger at his mother for the way she raised him. Several family members are late for the 11 A.M. service, so the Reverend R. E. Dinkins decides to wait a few minutes. Finally, Rosa Lee motions to Dinkins to go ahead anyway. Dinkins leads the dozen mourners in prayer, then asks anyone who wants to speak to come forward.

Richard rises. "Bobby has taken care of me and all my brothers. He had a good life, and he did the best that he could. I'll never forget him."

A female relative delivers a more pointed message. "To the family, I would like to say, be not ashamed of your son or your brother. God had him here for some reason, some purpose in life." She looks toward Rosa Lee. "As he sleeps away, it is time for you all to get your act together. Get your act together, acknowledge the Lord, and serve Him!"

A hush falls over the room. Now it is Rosa Lee's turn.

"First, I'd like to say, thank God for giving me the strength to be and to get up here." She pauses, then cries out: "Bobby!"

His name echoes throughout the silent parlor.

"I love you, Son," she says, "and so do your brothers and your sisters. But I know now that you are in a better place. All of us will always love you. Take care of him, God, 'cause he was my oldest. Thank you."

Rosa Lee has a plan for persuading Judge Long to release Patty on probation. The day before the sentencing, she delivers two letters to Long's chambers—one from her doctor, which details her deteriorating medical condition, and the other a personal plea that her seventeen-year-old granddaughter wrote for her, imploring the judge to let Patty come home to take care of her. When I remind her that she left her old apartment to get away from Patty's drug-addicted lifestyle, she waves me away.

When I pick up Rosa Lee on the afternoon of May 10, 1994, she is nervous, almost shaking. She is still weak from her latest bout of pneumonia, which put her in the hospital for two weeks, and she uses a cane to walk from my car to the courtroom.

It is close to 5 P.M. by the time Patty's case is called. Patty is brought from the lockup. She looks healthier than she has in years. Eighteen months in jail, away from regular drug use, has given her body a chance to recover. She has lost the sallow, drug-induced pallor that I remember. She sees Rosa Lee and breaks into a smile.

I whisper to Rosa Lee that the prosecutor's recommendation could be crucial in deciding Patty's sentence. The judge will want to know if Patty has held up her end of the plea bargain.

All of the defendants in the case have pleaded guilty before trial, so Patty never had to testify in open court. Prosecutor Pasichow tells Long, "I feel absolutely compelled to let the court know that she's been cooperative." Patty's role in Priester's murder, Pasichow says, "really comes down to, in part and to a large extent, Ms. Cunningham's greed in terms of her addiction, in terms of her need for money, and in terms of the type of lifestyle that, unfortunately, Ms. Cunningham was living at the time." That doesn't excuse her actions, Pasichow says. "What she did was set in motion something that she now regrets, but something that she really could have stopped."

As prosecutors' statements go, this is a pretty mild one. Pasichow could have asked Long to sentence Patty to the maximum time in prison, but she asked only for an "appropriate" sentence.

"Ms. Cunningham," the judge finally says, "this is your opportunity to speak to the court."

Patty stands. The words rush out. She tells Long that she agreed to let the robbers into Priester's apartment only because she was afraid that they were going to hurt her. "I'm really sorry for what happened to Mr. Priester. Because I loved him too. A lot! And I ask him every night to forgive me for what happened. And if I could have changed it, I would—

"This is the first time—this is the first time that I ever been without drugs this long. And it feels really good to me. It gives me a chance to get my life together, make my life much better. So I'm asking to be put on probation."

But Long is clearly in no mood for redemption. She is too troubled by the statement of facts on Priester's murder.

After Patty left Priester at the apartment that night, the robbers repeatedly asked Priester, "Where is the money at?" Priester pleaded with them to leave him alone. The robbers gagged him, handcuffed him, and bound him at the knees and ankles with belts and ropes. All four robbers took turns hitting Priester in the face with a heavy wine bottle and a brass ornament. The robbers tied a hood tightly over his face and shot him in the head. As far as the police could determine, the assailants left without finding any money in Priester's apartment.

"What they did was just completely unnecessary," Long says

to Patty. "Completely unnecessary. But they did it anyway. And I think that when you decided to let them in the house and made it possible for them to get into the house, you knew that you were doing a favor for some pretty bad people. . . .

"It's bad enough that people do this to total strangers," Long continues, "but there is no real way to excuse what you did to someone who is a friend to you."

Long announces Patty's sentence: one to three years for the conspiracy conviction and seven to twenty-one years on the burglary conviction, to be served consecutively. "You should pay a price for what you did, and you should not basically just get off the hook simply because you and your mother are in bad health," Long concludes.

A few hours later, we sit in my car in front of Rosa Lee's apartment building and rehash the sentencing. Rosa Lee is distraught. She wanted a chance to speak to the judge. As Patty's mother, she says, shouldn't she have had the opportunity to explain?

I had been warning her for months that Patty's lawyer might not let her say anything in court, that he might decide it would do Patty's cause more harm than good. But Rosa Lee kept rehearsing her speech, as if this were her trial, not Patty's. One day, months before Patty's sentencing, she gave me a preview of what she would say to the judge if she got a chance.

"I want to say, 'Judge Long, my name is Rosa Lee Cunningham. I just want to clear my conscience and my mind the way I feel about my daughter being in jail on account of I feel that I brought my child up wrong because I didn't know better. I didn't know no other way. Not only Patty, all of them children.

" 'I don't feel too good about it, Your Honor. I never have. . . . I wasn't thinking right and I wasn't thinking clearly. I just didn't want her to become hurt like me. I didn't want her to want things and couldn't get them like me. . . .

" 'Your Honor," she continued, "I love my children very much, but somewhere down the line, I didn't raise them right, and it is hurting the hell out of me."

It was a harsh assessment, and undoubtedly designed to elicit

Long's sympathy. Yet it was direct and honest in a way that went far beyond our first interviews six years earlier.

But then, Rosa Lee is not the same woman she was when we first met. In 1988, she still shoplifted regularly, sold heroin on the street, and used heroin and cocaine frequently while sharing dirty needles with Patty. Somehow, she was also taking care of her young grandchildren because their mother was strung out on crack.

Then Rosa Lee found herself paying a heavy price for her past. She learned she was carrying the virus that causes AIDS. She suffered a series of seizures after injecting heroin. She came close to dying from an overdose of seizure medication because she couldn't read the dosage instructions. Then came Patty's arrest for murder, followed by Bobby's death. Now she spends hours praying for herself, judging herself, endlessly asking questions for which there are no easy answers. She wants more than survival at this point: she wants peace from a life that offers almost none.

It is September 1994, four days before the series I have written about her life starts to run in the *Washington Post*. Rosa Lee has adjusted to life without Bobby and Patty. Her apartment remains a haven for those children with nowhere else to go. Richard and Ronnie are staying with her; Ducky, however, is back in Lorton serving time for theft.

Rosa Lee keeps herself busy by helping to take care of the family's newest generation—her great-grandson. The baby's father is Junior, who is also at Lorton. In August, a jury convicted Junior of armed robbery and possession of a firearm during an act of violence. The baby's mother is an illiterate, fifteen-year-old girl, a tenth grader. Rosa Lee looks after the infant on weekdays so the mother can go to school.

On school days, the baby's mother meets Rosa Lee at the McDonald's near the methadone clinic. On this Thursday morning, she handed Rosa Lee a still-warm bottle of formula, quickly washed down a sausage sandwich with soda, kissed her son, and left for school.

"You're a good-looking boy, you know that?" coos Rosa Lee as the twelve-week-old infant sucks his bottle. He finishes the bottle, and his eyes begin to droop.

She gently rocks the baby on her lap. "He's such a beautiful baby and so easy to look after," she says, stroking his cheek as he falls asleep.

Epilogue

OVERLEAF: *Rosa Lee and the author share a meal over an interview at Rosa Lee's favorite McDonald's* (© *Lucian Perkins*—The Washington Post).

FOR FOUR INTENSE YEARS, I followed Rosa Lee Cunningham, her children, and five of her estimated thirty-two grandchildren. I became absorbed by Rosa Lee's story and deeply troubled by her choices—the ones she made and the ones she saw available to her.

I recognize that there are many ways to look at Rosa Lee. There is something in her life story to confirm any political viewpoint—liberal, moderate, or conservative. Some may see her as a victim of hopeless circumstances, a woman born to a life of deprivation because of America's long history of discrimination and racism. Others may give her the benefit of the doubt in some cases but hold her personally accountable for much of what she did to herself, her children, and her grandchildren. A third group might say that Rosa Lee is a thief, a drug addict, a failed parent, a broken woman paying for her sins, and a woman who seemingly was so set on placing her children on the path to failure that it is amazing that even two of them manage to live conventional lives.

There is some truth in all these views, but none of them reflects the complexity of her life, or the complexity of the crisis in the nation's inner cities. Simple platitudes do not suffice to lay bare the genuine complexities of Rosa Lee's life and personality.

Simple solutions that may be offered are countered by the limited range of choices available to Rosa Lee and others like her.

We all like to simplify matters to conform with our beliefs and preconceptions. The reality, however, is often much more complicated and difficult to grapple with. For most people trapped in it or anyone who thinks about it, intergenerational poverty is a difficult reality to overcome.

Clearly, the choices Rosa Lee made early in her life pulled her down from a childhood on the upper edge of a bare existence into an adulthood of poverty coupled with criminal deviancy, putting her squarely in the underclass. But it is also just as clear that Rosa Lee does not believe that the occupational opportunities available to many African Americans beginning in the mid-1950s were also available to her. In her isolation from the main currents of American life, including the growing African American middle class, Rosa Lee is unaware that there has been a momentous expansion of opportunity and looks at the world through the eyes of her mother, a world where whites had everything and blacks had to scuffle for every little piece they could get.

Rosa Lee reveals this side of herself when questioning me about my upbringing in Harlem and the Bronx during the post-war years. She is always surprised by my answers: that my father started out as a clerk in the U.S. Post Office and rose to become a supervisor; that my mother, a registered nurse, started out as a visiting nurse for Harlem's welfare mothers and rose to become a supervisor in New York City's Health Department; that my parents sent my brother and me to private schools.

"You mean to tell me that they had black people doing that in them days?" she asks. After almost every revelation about my own history, Rosa Lee is disbelieving. "Mr. Dash, you are lying!" she declares. I insist that I am not, and that there is nothing exceptional about my family's history. The majority of African Americans who moved up into the middle class in the same period did so in the same manner, I tell her. Education was the route. Among my parents' generation, adults in the black middle class all over the country came to understand that a good education was available in only a few select public schools and that their children would be more likely to receive a superior education in a private college-preparatory school. Many parents sacrificed a better lifestyle for themselves in order to send their children to private schools.

"My father tells me he asked me a civics question one day when I was in junior high school," I tell Rosa Lee over breakfast one morning as she peppers me with questions about why my parents sent me to a private high school. "He says my answer was so far away from anything that made sense he was alarmed. He couldn't believe that New York City schools had deteriorated so badly in one generation, since he had been in school."

"You know, I didn't understand what you could do with an education," says Rosa Lee, repeating something she has told me several times before. "I really didn't push it with my children either. If they wanted to stay home in bed, I let them."

Washington's public school system failed her miserably, as it subsequently failed most of her children and a number of her grandchildren. Rosa Lee's illiteracy shuts her out of almost every entry-level position in the American job market.

When Rosa Lee was a young woman, pathways to achievement were opening up in Washington, D.C., just as they were in other cities, but she did not know it. Her exposure to middle-class African Americans was fragmentary, at best, and made no lasting impression. She had a limited understanding of the civil rights movement and its goals, and still does not see what was achieved except that blacks no longer have to ride in the back of the bus. Rosa Lee, like many of the black urban poor, was unprepared to take advantage of those new opportunities.

As Rosetta Wright's oldest daughter, Rosa Lee was a victim of both sexism and racism. She was deliberately raised in and trained to adhere to the rural South's rigid gender and racial roles, which guaranteed her domestic day work only. That was an employment path she rejected as leaving her open to the whims of white people, a position she refused to place herself in. Since at least the age of seven, after her only childhood visit to Rich Square, Rosa Lee has harbored a deep fear of white Americans. As a young woman, the last thing she wanted to do was work inside their homes. She is so defeated she won't even register to vote, feeling that going to the polls will not make one iota of difference in her life.

Rosa Lee's story—that of one woman and one family over six generations—is critical. For if we, as a society, are ever to come up with viable solutions to poverty, we must agree on what the facts are, regardless of our political viewpoints, before we can offer those trapped in poverty a way out. There have been other studies of families like Rosa Lee's, but that does not exempt any of us from examining poverty's impact on families again and again. We need to learn all we can, in any way we can.

Viable solutions to poverty will never be simple. As Rosa Lee's story shows, immense difficulties await any effort to bring an end to poverty, illiteracy, drug abuse, and criminal activity.

In the poorest neighborhoods, these problems are woven together so tightly that there's no way to separate the individual threads, especially in those communities overwhelmed by drug abuse. Reforming welfare doesn't stop drug trafficking; better policing doesn't end illiteracy; providing job training doesn't teach a young man or woman why it's wrong to steal.

But *complex* does not mean *intractable*. Rosa Lee's sons Alvin and Eric, for example, individually rejected their mother's lifestyle while they were still in elementary school—Alvin out of shame and humiliation about living on welfare, Eric out of anger and disgust at his mother's shoplifting. At a crucial juncture in their adolescent lives, each benefited from the personal interest of an adult and ended up rejecting the lure of the street. They are a testament to what can be achieved in the most dire circumstances. So are eight of Rosa Lee's ten brothers and sisters, who moved from poverty into the working and middle classes. They, like many others who grew up poor, learned the importance and value of personal responsibility, and it gave them the edge they needed to invent a different way to live.

Only three of Rosetta Wright's eleven children fell into the underclass: Rosa Lee, a younger brother, and a younger sister. We can learn a great deal if we remain willing to look at their lives and the lives of people like them.

Behind the poignant stories about Rosa Lee and her family are the grim statistics of a growing underclass mired in petty crime, illicit drugs, the sexual abuse and neglect of children, mayhem, violence, and murder.

• In the past generation, America's urban underclass population has tripled in size—to an estimated 2.7 million people, according to Urban Institute studies. By the time of the 1990 census, the underclass was growing at a rate of 8 percent per decade. America's history of racial discrimination has had a disproportionate impact on black Americans, who make up 57 percent of the underclass. Whites and Hispanics compose 20 percent each. The remaining 3 percent is made up of Asians and Native Americans.

• Members of families like Rosa Lee's, in which criminal behavior is "a continuation from generation to generation," make up 15 to 20 percent of prison populations, but are responsible for 60 to 75 percent of crime, says Jasper Ormond, a clinical psychologist formerly with Washington's Department of Corrections. "That's why it's such a significant group to focus on," he adds. "Poverty is the underlying force. Crime has been seen as a way out of poverty."

• Of the 10,000-odd inmates that make up Washington's prison population at any given time, half are criminal recidivists—men and woman repeatedly arrested for new crimes a short time after being paroled on previous convictions. Going to prison has no measurable impact on their behavior. When they leave prison, they are in the same predicament they were in when first arrested.

Males make up more than 90 percent of Washington's prison population, and the average male inmate is between the ages of eighteen and twenty-four, grew up in the city's poorest neighborhoods, dropped out of school before completing high school, and reads just above the third-grade level no matter what grade he reached before dropping out. The statistics about education give us a clue about where one of the major problems lies. Rosa Lee's grandson Junior, who completed the tenth grade and yet barely reads and writes, fits exactly into this category. Junior, like most of his fellow prison inmates, stopped learning by the fourth grade. Between the ages of eight and nine, something happens to these boys growing up in urban poverty that leaves too many of them educationally crippled before they reach adolescence. We have to understand what is happening and intervene. Most public school systems serving poor urban communities are turning out large numbers of illiterate boys. These youths see crime as their only way to survive. Significantly, fully literate high school graduates are a rarity in the nation's prison systems.

• One measure of underclass growth is teenage childbearing in poor urban communities. Nationally, rates among unmarried African American girls ages fifteen to seventeen rose from 67 births to every 1,000 girls in 1983 up to almost 77 births to every 1,000 girls a decade later. Among white girls of the same ages, the figures are 13.5 for every 1,000 in 1983 up to 22 for every 1,000 by 1993.

• Foster care is becoming increasingly dominated by minority children, because African American and Hispanic children are entering and being retained in foster care at higher rates than whites. Moreover, increasing numbers of physically and sexually abused children from poor urban communities are ending up in foster care, which is no safe haven.

According to Toshio Tatara, director of research for the American Public Welfare Association, in the years since 1982, the number of children in foster care nationwide has climbed from 260,000 to 442,000—a 70-percent increase. "There is no single answer to account for the increase," says Tatara. But after 1986, he adds, "parental drug abuse" caused by widespread use of crack cocaine "is one factor" in children being taken away from their parents and placed in foster care.

Ronald B. Mincy, the director of poverty programs for the Ford Foundation, says the overwhelming number of children who are sexually and physically abused before they come into the foster care system are coming out of underclass urban neighborhoods. "You also find a lot of child abuse in the foster care system," adds Mincy. "The number of black children in foster care is extremely high, and they tend to remain in foster care because of the low rates of adoption. One of the real dirty little secrets of the foster care system is that those children are often the victims of rape."

Families like Rosa Lee's are not difficult to find. At the start of my research, I interviewed twenty men and twenty women, heads or members of criminal recidivist families, in the D.C. jail. All forty had similar family histories of drug abuse, repeated imprisonment, the abuse of children, chronic unemployment, and marginal educations extending over at least three generations. I selected four families to follow. From this small group, I gradually focused on Rosa Lee's family alone. Just keeping up with four living generations in her family occupied me full time for the entire four years. Above all, I realized that most recidivists, men and women, become parents as teenagers, but that we never hear about what happens to their offspring as the parents cycle through repeated incarcerations. I wanted to know what these children face as their parents are sent off to jail.

In 1994, the *Washington Post* published "Rosa Lee's Story: Poverty and Survival in Washington" on its front page every day from September 18 through 25. Over those eight days, about 4,600 readers called a special telephone line at the *Post* that was set up to allow readers to leave their reactions as recorded remarks. About half of the callers praised the story, while about a quarter had a wide variety of criticisms. The remainder provided a range of observations, some individuals offering both negative and positive comments. In addition, the *Post* editorial page received numerous letters about *Rosa Lee's Story.* Many readers also called or wrote to me directly. In the weeks following publication of the series, I met with professional and university groups and appeared on a number of radio and television talk shows where I encountered a similarly diverse range of praise and criticism.

Although the great majority of responses to the series were positive, it came as no surprise to me that the articles disturbed and angered some readers, both white and black. Of the African

American callers, for example, about a third typified a part of the black middle class that reacts angrily to any graphic story in the media about the lives of blacks trapped in poverty. Many of these people feel that by writing about Rosa Lee and her family I am perpetuating stereotypes about African Americans. They argue that white Americans are generally incapable of perceiving class differences among blacks and are quick to ascribe antisocial underclass behavior to all African Americans.

These middle-class blacks react with visceral rage to a public, close-up look at African Americans in poverty and view such efforts as an assault on their hard-earned status and material well-being, something they fear can be taken away from them. A number of them are embarrassed about the circumstances and lifestyles of the black underclass, although African Americans have had nothing to do with its creation. While they recognize on an intellectual level that America's long history of discrimination and segregation, in terms of unequal access to jobs, denial of quality education, and the de facto restriction of blacks to isolated urban ghettos, is the root cause for disproportionate numbers of African Americans suffering in poverty, on an emotional level they are defensive about those blacks mired in generation after generation of welfare dependence.

The black sociologist E. Franklin Frazier captured their defensiveness in his 1957 classic, *Black Bourgeoisie*. "Since the world of make-believe cannot insulate the black bourgeoisie completely from the world of reality," wrote Frazier, "the members of this class exhibit considerable confusion and conflict in their personalities. Their emotional and mental conflicts arise partly from their constant striving for status within the Negro world, as well as in the estimation of whites." Four decades after Frazier wrote those words, much of that African American middle-class striving and defensiveness remains unchanged.

One African American reader of Rosa Lee's story expressed one of the black middle-class's most pervasive fears, saying, "If you walk down the street and you're black, everyone thinks you're a criminal." Several of the callers felt that a black journalist should concentrate on people who grew up in circum-

stances like Rosa Lee's and became brain surgeons. Some readers felt I had made Rosa Lee out to be a hero. Others wanted to
know why I hadn't written about Appalachian whites trapped in
the rural underclass for generations before and after blacks were
freed from slavery by the Civil War. All in all, my critics felt that
by devoting eight days to an in-depth look at a family of welfare-
dependent petty criminals, the *Post* had given this growing urban
crisis the wrong kind of attention.

My answer to all these complaints is simple. I wrote about
Rosa Lee and her family because I am a black journalist uncomfortable and alarmed by the growing black underclass trapped in
urban poverty, filling America's prisons, and shooting each other
on the street rather than finishing high school. I was interested in
writing about the crisis in all its stark reality, and the only way
to reveal that reality was to focus on one family. My precise
intention in writing the series and this book is to make the reader
as uncomfortable and alarmed as I am.

Ronald Mincy, the Ford Foundation poverty expert, feels that
stories like Rosa Lee's play an important role in informing the
public about the realities of underclass life. Mincy believes the
crisis of poverty and crime in our cities needs to be written about
in a way that people can understand. He has studied it statisti-
cally and has an intimate understanding that the problem is
growing, not receding.

Mincy's own story is the type of success saga a significant
number of middle-class blacks prefer to read about. Mincy over-
came tremendous odds. He and his two brothers were raised by
their single mother in the South Bronx in the Patterson public
housing project, not far from the East Harlem neighborhood
where I grew up. Mincy earned a doctorate in economics from
the Massachusetts Institute of Technology. He, his wife, and two
sons live in Harlem out of a commitment to making a change
where change is most needed.

Every evening Mincy leaves his midtown Manhattan office
and travels north four miles into a large swath of real estate with
rows of boarded-up and deteriorated nineteenth-century tene-
ments. Nearing his West 122nd Street home, Mincy passes

through a street-corner drug market brazenly operated by the newest male generation of Harlem's underclass. "As I round the corner, there are drug deals happening on the corner," says Mincy. The kids attending the nearby junior high school "are coming in and out of that all the time."

This scene is replicated on street corners in every large and small city in America. The adolescent drug sellers and their destitute clients are just the observable symptoms of continuing inner-city decay. This decay is intricately interwoven with other dead-end ingredients of life within America's bottom tier of poverty: adolescent childbearing, child abuse and neglect, foster care, dropping out of school, welfare dependence, single parenthood, chronic unemployment, and elderly people who are afraid to leave their homes because of neighborhood crime and violence. "In most cases, there is not a father in these households," continues Mincy. "There is not even a positive older brother! That is a situation that is tragic. It is an intergenerational thing."

Reams of poverty statistics cross Mincy's desk every week, but the tales that drive his search for prescriptions are the stories he reads every day in newspapers. A *Washington Post* story about a fourteen-year-old boy who anticipates dying by age seventeen still haunts him. This, Mincy says, "is usually the only picture" the public gets. Mincy argues that in reading the life stories of Rosa Lee Cunningham and her family, some readers "will realize that in addition to sort of being horrifying, this is also tragic. Some will be struck by a sort of compassion" for the growing number of people trapped in debilitating poverty and repeated patterns of criminal behavior.

Mincy, other poverty experts, and municipal judges I have interviewed all tell me that, among families living in extreme poverty, stories like that of Rosa Lee's family are not uncommon. That is why I wrote about her. We all need to know that.

While the series is running, I call Rosa Lee each day. She is happy. The staff at the methadone clinic tells her how brave she is to tell her story in so much detail. Rosa Lee's drug buddies at McDonald's treat her like a celebrity, buying her breakfast and asking her endless questions about each day's installment. Rosa Lee gladly soaks up all the attention.

A couple of days after the series ends in late September, we meet for breakfast. Parts of the series have been read to her by friends and a granddaughter who attends high school, she tells me, and she has one complaint.

"You give Cheetah too much credit," she sputters, using Eric's nickname.

"Is that your only complaint?" I laugh. "I think I treated Eric fairly. When I met him, he had a new wife, a stepdaughter, a baby daughter, his eight-year-old son, and two of your grandchildren living with him in a three-bedroom apartment. He rescued the two grandchildren after you got busted at 14th and W. You're just angry with him because he confronts you about his childhood and your behavior. I'm not in that."

"'I'm not in that,'" Rosa Lee repeats, mimicking me. "I say you give him too much credit. He's not as good as you made him out to be."

I laugh again and we agree to disagree on that one point.

In the following months, Rosa Lee does a lot of public speaking around Washington. Her audiences include drug treatment officials and physicians at her methadone clinic and other drug treatment programs, as well as parishioners at numerous churches. Because of the photos that ran with the series, strangers recognize her in McDonald's and on the street. Most tell her that they learned something from reading her story. Some tell her that they did not like her story and wished she hadn't cooperated with me. Rosa Lee beams when she tells me about the supportive strangers who come up to her. She dismisses her critics with a sneer, a wave of her hand, and a profane characterization.

Several of her youngest siblings let her know that they did not like what she told me about Rosetta and contended it was untrue. "What do they know, Mr. Dash?" she says angrily. "They weren't even born when I was eighteen and my mother had already whipped my butt since I was little. And kept on whipping it, too."

We are having lunch at an H Street restaurant one day in mid-January 1995 with the fifteen-year-old mother of Junior's seven-month-old son. The baby is sleeping in his stroller. Rosa Lee tells me she has been collecting a lot of money when she speaks at churches. "After I talk about my life, people come up to me and slip five and ten dollar bills into my hand," she says. "They tell me to have faith in God and everything will be all right."

"How much have you collected?" I ask.

"Why do you want to know?" Rosa Lee demands. "You're not going to put *that* in the *Washington Post,* are you?"

"No," I tease. "I'm your agent. I get ten percent of everything you collect."

Rosa Lee and the teenage mother laugh for several moments. The girl has been around the great-grandmother of her son long enough to guess what Rosa Lee's reaction will be when she stops laughing. Wiping tears from her eyes, Rosa Lee finally stops long enough to get out her response. "Well, buddy, if that's the case, you'll never know how much I've collected."

In March, Rosa Lee rejoins Mount Joy Baptist Church after an absence of almost three decades. She is welcomed by the minister and the congregation like a long-lost sister. Most tell her that they read the *Post* series and her past is of no importance to them. Many of the older members remember Rosa Lee, having been childhood friends or acquaintances when she was a junior usher. Rosa Lee speaks at the service, and the whole reunion is filmed for a *Frontline* program called "The Confessions of Rosa Lee."

Immediately after the series was published, I had dissolved the professional barrier I had maintained between Rosa Lee and me throughout our relationship. Now I give her personal advice whenever she asks. I've also given her my home telephone number, and I meet her at McDonald's several mornings a month. We generally talk over the phone several times a week.

We've become genuine friends, which is a rare occurrence for reporters who cover the lives of poor people. Our lives and the worlds we live in are very different, but we were able to bridge that difference. This happened to me once before, with several teenagers I interviewed over a seventeen-month period for a project on adolescent childbearing in the mid-1980s. I became an adviser for them, too, after that project was published. Now that they are adults, I hear from them only infrequently. It's different with Rosa Lee. I know she relies on me to listen to her and help her through her daily crises.

One hitch develops early on in this more personal relationship. Although her dose is up to eighty-five milligrams of methadone a day, she wakes up about 5:00 A.M. when the synthetic drug wears off and her abdominal cramps begin. The clinic doesn't open until 7:30, so Rosa Lee is wide awake with nothing to do for a couple of hours. Within days of my giving her my home number, she starts calling me about six o'clock in the morning to talk.

After several calls at this hour, I sleepily complain, "Rose, you are the only person on the face of the earth who will call someone at six in the morning to chat!" She laughs, but thereafter she generally calls me in the afternoon to leave a message on my home voice mail or, almost like clockwork, between 8:30 and 9:00 at night—after her favorite television shows are over. She's usually in bed by 9:30.

When the telephone rings on April 11, I look up at the clock. It's about ten minutes before 6 P.M., so it's not Rosa Lee, I think. The voice that answers my greeting, however, is hers.

"Mr. Dash," she says in a sad, dry voice, "Reco is dead! Shot dead this afternoon."

Rosa Lee's fifteen-year-old grandson, Reco Leon "Suave" Cunningham, was the same boy she had taught how to shoplift when he was eleven, the same one who had acted as a lookout for Junior when Junior had a beef with a drug dealer who was trying to collect on one of Patty's debts, and the same one who attended Junior's sentencing for his first armed robbery conviction. I had first met Reco in May 1988 when he was eight years old and living with his uncle Eric. Then he was an open, bubbly, and gregarious kid who giggled and laughed at almost anything. Recalling the day I met him, it is inconceivable that he is dead. How can he be dead? He hasn't lived yet.

Still, his premature death didn't come as a complete surprise to either Rosa Lee or me. Junior was Reco's idol and role model. Junior, Rosa Lee, and another adolescent cousin had kept me up to date on Reco's gradual entry into Washington Highlands' underworld of drugs, guns, and feuding neighborhood crews. Reco, just like Junior, was following the path of too many black boys growing up in poverty today.

Like Junior, by the age of eleven Reco was hanging out with older neighborhood boys whom he wanted to emulate. One day, in front of Rosa Lee's building, Reco watched Junior and the boys they both hung out with beat a woman bloody over a six-dollar crack debt. On another occasion, he and Rosa Lee watched the same group of boys beat another boy unconscious over a hundred-dollar drug debt. After that beating, Rosa Lee tried to convince Reco that he shouldn't associate with those boys or soon he would be beating up people in the same manner. "He just stood there," Rosa Lee recalls about Reco's response to her warning. "He didn't show nothing." Reco had moved into cool pose.

By this time, Reco was already holding older boys' crack stashes for them overnight. This is a common practice in drug-plagued neighborhoods all over the country, because a younger boy faces less severe penalties if the police catch him with drugs.

When he was thirteen, Reco became a victim of street violence for the first time. Rosa Lee told me that Reco was shot in the leg by another youth. She didn't know the cause of the altercation, just that the other boy had been "in Reco's face" when he shot Reco. Taken to D.C. General Hospital, Reco refused to tell police officers who shot him. "He's living by the street code now," Rosa Lee told me. "He won't snitch."

Not long thereafter, Reco witnessed another shooting incident, this time involving a feud between two neighborhood crews. Seventeen-year-old Little Man, who used to sell crack on credit to Reco's aunt Patty, was shot one day while walking with Reco. While both escaped, their sixteen-year-old assailant was arrested, and Reco became a witness in the boy's prosecution. In the course of bringing the assailant to trial, Reco and Little Man talked frequently with Assistant U.S. Attorney Oscar A. Mayers, Jr. The prosecutor remembers Reco as "a follower, very young and immature." Reco only cooperated with Mayers at Little Man's insistence, since both were afraid that if the assailant weren't convicted he would kill them.

The shooting, however, did not deter Reco from dealing drugs himself, Rosa Lee and other members of her family told me. With some of his earnings, he bought a late-model Oldsmobile Cutlass that he was too young to drive legally. He had dropped out of junior high school after punching a teacher in the face and being suspended. Drug dealing was his only job.

Reco's allegiance to his crew, rather than his drug dealing per se, was what led to his death. In fact, his death was precipitated by a continuation of the feud that had resulted in the shooting of Little Man. Mayers sketched the outline of what happened the day Reco was killed:

Around 4:25 P.M., Reco and a nineteen-year-old member of his crew, who was wearing a ski mask and armed with a .38 caliber revolver, drove up behind a white 1979 Lincoln Town Car in Washington Highlands. Reco was driving his Cutlass. Reco's passenger shot out the back window of the Lincoln, and Reco then drove around in front of it. The driver of the luxury car—a member of a rival neighborhood crew—was untouched by the gunfire and gave chase. Witnesses said there was a gun battle between the two cars for eight or nine blocks. Reco lost control of his car, and it ran up onto the sidewalk. The driver of the Lincoln pulled up alongside Reco's car. Reco and the gunman in his car, who was by now out of ammunition, got out and ran, and before long the other driver shot Reco once in the back. Then Reco's companion fell down, and the other driver stood over him while shooting him in the head four times with a .45 caliber semiautomatic pistol. The Lincoln driver then ran, leaving his car next to Reco's Cutlass. Reco, who was breathing when the ambulance arrived, was pronounced dead at D.C. General Hospital at about 5 P.M.

"It appears that Reco and the other boy were trying to do a hit on the driver in the Lincoln," said Mayers. "It was a botched hit! Reco wanted to be a gangster, but he was a kid. From what I know about him when I talked to him, Reco just wasn't the type of person who had what they call the heart to be a ruthless gangster."

I sit several rows behind Reco's family during the morning wake. The funeral home is crowded with several hundred mourners. Exactly one week has passed since he was killed. This is the second funeral I've attended for a member of Rosa Lee's family. Bobby died of AIDS fifteen months ago at age forty-three. At the time, I had thought that Bobby was too young to die, but now here I am at a fifteen-year-old boy's funeral. I still have not emotionally accepted his death. He was just a kid.

A teenage girl carrying her baby comes up to the open casket and begins to cry. "Why did they have to shoot him?" she asks out loud of no one in particular. Suddenly, she begins to shake and cry uncontrollably while holding on to the side of the casket. The coffin begins to tip. It's in danger of tipping over until two adults rush up to steady it. A woman rescues the girl's baby. The man grabs the girl, embraces her, and she collapses into his arms, sobbing.

There are very few dry eyes in the parlor as the couple walks the girl to a seat in the back of the room. Reco's mother and his older sister cry quietly. Alvin, the family anchor, is here. Standing near him in the front is Ben Wright. Reco's mother stands and begins crying over her son's body, trying to hug him. Eric pulls her gently away from the casket, makes her sit down. Reco's buddies are also here. Six of them will be pallbearers. I recognize one of them and greet him. They are dry-eyed, their faces revealing no emotion.

My eyes are blurry with tears as I try to search for some deep meaning behind it all. I don't find anything but more pain for Rosa Lee's family and the many families like hers. This ritual of burying adolescent black males is not something that is going to end soon.

When I arrived for the beginning of the 10 A.M. service, I had scanned the room for Rosa Lee and was surprised when I couldn't find her. Then someone tells me she was taken to Howard Hospital in an ambulance at 4 o'clock this morning suffering another bout of pneumonia. I'm not overly concerned. I make a mental note that this is her seventeenth hospitalization in seven years from either seizures or AIDS-related pneumonia. She has bounced back every time. I just talked to her yesterday and told her I would meet her at Reco's funeral. She was her usual feisty self. I'll go by to see her in the hospital this evening.

The wake lasts about an hour, then the casket is closed and a minister conducts a forty-five-minute prayer service. A blocks-long line of cars follows the hearse out to a suburban Maryland cemetery. A short prayer service is said over the casket, and then the mourners leave, headed in their individual directions.

When I arrive at the *Post* at about 1:30 P.M., the newsroom is all abuzz with a rumor that photographer Lucian Perkins and I have won a Pulitzer Prize for "Rosa Lee's Story." At 3 P.M., an Associated Press news wire story announces that we have indeed won a Pulitzer, in the Explanatory Journalism category. Reco's funeral has put a damper on the celebration for me, but I hang around the office for a short while before heading over to Howard Hospital. At the patient information desk, I ask for Rosa Lee's room number. The receptionist flips through a Rolodex looking for her name. She looks up at me. "Miss Cunningham is in ICU, the intensive care unit," she says.

I hurry to the fifth floor and follow the red lines on the linoleum tiles that lead to ICU. Through the glass window in the door closing off Rosa Lee's cubicle, I can see she is propped up in her bed and unconscious. She is on a breathing machine, a large tube strapped into her mouth, and oxygen is being pumped into her lungs. Her chest heaves with each push of the machine. Rosa Lee is fighting for her life. A sign on the door says only family members are allowed inside the cubicle. A nurse asks me if I am a family member. "No, just a friend," I respond.

Rosa Lee remains unconscious over the next two weeks. The nurses become accustomed to my coming by and standing outside the door. Finally, in early May, I come to the hospital to see her around 7 P.M. and run into Alvin standing outside the cubi-

cle. He has just gotten off work and is still in his bus driver's uniform. Rosa Lee is awake and breathing on her own. I enter the
cubicle with Alvin. Rosa Lee is so weak she can't lift her arms,
but she smiles and is able to give weak yes and no replies to my
questions about how she is feeling. When I leave, I run into Eric,
who is sitting in a nearby waiting room with a family friend.

Several days later, Rosa Lee is transferred to a regular hospital room. Now, she has lots of visitors—her current boyfriend is
there every day, her children, other family members, and
friends—and they bring cards and flowers. When I visit her, her
main complaint is severe pain in her lower legs and feet. Rosa
Lee makes sure that I and all of her other visitors massage her
legs and feet, giving her some relief from the pain.

In late June, Alvin tells me that Howard Hospital's physicians
have told him that they have done all they can for his mother. If
she is to fully recover from her latest round with AIDS, Alvin
says, it will be up to her and God.

I go to see Rosa Lee on the afternoon of July 4th. She has
taken a turn for the worse. She is comatose, and her breathing is
shallow. At half past seven in the morning three days later, Eric
calls to tell me that Rosa Lee died in her sleep at two-thirty.

For me, though, Rosa Lee's story does not end with her death. I
return to Rich Square twice in November 1995 to do more interviews with the people who knew Rosa Lee's parents and grandparents before they migrated from the area sixty-three years earlier. There is also some unfinished business I am trying to wrap
up. I am determined to find out what happened to Rosa Lee's
older sister. Even locate her, if I can.

Over lunch in Hilda Tann's kitchen, I finally learn what happened to Geneva, the child Rosetta Wright gave birth to in 1930.
Mamie Barnes, the woman who attended Cumbo School with
Rosetta, is also present. Rosa Lee and I had told Hilda that
twice, when we raised the subject of Rosetta's first daughter with
Daisy Debreaux two years earlier, Daisy had just looked out the
open door of her house and refused to say anything.

Months later, while Daisy was visiting Hilda, "I picked it out of her," Hilda says, laughing. Daisy was slow to respond, but she finally told Hilda, "Well, you know how folks is. When the white man wants a colored woman, they would put them over in another field from the other folks." In 1931, about a year after Rosetta gave birth to Geneva, she was again assigned to work in a field away from the rest of her family. It was common for mothers to take their babies to the field with them, and Rosetta took Geneva. A white man, the father of the child, came and took the baby away from Rosetta.

"They don't know who got her or where she went at," Hilda tells me. "Know she disappeared. This white man wanted the child to go to another man's house. Seem like these white folks didn't have no children and they wanted a child. Rosetta knew they were going to take this child and wasn't nothing she or her family could do about it."

" 'Cause you couldn't," continues Hilda, when I question her. "We didn't have no say in nothing. The white folks had the whole say. The [black sharecroppers] were working as slaves, don't care what they say about freedom after the Civil War. Rosetta never saw the child no more." Daisy didn't tell Rosa Lee what happened to Geneva, says Hilda, because "she figured if Rosa Lee's mother never told her, it weren't her place to tell Rosa Lee."

Mamie later tells me that Rosetta's experience was not an uncommon one for black girls working on the farms around Rich Square from the post–Civil War period up through the 1930s. "It was terrible," she says, with feeling. "If the [white overseers] don't have no children themselves, they'd take the one they had with you. They would tell the child that they adopted her from black folks. Or the parents died. She wouldn't know no more. I got some cousins that happened to." If the child stayed in the area, someone might tell her years later, when she was an adult, who her real mother was. But that was not going to happen after Rosetta moved to Washington, and the child might have been moved away as well.

What if Thadeous Lawrence had gone to the authorities and accused the man of raping Rosetta? I ask, knowing full well what the answer will be.

"Oh, good gracious," replies Mamie. "They would have scandalized her! The white man would have said he never touched that *black* girl! The white bosses could do what they wanted."

When Mamie was a young girl in the 1920s, her parents warned her to never let herself be alone with a white overseer. "I wouldn't get nowhere near a white man, if there weren't nobody there but me," she recalls. "They were good for getting young girls, them grown men. I mean it!"

I wonder out loud if we could find Geneva today. She could still be alive.

"True, but she probably was never told the truth about her people," says Mamie. "He [her father] could've changed the name, too, so you'd never find her."

Gene Bennett, forty-five, one of three white brothers whose late father bought the Bishop and Powell Plantation in the early 1950s, was not surprised when I told him the story of Rosetta's daughter. At the end of a long conversation outside the farm's two-story office, Bennett said simply that in the period when Rosetta and her family lived on the Bishop and Powell Plantation, the black sharecroppers "were treated like property."

I also spoke with Jasper "Bud" Jacobs, a black laborer who still works on the Bishop and Powell Plantation. He moved onto the farm with his parents at age eight in 1930. Through mud that cakes the soles of our shoes, he takes me to the site of Thadeous Lawrence's sharecropping shack and to the place where Charlie Lawrence shot the white overseer Herman Chapel in 1922. He's able to recount the details of the killing as if it happened last year, although it occurred the year he was born.

Bud doesn't know which white boss was the father of Rosetta's first child. "I was too young back then," he says. "But there's a lot you could learn if the trees and land could talk. It was close to slavery around here in the 1930s. The black people who could leave, ran!"

In January 1996, I visit Patty and Junior in Washington's prison system. In October 1994, Junior received a fifteen- to forty-five-year sentence for his second armed-robbery conviction. Both mother and son are biding their time before they're eligible for parole. Patty's first possible parole hearing date is October 1998 and Junior thinks his is sometime in 1999. They aren't prepared to do anything more or less, if and when they are paroled, than what they were doing when sentenced.

Ronnie is living with his wife's mother, Patty tells me, and Ducky is in the D.C. jail on another theft charge. "He wants to come live with me when he gets out, but I don't know where I'm gonna be living," she says. "So how am I going to take care of him? Ducky has to learn to take care of himself!"

Alvin and Eric are still doing well, Alvin driving a Metrobus and Eric working for the National Park Service.

In March 1995, a Superior Court judge sent Richard to a three-year inpatient drug-treatment center in Denver, Colorado. Alvin bought him the airplane ticket.

Rosa Lee Cunningham was a very powerful human being whose life and understanding of the world she lived in were severely restricted by the circumstances of her birth. She was caught up in a tragedy for which, it can be reasonably argued, she was partially at fault, but, at the same time, one that was foreordained. Unlike most of her brothers and sisters, who benefited from their grandparents' and parents' migration to Washington, Rosa Lee was unable to break free of her family's transplanted class, culture, and isolation.

During my many discussions and interactions with Rosa Lee and her family, I recognized in the family's history and daily life matters that two distinguished scholars had written about, independently at different periods, on the eve of America's entry into World War II and at the outset of the tumultuous 1960s. The perceptions and analyses of Charles Spurgeon Johnson and Gunnar Myrdal prefigure what I learned and saw firsthand.

Johnson—the son of an emancipated slave, a sociologist as well as a civil rights leader, and the first black president of Fisk University in Nashville, Tennessee—captured the difficult isolation of Rosa Lee's forebears in his 1941 book, *Growing Up in the Black Belt: Negro Youth in the Rural South*. Published in

Washington, D.C., the year Rosa Lee turned five years old, John-son's *Black Belt* gives an intricate breakdown of the class and social divisions among rural black Americans in the South extending back to slavery, the era when African Americans were divided, from the top, into "free coloreds," house servants, and field hands.

Following Emancipation, there developed a tiny upper class of black landowners, doctors, teachers, and school principals. A superior education was the distinguishing characteristic of this class. The next layer underneath was a small middle class, usu-ally consisting of church and community leaders who had an equally high regard for education and a desire to escape the stigma of low status that their skin color gave them in the larger white society. "Their children avoid contact with whites and seek economic independence in professional careers," wrote Johnson. These people and their children became small shop proprietors, small farm owners and renters, skilled artisans, and white-collar workers.

Within a two-tiered lower-class structure, the upper-lower class formed "the great bulk of the rural Negro population," according to Johnson. These people were unskilled and semi-skilled workers, personal and domestic workers "earning barely enough to live and not enough to live comfortably." Occupying the bottom rung of this hierarchy was the lower-lower class, which in contemporary parlance would be called the rural underclass. Johnson's definition of this lower-lower class fits the description of the "river" and "swamp" blacks who lived in pockets of extreme isolation along the banks of the Roanoke River south of Rich Square, North Carolina, and worked on the cotton plantations. Johnson could well have been writing about Rosa Lee's grandparents and mother when he wrote: "The lower-lower class is made up of individuals who lack most of the major characteristics [of the upper and middle classes], and who recognize the other classes as different and having more advan-tages. They have little or no education and skill, although they may be hard working. Their standard of living is very low and their resources are meager. They are tenants, sharecroppers, and laborers on the farms, and the unskilled laborers and domestic servants in the towns. They add to the low economic level a thorough cultural poverty with confused values. Frequently they are condemned to permanent economic incompetence because of their family structure. In this class are also the chronic relief cases," people who today would be described as welfare dependent.

The Swedish economist Gunnar Myrdal is most famous for his seminal work on the problems of racism in the United States, *An American Dilemma,* published in 1944. But in later years he turned his attention to the people who lived lives like Rosa Lee's. Myrdal was the first to identify the emergent "underclass" among twentieth-century American groups of black rural-to-city migrants, poor "hillbilly" whites, and Hispanic migrant farm laborers. In *Challenge to Affluence,* published in 1962, a year after Rosa Lee had given birth to her eighth child, he argued that large numbers of people from all three groups were permanently shut out from participating in American society, and that "the largest and still most handicapped minority group in America is that of the Negroes." He prophetically described what would happen to succeeding generations of all three groups, something we've seen with most of Rosa Lee's children, some of her grandchildren, and, very possibly, a great-grandson.

"In [American] society at large there is more equality of opportunity today than there ever was," wrote Myrdal. "But for the bottom layer there is less or none." Ominously, Myrdal added, "That class line becomes demarcated almost as a caste line, since the children in this class tend to become as poorly endowed as their parents." Myrdal concluded that as America moved into a technological age, where a good education would be a prerequisite for well-paid employment, and *"as less and less work is required of the type the people in the urban and rural slums can offer, they will be increasingly isolated and exposed to unemployment, to underemployment, and to plain exploitation"* [italics Myrdal's].

Rereading Johnson and Myrdal, it is obvious to me that what happened to Rosa Lee, and continues with three generations of her direct descendants, is tied much more strongly to the low class and caste level to which her family was relegated before she was born than to her many admittedly bad choices. Even given the relative success of eight of her ten brothers and sisters in overcoming these societal barriers, the opportunities to move up are fewer and the paths narrower for Rosa Lee's grandchildren and great-grandchildren. Without some major intervention, Rosa Lee's descendants, locked into the bottom of American society, are more likely to make the same set of choices Rosa Lee made.

My effort to understand the opportunities available to and the choices made by Rosa Lee and others trapped in the under-class—so that we all may be better able to address the crisis they represent—continues to this day and may even consume the rest of my professional career. But being a reporter, I am always fascinated by the details. So, even after having spent four years with Rosa Lee and her family, many times while working on this book I wanted to pick up the telephone and ask her again to expand on some detail she had told me about her daily life or her past. I was surprised at how long it took me to accept that she was dead and that we would never be able to talk with each other again. In the course of the writing, though, I often heard her voice as clearly as if she were sitting in front of me.

On my way to Virginia or downtown Washington, I sometimes drive by the McDonald's where Rosa Lee and I spent so much time together. Whenever I do, I think about her. She granted me unlimited access to a way of life that is an enigma to most Americans, eagerly consenting to my reporting on her life so that others might learn from her story. More than that, I liked her, and, now, I miss her.

Acknowledgments

MANY PEOPLE made direct and indirect contributions to this book, some knowingly and others unknowingly, over the course of hours, months and years of discussions about the African American condition, past and present. I would like to thank them all.

Among them, the most important person was Rosa Lee Cunningham, who stuck with the project, even though the many repeated interviews constantly brought to the surface unresolved feelings of shame for her personal misdeeds and confronted her with her responsibility for a lot of the destructive behaviour of most of her children and some of her grandchildren. My greatest hope was to get the book completed before she died, but the AIDS virus killed her as I was starting it. I regret that I will never be able to hand her a copy.

Robert Earl 'Bobby' Wright promised Rosa Lee that when the book was done, he would read it to her chapter by chapter, but he, too, died of AIDS, while I was still reporting the series for the *Washington Post*. All of Rosa Lee's children made crucial contributions about their personal lives and the family's history. Besides Bobby, they are Ronald Earl 'Ronnie' Wright, Alvin Cunningham, Richard Cunningham, Eric Wright, Donna Denise 'Patty' Wright (alias Patty Cunningham), Donald David 'Ducky' Wright and Rosa Lee's youngest daughter.

My editors at the *Washington Post* made the largest contribution to this book by allowing me the time and giving me the resources to do the series on Rosa Lee and her family. Steve Luxenburg, my editor on the *Post*'s investigative desk made the most significant contribution. He proposed writing the dialogue between Rosa Lee and me in the present tense, not an easy task when you're constantly bouncing between the past and present. While the book contains twice the amount of information that was in the series, much of Steve's format and structure was adopted for the book. The major changes in the book are the placement of the family's history, which was spread out over more pieces in the series and the addition of three new sections.

Photographer Lucian Perkins came into the project in the late fall of 1990 thinking it would all be done by 1991. Over the years, most of the family came to regard him as an unobtrusive fixture and were candid in their everyday behaviour while he shot rolls of film. Photographer Keith Jenkins worked on the project in the summer of 1993 when Lucian was in Russia. Although he hadn't as much time to establish the same rapport, he produced as excellent a set of photographs as Lucian.

Frontline producer June Cross really captured Rosa Lee in the television documentary 'The Confessions of Rosa Lee' and found two of Rosa Lee's elementary school teachers, people I had mistakenly thought were dead.

Sarah Flynn and Paul Golob saved me from myself by excising an overwhelming mass of detail. If this book is helpful to the reader, it is largely because of Sarah's and Paul's dedicated efforts to make it one of the best of its genre. I am grateful to them both.

Leon Dash
Maryland, 1996